CAREER CHESS

MAXIMILIAN A. LEROUX

In memory of Grace Chen

CONTENTS

ACKNOWLEDGMENTS

Thanks to Lie Luo for encouraging me to write this book. Thanks to Sascha Matuszak for guidance on better writing. Thanks to my father, Heinz Thoma, for the inspiration to strive for personal independence; and for comments and edits in this book. Thanks to my brother Sebastian for recommendations of literature and cultural sources, explanations on different human epochs, and great road trips. Thanks to Grandmaster Suk Jun Kim and Master Kathryn Yang for instructing me in Taekwondo practice. Thanks to Dario Casella for being a living encyclopedia of Ancient Greek and Roman quotations. Thanks to Louise Mason for line editing and localizing German proverbs into English language. Thanks to Robert Heinrich for proof reading and final comments; for helping me to get this book done after a decade. Thanks to Chad W. Adams for the author portrait. Thanks to Eloïse Boulerne and Kirsi Kahikko for the book cover idea. Thanks to Jeannette Zeuner for type setting, formatting and final cover design. Thanks to Pasi Auranen for building a company with me to make a dream become true. Thanks to my mother, Leena, for being an anchor throughout my life. And very special thanks to my wife Meredith for being my Sherpa, and for her patience and support.

FOREWORD

"I pay no attention whatever to anybody's praise or blame.
I simply follow my own feelings."

WOLFGANG AMADEUS MOZART (1756–1791)

Career is more than just work. It's part of a lifelong journey of discovery, learning, a mean and an end to happiness. Do a job you love you and never work a day in your life, Confucius said over two thousand years ago. That hasn't changed yet, but it seems forgotten.

Life, liberty and the pursuit of happiness has become a rat race for money and social sex appeal. Like hamsters on a treadmill, we are chasing the corporate carrot with a false sense of success and security. Without any real need.

Freedom is the capability to "live a life that you know to value because of your own reasons" as Economics Nobel Prize winner Amartya Sen (*1933) described it.[1] Instead, many people have fallen for the so-called work-life-balance myth. This concept tries to justify work as a necessary evil which would be balanced out by joy in life.

How about finding meaningful work? Wouldn't it be nice if work was fun and led to success? Some people seem to be afraid of that. The main stream idea of a career aims for certain job titles and company brand names. Today, success in a career is measured by the abi-

---

1 SEN, A. (1999), P. 29

lity to buy a lot of things. Maybe people have grown so used to it that they are afraid to see career as a mean to happiness, not as an end.

I started my own career in the exact same way though: Masters Degree in Economics, learned a few languages, traveled the world, volunteered, worked during semester breaks in several large companies, and I ran for public office at the age of 20 and was elected twice. I tried to do it all by the book. It was exciting, and I believed it was necessary to kick start my career and stand out of the crowd. I began my career full of enthusiasm, just like most young professionals. Very soon though I was stunned that talent and hard work alone weren't enough. At times they didn't seem necessary at all. Looking around me I was surprised to observe quite a few inept leaders, some of which were complete idiots. There must have been other reasons than talent that lifted them into their positions.

Why do some people who seem to have no skill make it, and others don't? How can *I* make my way up? Attempting to analyze this initial challenge, I buried myself in career literature looking in vain for an answer. Mostly I found the same top-down approach from the perspective of a hiring manager or heroic stories on how someone else made it. Overall, it felt that career literature missed something.

Career seemed to be narrowed down to an exhaustive hustle for money and job titles with no end. Yet, everyone follows some logic and some belief on how to make a successful career. And that was the clue I needed: it's all a game! Life is a big chess game with each figure on the field coming with specific abilities and power; and all playing by certain rules.

Game Theory, a discipline within economic sciences, says that all human interaction is a game. And we are in the middle of it. Seeing it as a game, with a good sense of humor and a spirit of adventure, you will be able to get on top of your career and your pursuit of happiness.

As humans we live in packs and are dependent on one another. We want space for our personal freedom. We want to influence others, but do not like to be controlled. This is the tug-of-war through our entire life. This is what makes corporate politics a quest for what-is-in-it-for-me.

Friedrich Nietzsche (1844–1900) said: "The individual has always had to struggle to keep from being overwhelmed by the tribe. If you try it, you will be lonely often, and sometimes frightened. But no price is too high to pay for the privilege of owning yourself."

To be free means to not be afraid and to have the courage to use your own reasoning. Freedom and happiness are two sides of the same coin. Taking charge of your own life is therefore the initial start to success.

A good plan is half the victory. Once you realize that the world is not about you, even a difficult boss, a rigid hierarchy, or an overwhelming bureaucracy are just some of the hurdles you'll have to take in order to get where you want. You can learn how to deal with any situation in life by analyzing and seeing it within the context of the environment it happens.

Sun Tzu (544–496 B.C.), the ancient Chinese general and creator of the *Art of War*, said that "if you know the enemy and know yourself, you need not fear the result of a hundred battles." Observing the behavior and the incentives that trigger specific behavior, understanding your battlefield, are the key to winning the corporate career game.

I have elaborated a methodology on how to plan for success. I applied it with success and then stumbled over new challenges. This led me to questioning why all career development mattered in the first place?

Let's take money out of the equation for a moment. We all need an income to pay our bills and we have to work hard for success. However, if we stop following a career for the money, but to gain freedom and happiness it unleashes the energy you need to ultimately become successful. And the money will come with it. We should take a breath and think for a moment what kind of life we want to lead for our own good reasons.

In the first ten years of my professional career I had three jobs. In the first couple of jobs I was promoted before I was laid off. In the third one I made more money than in any job I ever had, yet I couldn't wait to leave.

Ultimately I came to realize that I needed to become an entrepreneur to find happiness. While I'm using my personal story to describe the path of a young freedom loving man through his endeavors, I didn't want to write a me-too version of a ten-steps-to-success- or a this-is-how-I-did-it book. Instead I have embedded different type of challenges in a hand book following a path of enlightenment. I'm using the help of economic sciences, and the wisdom of the greatest thinkers in history to create an analytical view of the world and derive a strategy and actions from it.

I have lived in many countries among different cultures. I was on the hunt for adventure and gathered experience around the world. It was a constant multifaceted rollercoaster. Since I couldn't find the *one* book that would have all the answers, I followed the advice of the medieval Benedictine monk Rabanus Maurus (780–856): "Exercise yourself through reading and then pen something of use yourself."

I spent almost a decade working on this book, and there have been several versions of it. At times it was quite bitter. The happier I was, so was the manuscript. It was a work in progress. Just like real life. To write a book is a big step outside of oneself, to reflect and summarize your thoughts and experience. I found a middle way of building a career and success without the constant worry about social approval and without taking myself and everything else too serious all the time. The working title of this book throughout the years has been:

"The intelligent hippy! Live free and make money at the same time."

INTRODUCTION TO CAREER CHESS

*"Enlightenment is man's emergence
from his self-imposed immaturity."*

IMMANUEL KANT (1724–1804)

The world today has more opportunities for individuals than humans have ever experienced throughout the history of mankind. It's up to every individual to take advantage of a world full of options. This world of opportunity doesn't trickle down on a career path as easy as the download of a Smartphone app. In a fast-paced world in which progress in technology and innovation speeds up like the expansion of the universe, the new human challenge is how to keep up with change and how to avoid getting rolled over by the bus of globalized shareholder value while trying to build a stress-free happy life.

The opportunities are getting bigger and broader for a greater number of people. And with it the challenges. The possibility to travel the world with ease and use technology in all situations have shaped a different way of how we live and work. All generations experience the shifted attitude towards work, especially the chase for quick success. Everyone has to adapt to this world in order to not get uncoupled from the train to the future. A new generation of globetrotters grew up into a world of sheer endless opportunities surrounded by technology. This generation of millennials enters into a work environment with new expectations and yet encounter old habits and traditional hierarchies. Many are able to get a ton of experience, yet the way up feels just as difficult as it has always been.

Born in the late 1970s I enjoyed a wonderful childhood in absence of the Internet, mobile phones and no big brother watching me, except for my biological one. However, I don't second the general opinion that millennials would only look for instant gratification. Firstly, people have always looked for gratification, only the digital age makes it possible to receive this instantly. Secondly, in my genetically optimistic composition, I see that a generation with a plight to find meaningful work has evolved. In the opposite it seems that real gratification has gotten lost somewhat, and it cannot be compensated by digital thumbs up. We are living in a short-term economy, an economy that deems anyone replaceable. This only enforces the behavior to look for quicker success, and live in the here and now, rather planning for an uncertain future. Maybe people live more by what the economist John Maynard Keynes (1883–1946) said: "On the long run we are all dead."

When the challenges fade and the learning curve flattens, people want to leave their jobs. Today, many people, young and old, expect more from a job than to be solely a source of money. On the flipside, the reality of the world's economy is short-lived like the newest tech-gadgets or popular mobile apps. Things come and go faster, so can your job. Quick revenues with simple ideas, outsourced technology and monetization strategies packed in colorful marketing are the formula for startups sprouting everywhere. Funded by organized venture capital looking to cash out 3–5 years after their investment, many businesses are set up to be short-lived. In large corporations then, human resources are commodities like any other parts of the supply chain. Predictions of future job security in a person's career are as accurate as weather forecasts. Like with the weather you cannot change it, but you can come prepared.

The challenge how to get where we want to be in the world today is a new type of struggle. We all need a paycheck to pay for the lifestyle that we want to have, and everything I hear tells me I can and should achieve my dreams, but the reality is nothing like that at all. The rules, that hard work and skill alone will get you there, have no substance in reality. It requires something more than that.

I have often asked myself why do we need a career anyway? What purpose does it fulfill to jump from job to job and growing your responsibility? Some of my success stories and moments of happiness came by co-incident, when I seized an opportunity as it came along. I learned that the convergence of the pursuit of happiness on the one hand, and career advancement on the other, while they are two separate things, in a reciprocal enhancement they become the most long-lasting and meaningful path for life. The longing of living a happy life is the impetus to follow a certain career, it creates zealousness and happiness and turns into work enthusiasm. When one treats career as a mean for a happy life, not an end that's limited to making money, and career development as in making more money, then Monday mornings become the best moments of the week. I will prove that it's possible. I had stumbled upon happiness and a strategy for success in a corporate world. I had figured something out and applied it, and applied it again, and it worked. Initially it was merely an accident, and so I tried to reverse engineer what happened, and find a methodology. This process turned into the idea to write this book.

It was the winter of 2007 in Helsinki, Finland. I had just returned from a year and a half living and working first in Brazil and then the United States. In the few months since my return, I had developed a habit of after work dinners with my Chinese friend Lie Luo. We often went to an Italian restaurant called La Famiglia. It has a nice atmosphere, is affordable and allows for comfortable, private conversations. It's in the heart of the city center, and we usually took the Metro to get there.

La Famiglia is a great place to share a bottle of red table wine and talk about life. In the dark winter of Finland, this place provides the warm atmosphere I needed to let my thoughts drift and temporarily take leave of my current reality. Instead of thinking about how cold the walk would be from the restaurant to the Metro station, we dove into long conversations. We spent hours dreaming of different places to travel to, how to attain our life goals. We were young professionals with just a few years of work experience. Still full of energy and enthusiasm despite a sobering taste of the corporate world and its hierarchies and irrational decision making processes.

Lie and I had worked together for a game developer for mobile phones, back in 2004. In 2005, after only a year selling mobile games to the Asia Pacific market, Lie had moved on to Rovio, the eventual creators of Angry Birds. But that was yet a few years into the future.

The founders of Rovio had asked me to join their team, attaching some company shares to the offer. That was just a little after Lie had joined them. I had been a sales manager for Digital Chocolate selling into key accounts in German speaking markets. Rovio was looking to have me do something similar. Lie, being Chinese, was selling to Asia-Pacific. It seemed to make a lot of sense for Digital Chocolate to have a native German on the sales team to cover German markets and a native Chinese covering China. The growing frustration both of us felt in 2005 was that, regardless of our completely different cultural background, we had the sensation that the company we worked for only cared for us as long as we had a skill that they really needed. It wasn't about our potential to help the company grow, it was only about one particular skill that they wanted. Their own immediate need of selling to customers in specific markets always came before our desires for new challenges.

In 2005, Lie had started a discussion with Digital Chocolate's CEO, Trip Hawkins, former founder of games giant Electronic Arts. Lie told Trip that he didn't feel the company was offering enough of a career path. Trip Hawkins argument threads like this:

- Lie was a perfect fit for the position.
- Lie's company shares would be worth a lot one day.

Ten years later the shares that Lie and I both own at Digital Chocolate are still worthless. All we have are memories of good times with fun people in a growing startup. Moneywise there was never anything attractive for us there, neither the salary, nor the potential bonus. Initially that didn't matter, because we were a hands-on part of the growth, which was very rewarding. We could see how our own efforts and late hours at work translated into success. It was exciting to be part of a growing company. Inevitably at some point came the question of what's next? Trip Hawkins was trying to repeat for Lie arguments that made sense to Trip Hawkins, rather than trying to understand what Lie's real concerns were. In fact, Trip's arguments were from an organizational perspective: Because it makes so much sense for *us* to have you on board, it should also make sense to *you*. Our happiness is your happiness. We have given you a job that is a perfect match for your skills, you should be excited. In addition, he thought future money would be the main motivation for anyone staying on.

Why does money alone not motivate? I'm in an international business, I want to be more than just "the German". I want more than just the empty promise of getting monetary pay-off some day. And the same applied to Lie. This did not resonate with the executives. Trip was taking a trickle down approach while we expected team empowerment for growth.

So why do people usually leave their jobs? In a job interview I once had, a seasoned human resources professional with 30 years of experience, his name was Herman, explained to me his view on the topic:

1. People leave their jobs if they do not get the tools they need in order to perform their jobs, like a graphic artists who doesn't get the graphics program for his computer that he needs, because the finance director wouldn't approve the purchase of the software. If you cannot do what you are hired to do you will end up leaving.
2. Anyone who has a problem with his boss will eventually leave.
3. If you feel that you are not getting paid enough.

An important argument in the 21st century though is the 4th reason, which Herman did not mention: If you don't see a future path on where your journey is going, you will take destiny into your own hands. Any company will lose their best people if they are unable to outline a tangible career path, mediocrity stays behind and establishes the company culture.

It's a simple box into which people are placed and it follows the logic of an organization: You are Chinese so go sell into the Chinese market and one day your shares will be worth a lot of money.

If you are the perfect fit for a job, then the company wants you to believe it must be meant for you.

I was born in Augsburg Germany and grew up in Frankfurt. I am aslo half Finnish and spent all of my summers on the Finnish country side in a lake cabin. Drawn to Finland by its people and culture, its magnificent landscape of endless forests and countless number of lakes, as well as four distinct picture-book seasons, I moved to Helsinki right after graduating from University. Finland was my place of choice to start a career and eventually raise a family. Throughout my life I have travelled all over the world. At that point, my home town appeared smaller and smaller each time I returned from a trip abroad. My thirst for exploration was not satisfied and I felt the itch to go somewhere else. There was still so much more to see in the world. I chose Finland, because there I have family and friends, and next to my German passport. I am also a citizen of Finland. It was somewhat new and somewhat home. This was where I was hoping to start a career. In the end I wasn't running away from my hometown to look for a better life, but to look for an opportunity in a country I love. I wasn't trying to escape. In addition, Finland is a small export oriented country. With my experience and language skills I felt that I was going to find a quicker way into an international career path.

It wasn't as easy as I had hoped, but finally in the late fall of 2004 I found the job at Digital Chocolate. I told my friends in Germany that I had found a job, because I speak German. Everyone nodded and said: "Oh yeah, that makes a lot of sense."

With no post-graduate work experience I had to take advantage of my main competitive advantage on the job market: German language skills. After all, about 12% of Finnish exports go to Germany, and 14% of imports come from there. This makes Germany the largest trade partner of Finland. After living off 200€ a month for half a year I grew impatient. I was desperate to start a career and I didn't want to be broke anymore, I needed a real income. I had tried to land a job in anything that I was interested in and felt skilled for, without success. One day I decided to give in and accept what "made sense" to everyone and started to only look for jobs that required German language skills. And from that moment on, job interviews kept coming.

Eventually it worked and I started as a Key Account Manager for German Speaking countries at Digital Chocolate. Lie had been in a similar situation as I and had followed the same tactic, knowing that if he'd play the Chinese card, he would eventually land a job. That is how we became colleagues and friends. The reason both of us took the job was to get a paycheck by offering what someone else needed, hoping to be able to show our full potential once we were an insider. It turned out to be more than income, but also a fun environment to work in. Unfortunately it didn't seem to transform into a career path. It looked like we were doomed to do the same job forever unless we did something about it.

Lie left Digital Chocolate in 2005, because he couldn't see a career path for himself. I wanted to leave, because of all four reasons: I had a lot of international experience, but I could not take advantage of it. My manager did not inspire me, he was rather demotivating and I did not feel like I was paid enough compared to the revenue I created. But most of all, just like Lie, I wanted to leave, because of the lack of a true career path.

I felt that corporate hierarchies are rigid and irrational. The only way to get somewhere was to force change one way or the other.

"Diligence is the mother of good fortune", *Don Quijote's* creator Miguel de Cervantes (1547–1616) said, "and idleness, its opposite, never brought a man to the goal of any of his best wishes." Idleness doesn't lead to progress, so I did not try to talk myself into liking the status quo in the hopes for some outer force changing things for the better. I went to HR and told them something better happens soon or I was leaving. I did not want to be pigeon-holed, forever the German who sells to German markets. I emphasized that I wasn't requesting any immediate changes, but a serious conversation with measurable, defined milestones on where my career could be heading to and how. The only answer I constantly heard was that the future was bright and full of opportunities and that I only needed to hang on for a while. In the meantime, as some of the Ex-Digital Chocolate employees were building their new company, Rovio, I started to warm to the idea of moving on. The company I worked at wasn't doing anything for me and Rovio was going to welcome me with shares to the company.

It all built up to a big gamble. I quit, or better I tried to quit. Rovio offered me a job and I gave my notice to Ilkka Paananen, the Managing Director of Europe at Digital Chocolate at the time. I respect him a lot and he had been the one who hired me in the first place. Handing my resignation to my immediate boss, I felt, could be seen as if I was recognizing him as such, which I didn't. He just happened to be appointed in that position, yet he didn't earn that respect.

Since he was also traveling at that time he called me to say:

"I heard the bad news."

"I am moving forward in my career, what is so bad about that?"

"Yes, but you are leaving us!"

"I don't really want to leave you, but you haven't given me a choice. I have been openly asking for a career path and opportunities for over six months now. I wanted to know where I could be in a year from now, but all I heard were vague promises and calls to hang in a little longer. I lost the confidence that you really mean it. I had to make the decision on my own, since you are obviously not making one on my behalf."

"What do you want?" he asked.

"I don't think you have anything for me."

"No, no, tell me what you want."

I had lived for two years in South America and have a great passion for that region of the world, so I said:

"There is a large market for us in South America, there are hundreds of millions of users that we can reach. We have no business there yet. If you send me to South America as an ex-pat to build that market, I will stay."

I had long dreamed of being an ex-pat somewhere in the world, preferably in South America, but I didn't think that they would go for it. In that moment I was so fed up, I just wanted to leave. My manager kept asking what I wanted so I said anything to just shut him up and we could all move on.

"When are you going to sign the contract with Rovio?" he wanted to know.

"Tomorrow at 9 a.m. in the morning."

"Can we two meet at 8 a.m. in the office?"

"I don't know what the point of that is, but I will be there at 8 a.m."

The next morning I walked into the office thinking I was going to have a random conversation and then sign with the competition an hour later. My manager by appointment said:

"If you are going to stay with us we will send you to South America. Pick which country you want to go to."

"Brazil?"

"OK, you can go to Brazil."

I was completely unprepared to make this life changing decision; especially because I really loved my life in Finland. I had no intention of leaving, I just wanted a job with a future. There was an opportunity, unexpected and bigger than expected, yet with the trade-off to leave Finland behind. Equally concerned about going away I was afraid that one day in the future I would regret not to face a new frontier and to go for something I had always wanted. Since I only had a few minutes to make a decision I need to follow my gut feeling.

I took the chance and moved to São Paulo in Brazil only a couple of months later. Looking back you can always find "would-have" moments in your life. I couldn't have known that Rovio would one day launch Angry Birds, but to this day I believe I made the right decision. I may not have stayed long enough at Rovio anyway. In the moment I made that decision it was irrelevant and therefore in the aftermath it doesn't count either.

My father always says that "the worst things in life are the missed opportunities, they will haunt you forever."

Making no decision means to choose the status quo. This can also be a missed opportunity since the wrong decisions can still be better than the status quo. Idleness and fear of the unknown lead people to constantly talking themselves into liking their lives. In self-condolence they may call it destiny, but "destiny is an invention of the cowards," as the Italian author and politician Ignazio Silone (1900–1978) precisely said.

The decision for Brazil was an inflection point; a moment which altered the course of my life. Deciding between working in a similar job in a country I love or an exciting opportunity in a company I was fed up with was enough material for eternal hesitation. When the clock was ticking I had to come to a conclusion, before destiny decided on my behalf. Instead of getting into a Hamlet-style debate with myself about "to be or not to be"[2], I took decisive action and just did it. No regrets, I decided.

Howard Stevenson (*1941), a prominent figure of Harvard Business School has very precise words for the moment I had just lived through: "Very few people see inflection points as the opportunities they often are: catalyst for changing their lives; moments when a person can modify the trajectory he or she is on and redirect it in a more desirable direction. An inflection point is one of those periodic windows of opportunity when a person can pause, reflect, and ask: 'Self, do I want to continue on this path or is now the moment to change directions?'"[3]

---

2 SHAKESPEARE, W. (1603), HAMLET, ACT III, SCENE 1

3 SINOWAY, E. (2012), P. 25

In Greek mythology inflection points were worshiped as *Kairos*. Kairos was the Greek God of opportunity and is now used as a philosophical term for a perfect moment for a decision that steers life into a different direction. "Inflection points change the way we think about things. They present an opportunity that only occurs periodically. And they possess a kind of latent motivational energy, which, when recognized and harnessed, can unleash potential that one wouldn't seize otherwise."[4] The recognition of an inflection point is important, realizing that you are actually standing at a cross-roads and you can either keep walking, or look around and see what other path you could take. It doesn't mean you should turn your life upside down each time you have an opportunity to do so, but to realize that life is not a one-way street. Inflection points can appear in different ways: subtle and hidden, or obvious and even scary. They can happen co-incidentally, unwanted, forced by others or you can push for them yourself.

How should we deal with inflection points? Franklin D. Roosevelt (1882–1945) said in his first inaugural speech that the "only thing we have to fear is fear itself." We have to see it as Kairos in the ancient Greek way, as something to be worshipped, not to be feared. Kairos is an opportunity, not an obligation. Opportunities are not the question whether you want to do something or not, but to decide between the status quo and another option. Maybe an arising opportunity is not what you had dreamed of, but it can still be much more exciting than the status quo. And sometime to pass on an opportunity can also be the better decision

If you always do what you have always done, you will always get what you have always got. The corporate world doesn't work the way I expected it to before entering in it. The story that the world tells you on how we can be successful is a lie. But people want to believe that story. If you do not wake up to realizing that you might be chasing that carrot forever then you will always be frustrated. Insanity is to do the exact same thing over and over hoping for a different outcome. Albert

---

4 SINOWAY, E. (2012), P. 24

Einstein (1879–1955) said that insanity was to do the exact same thing over and over and hoping for a different outcome.

Some people tend to think too much about the *what if's* of an opportunity rather than asking themselves *what if I stick to the status quo?* A German proverb says "von nichts kommt nichts" – from nothing comes nothing. You can translate that into a modern business language by saying that from no input comes no output. It is important to make independent decisions, including the wrong decisions, in order to gain experience and grow as a person. Making mistakes is better than not making anything. The Romans said "errare humanum est" – to err is to be human.

In December of 2005 I became an ex-pat in Brazil. Something I had always wanted: Sent by a company to a foreign country using my expertise to build something new. I moved to São Paulo, a city of 18 million people. Brazilians are among the friendliest and most welcoming people I have met in over 40 countries that I have traveled to. I was able to make long-lasting friendships, travel to interesting places, learn fluent Portuguese and create fantastic memories. I went to countless beaches, spent carnival in Brazil, saw the rain forest. It's a diverse and fascinating place.

As much fun as my life in Brazil was, so was my job. Building up the business from scratch on a whole continent was a very rewarding sensation filled with a feeling of accomplishment. I felt like a pioneer. I was wearing many hats, from the legal aspects of doing local business as a foreign company to elaborate and execute a channel strategy, creating technology partnerships and localizing marketing content. On a daily basis I spoke Spanish and Portuguese with business partners, while communicating back to Finland and the United States. Think global, act local! I was there: I was living the international career that I had dreamed of. It felt great.

Unfortunately it wasn't about to last long. I thought I was on a high-speed career train while doing what I enjoyed. Soon my new boss reeled me back into the corporate line. As if he had unwillingly agreed on his first week on the job, to send me to South America, the support I had received had been half-hearted from the beginning. Only half a year later, as my work started to bear fruits, my manager suggested that I could be moving to the Unites States and join the North American sales team, while continuing to work with South America remotely. I had wanted to stay longer in Brazil, but the corporate strategy was elsewhere and there wasn't enough room for what I wanted anymore. Or maybe it had never really been there, I wondered? As I learned that the days in São Paulo were numbered, I was between leaving the company on a 2nd try and return to Finland or to gamble again. As I realized the 2nd time around that what I wanted didn't matter too much, my loyalty towards Digital Chocolate was winding down. I didn't feel like I would ever get out of the sales role into managing a territory for real and building a team. After only six months of business development on an entire continent, they wanted me to go back to manage key accounts? That was not a career plan to me.

It was the moment I came to believe that I may not have been sent abroad for my skills alone, but much rather because the CEO had wanted to stop the leaking of good employees from Digital Chocolate to Rovio. That realization felt like betrayal. Niccolo Machiavelli (1469–1527) stated in his famous work *The Prince* that "a prince never lacks legitimate reason to break his promises."[5] My ex-boss had only helped me to help himself, not because he cared for the market entry in South America or my career.

He helped me to help himself. This was *the* key understanding of my back analysis. And quite useful for the future, since that's not an isolated case in the world. Essentially the company, more specific, the decision makers made my ex-pat tenure in Brazil happen because of themselves. Out of a mixture of emotion, business rational, and cold calculus in presence of a competitor that attracted the company's personnel. In that moment my skills and experience were merely needed to justify the decision, not the cause of it. It was when opportunity met preparation. This was what I needed to replicate in the future.

---

5 MACHIAVELLI, N. (1532), CHAPTER 18

I decided to gamble again. Instead of moving to the company's headquarters in the Silicon Valley I made a case for myself to move to New York City. In my head it was only a matter of time until I'd leave Digital Chocolate for real, so I wanted to see how much I could squeeze out. The best arguments I had were the time difference to my Canadian customer in the north, my Latino customers in the South and only 7 instead of 10 hours difference to Finland. I still needed to work a lot with engineers there, which would have made my life very tedious working from the West Coast of the United States. This argument worked and I could enjoy a once-in-a-lifetime opportunity to be part of the hustle and bustle of the Big Apple. The instrumental value of New York would be to highlight it later in my curriculum. Everyone loves New York, putting it into your life's story will get attention. I promise. And nobody ever regrets having that experience.

In October of 2006 I moved to the Big Apple and it took still one year until the company unsurprisingly began to decline: Too little time was spent on making things work, too many chiefs and too few Indians tried to keep the tribe going. Successful businesses spend less than 20% on strategy and over 80% on execution. In sales & marketing the company spend 80% in micromanaging and keeping people from being able to execute their jobs. At the time when a start-up requires manager's approval to send a customer a 20$ t-shirt, a company scrutinizes anything that draws people to work in emerging companies. Many people are attracted to startups by the idea that you spend more time on real work and you are hired to get things done. My assessment was that some people wanted to play big company with a startup that needed less rather than more processes. Throughout the year 2007 the company lagged behind its revenue goals and the Venture Capital investors demanded action. Tens of millions had been invested, however when former middle management people from large corporations get senior positions with high salaries, the outcome can be predicted. Running a big company culture in a small business is an early symptom that you are set up for failure. One example to prove this may be that the people who had made the greatest games and build up the business prior to the Silicon Valley take-over were Ilkka Paananen and Mikko Kodisoja. These two had moved on and together-er with a known team they built a billion dollar company, Supercell. Meanwhile Digital Chocolate had closed its doors. It was Ilkka's and Mikko's talent to create great products and great business acumen to meet the trend on the market. When others with lack of integrity and leadership skill took over the self-inflicted wounds led to self-destruction.

In that moment when I was amongst the crowd that were let go I felt relief. The micro-management was driving me nuts and I had only been hanging in there for the money and because New York was fun. The company had no future, I had no future, and I could only learn how not to run a business if anything. This was another light bulb moment: I was there for Sex and the City, not for the job. In other words I was treading water.

Nelson Mandela (1918–2013) believed that life wasn't a matter of how often we fall, but how often we get back up again. It was the winter of 2007, I was back in Finland and my friend Lie and I sat at dinner at La Famiglia. We thought back on what had happened, what it meant to us, how we reacted and what we had learned from it. The 2nd time being a job-seeker in Finland it only took a few weeks to find a new job. While I had been in the Americas, Lie had left Rovio. It had been more of the same for him. For a while the new job was fun, but then again not so much had changed for him. He had sold products to the same customers in Asia Pacific as before, just under a new name. Very often companies make a job "sound very interesting" only to have you do the same job, just for a little more money and the promise of a great future. It was proof enough for me that it was good not to go for Rovio when I had the chance, though I felt bad for Lie who seemed disappointed.

The next lesson learned was: Company's hire you to do the same you already do elsewhere. Some companies offer you a fancier title if you are willing to put on with the same job for a little longer. Taking the better title can help you to find a better job somewhere else since you are able to sell yourself as a more senior person then.

After a year and a half in Brazil and the United States I had not gained as much responsibility as I had hoped for and was promised when I shook hands with my previous team administrator. I did get the extra experience and all of the good things that come along with being an ex-pat. Yet, in terms of career I was very hungry and willing to aim much higher. I wanted to believe that there was a path for me.

Yet, in that sobering learning moment after the rise and fall within Digital Chocolate I felt like Dr. Faustus in Johann Wolfgang von Goethe's (1749–1832) masterpiece *Faust*. In his famous play the main protégé starts his appearance by sitting restless at his desk in his study:

"I have, alas! Philosophy, Medicine, Jurisprudence too,
And to my cost Theology,
With ardent labour, studied through.
And here I stand, with all my lore,
Poor fool, no wiser than before."[6]

This hits the nail on the head. I had studied a lot, learned a lot, worked hard, voiced what I was striving for, won some battles, got what I wanted, only to be put back into place and lastly ended up with a lay-off notice. Thanks for nothing.

Three years at Digital Chocolate and I had to start over again. So there Lie and I sat together over dinner, going over the challenges of being overqualified, under challenged, and pigeon-holed, and as a foreigner in a different country. We spoke of entrepreneurship, leadership, common beliefs of career advancement, meaningful work, and hierarchies. Two young people with a completely different background, but similar attitudes and hopes for life. Lie had left his job at Digital Chocolate to find himself with more of the same, yet some Angry Bird shares that might be worth something one day. I had gambled and received what I wanted, then again I didn't. In the back analysis that I did through our conversations at our weekly dinners, it

---

6 GOETHE, J. W. VON (1808), NIGHT

became clear to me that the events that happened included a certain pattern of human behavior. Things that we said and did triggered specific reactions. I believed that there must be a way to theoretically replicate what happened, and codify it into a handbook. This was how the idea of this book was born. Lie encouraged me to put my thought process into writing, and make a book out of it. The initial thought for this book was quite simple:

- Reason #4 why people leave their jobs, that if you don't see a future path, you will take destiny into your own hands.
- Kairos: how to recognize and seize a window of opportunity.
- How to escape irrationality and execute your career plan from the bottom up.

It turned into something far more complex. I spent the following seven years studying, thinking, discussing and writing this book. You have to read books to write books. From the initially simple idea of making a strategy book on how to make your way up, I jumped from reading one book to the next, indulging ancient philosophy and history, game theory, military strategy and diplomatic negotiations, conversation and rhetoric, sharpening my mind through martial arts, lots of traveling and observing the behavior of people, especially in the office environment. The initial simple question on how to make your way up had turned into a much broader and existential question:

How to live free in a corporate world? How can I make a career and do a meaningful job without having to sell out?

Life is more complex than the usual self-help book tries to make it out to be. Written from the perspective of the employer, the mainstream literature regarding career and success focuses too much on climbing ladders and how to impress leaders and hiring managers. This perspective from the top of an organization has no basis in reality. This view is strengthened by a celebrity culture in which quick success is celebrated as the common goal of any member in society. Under the assumption that everyone is striving for money and power, it oversimplifies the reality of our common goal down to a few steps. It boils down to the idea that by imitating the behavior of successful people, life would all come together. It assumes that the world of business is purely rational: the harder you work, the further you get. That leads to the belief that people who are on top of the hierarchy must be smarter and have worked harder. The ones below are in the need of guidance and still have to work more to be eligible for higher tasks. The irrationalities and illogical behavior you can see in reality are proof that this assumption cannot be upheld. And most of all: How can that help you in your own individual situation? If you only learn to use a hammer out of your toolbox you will soon see a nail in every problem.

Real life has shown me many times that skill alone is not sufficient to climb the ladder, and money is not the single driver of motivation. The pursuit of happiness and the aim to reach the level of your competence is.

In our situation with Lie our complex wish lists seemed like mission impossible: We both dreamed of a meaningful career, get paid what we deserve, earn the responsibilities that match our abilities and get challenged to the fullest extent. And to top it up we were both thinking about relocating again. Lie considered moving to Singapore, I was thinking about how to go to New York for a second round. The quest was how to get it all. Some people are quick on saying that you might be dreaming a little big. Henry Ford's (1863–1947) answer is that "it's better to try and fail than fail to try". To achieve greatness one has to be a dreamer. Otherwise you may be too scared by the size of the challenge you are about to take.

Decisions for life, liberty and the pursuit of happiness can be complex and have many operational and emotional impacts, and they depend heavily on the individual circumstances. Many times there are interdependencies with your life outside of work that affect your decisions. Single with a small rental apartment or married with kids and your spouse back in school? You would like to switch to a great job, but it pays less than you need. Decisions that affect your career also affect your entire life and often cannot be made in isolation. Career steps are not solely based on improving skills and working hard, but always goes hand in hand with other aspects of life and personal aspirations.

Life's purpose cannot be about money and promotions: Money is a mean and a job title is static and descriptive. Money doesn't have intrinsic value and can therefore not be the goal itself, but only a warmly welcomed side effect of success. Money has erroneously become a measurement of how much someone has "made it" in life. In the search for social approval, success is a façade behind which some people want to hide. Looking at the profile and background pictures of some social media presence, you often get to see beaches, mountains, and endless horizons with beautiful landscapes. They are the dream pictures, an outcry of the hope for a happy life and the space to move freely. At the same time the frequent updating of selfies having cocktails with good looking people and "checking in" to a fancy restaurant for everyone to follow over the Internet is only feeding into the rat race that burns everyone out.

The need for money has to be seen in correlation to what you need it for. The common self-help career advisory makes the wrong assumption about life goals and in the consequence gives the wrong advice.

We need a Neo-Renaissance with humanistic thinking and a rediscovery of ancient Greek and Roman teachings. In today's globally interconnected human society with an unpredictable economy, we should take a moment to think about whether what we are doing serves a real purpose. Aristotle (4th century B.C.) said over two thousand years ago:

"Happiness is the meaning and the purpose of life, the whole aim and end of human existence".

What has Aristotle's definition of "living well" to do with chasing the money carrot? Living well according to Aristotle does not mean in the first place to be well off financially, like having a house, a car and a big pay check. Living well is to be understood as a non-static attitude or activity. The good life is led by constant proficiency of living a life of practical reason and to live it consistently. Happiness is not a constant state of affairs, but a being-able-to-be-happy-with-oneself. I doubt that Aristotle meant by this a constant status-update on social media aiming to get a bunch of people giving you a virtual thumbs up.

We need practical liberty!

Practical liberty is the application of a concept of freedom into a strategic and tactical path to happiness and success; to build a bridge between what great thinkers of all times have expressed through philosophy and make it practical. It means to apply philosophical teachings, liberty and personal freedom into everyday life; applying the idea of living well to a daily routine. That is the quest of making philosophy work in reality.

"Know thyself" the Oracle of Delphi[7] said. To find out who you are, what makes you happy and live according to that is the quest for a successful life. Greek philosophy teaches us to appreciate our lives by reminding us about its finiteness and humans' unique capability to truly live a happy life. Animals live to eat and not get eaten, and to reproduce in order to secure the survival of their species. To work like a horse, buy a house and buy all the things society expects me to have only to send my children through the same cookie-cutter path through life doesn't differ much to the life of an animal. Doing something meaningful is what can make your life more human, something that you do for your own personal reasons, something that makes you happy in absence of everyone else, and that is unique to yourself. This will lead to real happiness and success.

One day during my time in a large corporation I lead a conference call with about a dozen participants on the call. I tried to discuss new joint business opportunities with the alliance partner and initiate the execution of some ideas. One person said: "Well, in this group I don't think we are capable of making this decision." I answered that I truly believe to be capable of making this decision, only that we are not entitled to do so. Dead silence followed for several seconds which felt like hours. Everyone knew I was right, but just didn't want to say

---

7 Delphi was the seat of the most important Greek temple and oracle of Apollo. The Delphic oracle was consulted on private matters and state affairs in ancient Greek times until the 6th century B.C.. See ENCYCLOPAEDIA BRITANNICA, DELPHI

anything in respect to hierarchy and obedience. This type of life could certainly not be the goal, if the only condolence for it was money.

As I was thinking about my career one of the imminent questions was: Why does it matter to me? Money and job title, and good looking resumes, what are those good for? To impress people maybe? I like to travel and I need money for that. I like to use *all* of *my skills. I want to be empowered to make decisions based on *my* reasoning. I don't want to waste my time creating presentations to get approval to obtain permission to do what I knew a long time ago had to be done. In addition I want to be paid what I am worth. I want to receive my pay for the value I provide to someone else and not as compensation for pain in a job that I dread going to. I don't want to enslave myself for my paycheck trying to convince myself that this would be how the world is meant to be.

Too many people buy things they don't want with money they don't have to impress people they don't like. Spending habits can force you to do a job that you don't like. Most people have the same disposable income at the end of each month, regardless of its size. Pay-raise and buy-raise often go hand in hand. With more income people also spend more, live in a larger place, upgrade their vacation, their car, and their food. Being able to afford things is nice, but having your entire salary budgeted out to fixed costs takes away your ability to move to other jobs if they don't pay you the same or more than you are already making. You might be forced to turn a job down even if you think that it would be what you would like to do. Expensive habits can create dependency. Add credit cards and other debt to the game and sweep away labor protection legislation, and you have a society of dependent citizens. Making money for something should be a joy and not a necessity for having overburdened yourself in which selling your soul to the devil is the only way to get out. I had to learn that the hard way myself.

Shouldn't this be common sense? It is unfortunate as Voltaire (1694–1778) noted that "common sense is not very common". In a celebrity culture in which quick money and access to more consumption is seen as an equivalent to a happy life, living within one's means might represent less quality of life than society expects from successful people. This explains why millions of people are willing to live above their means for a false sense of happiness today and the continuous obligation to pay for it in the future. Pay for it not with money only, but pay for it by having to work somewhere even if you hate it. Only to pay for things that were supposed to make you happy, or maybe just get you *likes*?

To be poor is no fun, but the opposite of being poor is more than just to have money. Benjamin Franklin (1706–1790) said that "a rich man is often just a poor man with a lot of money." When you know thyself, and have a found a way of life that you want to lead and you know what means you need to accomplish that, money starts to have actual value and the making of it becomes the making of the means instead of an end.

Personal freedom and independence are prerequisites of happiness. The more we try to live other people's lives or to get their approval for ours, the more we follow a trajectory of an empty promise for success, the less our lives become self-driven and born out of our own will. We end up spending our entire life pleasing the expectations of others and lose to be ourselves. If you aren't yourself, then how can *you* be happy at all?

Nothing has distracted me more on an everyday basis than the constant thought around the question of what liberty means in a corporate world. Jean-Jacques Rousseau (1712–1778) said:

"Man is born free, yet everywhere he is in chains." Rousseau continued: "One thinks himself the master of others, and still remains a greater slave then they. As long as people is compelled to obey, and obeys, it does well; as soon as it can shake off the yoke, and shakes it off, it does still better; for, regaining its liberty by the same right as took it away."

Rousseau believed that right is founded on conventions. If everyone is born free and equal, then people alienate their liberty only for their own advantage. And the strongest is never strong enough to be always the master, unless he transforms strength into right, and obedience into duty. Rousseau emphasizes, that "to yield to force is an act of necessity, not of will – at the most, an act of prudence. In what sense can it be duty?"[8]

---

8 ROUSSEAU, J.-J. (1762), Chapter I and III

If *this is how the world is* and *this is what you have to do to get by* are my actions then born out of my free will?

It seems like many employers think that they can do anything they want, because they pay for it. And employees are willing to just accept anything, because they need the money. I get the sensation that society is always willing to accept anything for just buzzwords including "business needs", "good for the economy", "shareholder value", "the global competition". Under the disguise of looking for the best future outcome you can do almost anything. And people eat out of your hands.

I was neither born into a rich family, nor did I go to an elite University that came with an alumni network that would kick start my career four levels higher than the average persons. I enjoyed free public education in Germany, applied for and was granted a scholarship for living expenses and study material. The scholarship granted by the Friedrich Naumann Foundation for Freedom also included financing of a year and a half of studying abroad, which I spend at the Universidad Nacional de Córdoba in Argentina. I built up my own network, I worked and studied a lot, and I was always driven to be self-reliant. Even while I was still a student I ran for public office in Frankfurt, and continued a full-time curriculum while serving in the City Council. I certainly wasn't lazy and I felt that I was successful on a personal level until I encountered the realities of a corporate life. Many of the things that mattered to me and that I was proud of didn't count to others. All a company cared was if I had the particular skill they were looking for. Work didn't feel to be mutually beneficial early on.

Over the years my approach to career development shaped into defining the starting point for all career related actions by the kind of life I want to lead and use this as a basis for decisions. You can call this applied enlightenment. If I spend at least half of my awake time every day at work, it is worth filling that time with something meaningful. This requires to detach from social expectations in order not to drive into a default future, out of personal control. Building and executing a personal strategy is based on a vision for a lifestyle and then breaking it down to the world as his in order to derive tangible actions from that. The way to get where one wants happens by taking the world as it is, especially anticipated human behavior and ways on influencing third party decisions and steering fate into your favor. Applying game theory, a sub discipline of economic sciences, and complementing it with the principles of the art of war, gets one further than trying to impress managers. Saying yes to everything or hope for good feedback for a resume is not a way to be in control of one's own future.

Many people have the same desires and similar aspirations, but different ways and opportunities to achieve them. There is no one perfect way, but a combination of the truth of your circumstances and finding the best way to deal with life as it happens.

Cervantes said: "Life is a chess game." Let's play chess. This strategic board game is about a thousand years old, while other more simple versions of this popular game were already played by Celtic, Germanic and Viking people between the 4th and 12th century A.D. called *tafl* or *hnfatafl*. Strategy games like chess are often the object of research, most notably in game theory.

To win a chess game a player elaborates a strategy that anticipates the opponents actions and reactions, and by a series of moves that forces this strategy onto the opponent. A good chess player can entice the opponent to make certain moves by thinking three steps ahead and distracting from his real intentions. A good player does this by thinking like the opponent and seeing the other one's alternatives from their perspective. Focusing on the outcome the moves on the chess board aim to lead the opponent to act in a certain way that allows to ultimately set him check mate, where he has no other options left but to accept his defeat.

According to Dale Carnegie (1888–1955) the best way to make someone do something is to make him want to do it. This advice has universal character and isn't exclusive for leaders on how to manage their subordinates. This also applies to your manager or investor alike: make them want to do it. Instead of pleasing others and doing what they say in the hopes for raise and promotions, I want to get out of the suppliant-thinking and take the bull by its horn and deal with challenges like a (chess) player rather than through sacrifice and prayer. To face any challenge, stand up and get on eye-level with it. There will always be third parties that will have influence over your life in one way or the other. But they are also just human beings with very natural human desire and behavior. Shaking off the yoke of self-imposed immaturity and putting a plan into action that imposes your strategy on the opponent are two parts of the same coin.

In 2007, shortly after Digital Chocolate made me redundant, I started in a new global business development role with Savox Communications, back in Finland. From the beginning it was my goal to gain another assignment in New York City at some point. This time it wasn't for being an ex-pat, but to be back with my girlfriend, Meredith, who I had met in the big apple. Since it wasn't planned as a time limited ex-pat agreement, but as a continuation of my career, I needed to get a promotion as well. How could I convince my employer to send me abroad? The starting point was to analyze the situation that had led Digital Chocolate to send me to Brazil, all while adhering to Sun Tzu wise words:

"Do not repeat the tactics that have gained you one victory, but let your method be regulated by the infinite variety of circumstances."

The events that happened at Digital Chocolate were circumstantial, but I was convinced that by thorough analysis I could elaborate a replicable methodology.

My plan was successful and In 2009 I relocated to New York again, Meredith and I got married. Since success did not last as long as I had hoped, life's rollercoaster took us to Austin, Texas until early 2014. After three years in a large corporation I took a voluntary separation package from Dell. We moved to Boston, where I finally started my own company, initially wanting to compete with Savox which then turned into something much bigger and better. The experiences since my conversations in the La Famiglia restaurant in 2007 until today have come to a book that turned out to be a work in progress and the study and work to write it has changed my own life in the same way as the book itself has been changing over the years. While this book is part of me and uses my experience to explain this approach to life and career, this book is not about me. It is my contribution to a discussion about work and life in the 21st century.

1 THE DIVISION OF LABOR

"If you know the enemy and know yourself,
you need not fear the result of a hundred battles."

SUN TZU (5TH CENTURY B.C.)

Quality prevails, but not whatever prevails is therefore of good quality. Talent and hard work are necessary for success, but do not guarantee it. On the flipside people who are successful don't always work hard or have any talent at all. The nature of corporations supports this phenomena.

In 2004 I graduated in Economic Sciences from the Goethe University in Frankfurt, Germany. Aiming to see more of the world, I moved to Finland that same year and started my first job in an international sales role with Digital Chocolate in Helsinki: a growing startup that developed and sold games for mobile phones in the times when there weren't any smartphones yet. A pioneer in it's industry.

Thrown into the cold water I first noticed the gap between theory and practice of economic sciences and the reality of the business world. The corporate world is far less rational as people try to make it look like.

I believe in the theory of a free market, that less regulation can lead to better outcomes for everyone. The economic model of a free market assumes equal distribution of information and rationally acting players. In reality we can observe that neither is the case. This can be considered a market failure.

1

In theory the quality and price of a product should speak for itself and the best product should become a market leader within its segment. Marketing aiming to differentiate your product from that of competitors is filling the gap of the market failure above:

Marketing exists to take advantage of the unequal distribution of information and the irrationality of the players.

Marketing is there to tell a story of a person, a product or company, to appeal to feelings and to create sympathy and identification, for example the coolness of electronic devices or fashionable clothing. It serves customer loyalty and retention. Ultimately the goal of marketing is to generate demand. Marketing can also be used to cover up bad quality for a while. If you discover enough new customers regularly, it may turn into a long term strategy. In case you are a company with a popular brand, you can launch new products or services often enough that the next new gadget is more important to the customers than the flaws of the old one. This way the company keeps making money with products that aren't great, but good enough. To keep up with the competition good enough may be sufficient to stay in business.

Marketing is everything from the company strategy, the product quality, the market positioning and customer service. Marketing is about how you want to be seen by others, how to engage and interact, create brand loyalty and returning customers. Marketing can also be used to distract from facts and make your brand shine in a different light. In a text book Machiavellian style it can be used to create more illusion than reality, blindfolding people by creating much ado about nothing.

This already starts with breakfast: in the cereal isle of a supermarket one can choose between a plethora of colorful boxes with happy people eating breakfast, enhanced with perfectly rendered photographs of deliciously looking morning goodness, decorated with fresh fruit and lots of sunshine. Relaxing or uplifting background music in the supermarket, comfortable lighting and friendly smiling staff will do the rest to make you buy. Only the one who takes the time to look at the ingredients that are written in fine print at an inconvenient location on the box will often discover the amount of unhealthy, cheap ingredients that were used to produce your diabetes enhancing start into the day.

In the micro-economics of companies we notice the same market failures: un-even distribution of information and non-rational acting players. There are a lot of unskilled white collar workers in leading positions. How can that happen? How do some of the smiling cereal boxes full of cheap ingredients make it to the top of the management totem pole? Do they market themselves better? Does sheer boldness lead some people to naturally play the game a little better? Is ignorance a bliss? Do others not see it or get it? Are they innocent bystanders that don't care? Or does nobody dare to look at the backside of someone's personal marketing? How come that even in times of recession people that should be made redundant first, stay in their positions, and others lose their jobs? Why do these people survive and go from one well paid position to the next feeding into the belief that they are so amazing? Possibly because the way the system functions allows for these labor market failures to happen.

Sun Tzu said: "If you know the enemy and know yourself, you need not fear the result of a hundred battles. If you know yourself but not the enemy, for every victory gained you will also suffer a defeat. If you know neither the enemy nor yourself, you will succumb in every battle." Hereby the "enemy" is not any person or institution. I want to use it figuratively as the overall challenge that has to be overcome. In other words, if you want to succeed in your quest you need to know what you are up for.

To be successful we need to understand how organizations function, understand our battlefield. Then we can build a strategy for personal success. How did corporations come about? Looking into the organization and dynamics of corporations we will be able to elaborate a methodology and a plan of action how to use the invisible, unwritten rules in your advantage to build a plan for success.

So what are corporations? Walt Disney (1901–1966) said: "I only hope that we never lose sight of one thing– that it was all started with a mouse."

People generally use the word corporation with a positive or negative undertone depending on what argument they try to make. Corporations are welcomed by local politicians as big employers in their communities. Governments welcome the business and income tax revenues that can be collected. Others, including unions, environmental groups, and certain political movements see corporations as institutions that exploit labor or threaten the environment. Small businesses can see them as their largest customers or their fiercest competitors. For individuals to be part of a corporation can mean a variety of things ranging from regular income, status or being part of something big. Many people dream of a job in a big corporation, especially if their products are fancy and cool. To form a part of a corporation can also be felt as an evil necessity in order to pay ones' bills. The reasons why people love or hate corporations and why they feel good or bad about working for one, is endless. Any company though, large or small, started with one person or a small group of people who decided to start a business. Even if it was simply drawing a cartoon of a mouse.

Not every inventor is a business man and not every business man knows how to invent things. A butcher who makes the most popular sausages in the neighborhood can be a successful small business person as a sole entrepreneur throughout his whole life. The butcher aiming to become a business magnate with a sausage factory and nationwide distribution will need more than sausage making skills. The necessity to find experts in specific disciplines of business are therefore part of any growing business. The development and growth of a company then, affects the individuals' roles and responsibilities and lay the ground for corporate politics.

On January 29th 1886 the German entrepreneur Karl Benz was granted a patent called "automobile fueled by gas" for his invention of the "Motorwagen", the world's first car. In 1926 Benz' company merged with Gottlieb Daimler's which then formed what is known worldwide as Mercedes Benz. In 2014 the corporation employed 279,972 people worldwide and earner revenues of €129,9 billion (around US$157 billion).[9]

---

9 DAIMLER AG (2014), ANNUAL REPORT

How does such a growth come about that creates a multi-billion corporation? In the process from a small to becoming a big company big tasks are broken down into many small ones. Then enough people are hired for each group of tasks to scale it to an enormous size. Only the division of labor can enable that something that started with one single invention turns into a worldwide operation. Dividing the production of goods into a step by step manufacturing process, and eventually elaborating the assembly line combined with the opening of new markets, was the tipping point for manufacturing of goods that enabled the exponential economic growth starting over 200 years ago. It represents the foundation of how large corporations came about.

The First Industrial Revolution was initiated in Britain in the years 1760 to 1830 and spread from there to other countries in the world: a multi-faceted change in economic activity that was made possible by the invention of machinery, the division of labor and access to new markets worldwide. With a world that had changed its face, the ground was set for more personal freedom, entrepreneurship and industrial growth. The industrial revolution was a true revolution, because the changes were not decided by an institution or government, they were driven by groups and individuals who explored, invented, innovated and changed the way we manufacture and sell goods. And an ever growing class of people forming the demand have led to the world's economy as we know it today.

In 1775, Adam Smith (1723–1790), Scottish moral philosopher and often seen as the "inventor" of modern economic sciences, published an *Inquiry into the Nature and Causes of the Wealth of Nations.* Two and a half centuries later it hasn't lost any of its remarkable character.

Smith believed in the "invisible hand" that guides an economic system based on individual self-interest.[10] His theory states that economic self-interest benefits society, leading people to put labor into their businesses, creating wealth for the entire society. Smith empha-

---

10 ENCYCLOPAEDIA BRITANNICA, SMITH, ADAM

sizes that the main cause for economic growth lies in in the division of labor.

The Wealth of Nations starts with Smith's famous passage describing the work flow of a pin maker: "A workman not educated to this business, nor acquainted with the use of machinery employed in it, could perhaps make one pin in a day, and certainly could not make twenty." Through the division of labor, Smith continues, the making of a pin can be divided into a number of specialized tasks, including drawing out the wire, straightening it, cutting, then pointing it and ultimately grinding the wire at the top for receiving the head. Smith says that the making of a pin in this manner, can be divided into 18 distinct operations: "I have seen a small manufactory of this kind, where ten men only were employed, and where some of them consequently performed two or three distinct operations…those ten persons, therefore, could make among them upwards of forty-eight thousand pins in a day." Smith concludes that "in every other art and manufacture, the effects of the division of labor are similar to what they are in this very trifling one, though, in many of them, the labor can neither be so much subdivided, nor reduced to so great a simplicity of operation. The division of labor, however, so far as it can be introduced, occasions, in every art, a proportionable increase of the productive powers of labor." According to Smith, the great increase in the quantity of work are based on three circumstances:

1. The increase of dexterity in every particular workman.
2. The time that is saved that is usually lost in passing from one type of work to another.
3. The invention and use of machines that enable one person to do the work of many. [11]

Before there was money, value had to be created through labor. "Every man is considered rich or poor depending to the degree in

---

11 SMITH, A. (1776), BOOK I, CHAPTER I

which he can afford to enjoy the necessaries, conveniences, and amusements of human life." Smith says. "However, after the division of labor has taken place, he can only produce a limited amount of the needed goods on his own and is relying on the work of others. Therefore a man is rich or poor depending on how much of his own work he can exchange for the needed goods or how much he can afford to obtain from others." Smith concludes that "labor was the first price, the original purchase – money that was paid for all things." Wealth, is therefore allowing a rich person to purchase command over other men's labor or the product of other men's labor.[12]

Money by itself doesn't mean power, but it can be converted into such. If you are in possession of monetary means that allow to invest in machinery you can convert that into power over people since everyone needs money to at least a minimum degree. The need for money and the little options for self-sufficiency is creating dependency. The larger the dependency on money becomes for a person, the easier it is to put the carrot in front of him. In that sense the day laborer or the white collar worker who is up to his ears in personal debt for living beyond his means, are equally dependent on the good will of the ones with money. This is how money can be converted into power and force others to work to pay for a living. The stress that one feels about their job can therefore also be felt as politics and conspiracy from others, but in reality it can be a home-made depression for knowing about one's dependency on regular income. Personal spending habits and social pressure can convert work's purpose increasingly and possibly solely into the source of income, rather than a place of personal challenge and learning. A place where the results of one's work lead to personal satisfaction and a sense of accomplishment: to feel good about yourself and proud of you work! Over consuming can force people even more into a quest to find increased income, instead of finding meaningful work.

In a nation of hunters, which Smith calls the lowest and rudest state of society, "every man is a warrior as well as a hunter". A warrior,

---

12 SMITH, A. (1776), BOOK I, CHAPTER V

at home or at war, maintains himself by his own labor.[13] The warrior is able to do anything on his own that he needs for a living, even if that is a primitive state of living by today's standards. Later when people settled as farmers they produced what they had to eat, they built their own house, raised animals and knew how to build and use very basic tools. Everyone had to know a little bit of everything in order to get by. In this sense an early stage startup entrepreneur has something of the early days farmer, combined with the spirit of a hunter: building on what he knows and looking for new opportunities.

Assuming there would be enough land and labor available a farmer could expand his self-sufficient existence into an agricultural business by cultivating more land with more people. With the extra labor basically paying itself through the increased income, the farmer can use the profits to build up capital that allows him to purchase machinery, silos and cooling systems and improved ways of transportation. Now add to that external effects that can benefit the farmer if he knows to take advantage of them. For example with the help of the discovery from Louis Pasteur (1822–1895) who developed the method of pasteurization, named after him, the farmer can preserve i.e. dairy products and prevent food-borne diseases. Excess milk can now be produced and stored. The opportunity to cool the products increases the radius to which the milk, cheese and yogurt can be delivered to. It's no longer farm-to-market, but farm-to-nationwide. In addition to the dairy products the new farm corporation can also start farming other products including wheat, hops, barley and potatoes. The wheat can be the basis for bread and other baked goods. Hops and barley are used to brew beer, potatoes are grown as animal food for pig farms and cow dung is distributed as fertilizer. And maybe the left over grains from the beer brewing process are used to bake high-end dog treats.

Now the corporation is involved in production and distribution of primary nutrition goods (dairy), value added products (bread & beer)

---

13 SMITH, A. (1776), BOOK V, CHAPTER I

a supplier for other farmers (animal food and fertilizer) and special-ty retail products (dog treats for pet stores). Any of these different business units are serving a different market with its own competi-tive environment, meeting different legal requirements, and different volatilities of prices. While a primary good like milk is depending on market prices, value added products, like beer or dog treats, can follow its own pricing strategy depending on product marketing. Beer can be sold as a mass market refreshment at a cheaper price or as a specialty brew for selected retail stores only. A simple farming opera-tion has then turned into a corporate business. It requires an increased specialization of the work force and a high division of labor: farming operations, machinery purchase and maintenance, warehousing, lo-gistics, finance, sales, marketing, legal, research & development. All of a sudden most people in this farming business don't have anything to do with the actual product, but rather with the handling of the business operations around it.

Just walk into the cereal aisle in a supermarket and ask yourself if the designer of a Corn Flakes package has actually ever seen the place where the corn is harvested and processed?

This imaginary example shows how the division of labor, inven-tion of machinery, discoveries in micro-biology and chemistry, such as innovation in the production process can lead to exponential growth of a business and how this growth requires an increasingly specialized work force.

We can conclude it with Walt Disney's words: it all started with a cow.

As a company grows from a single person craftsmanship or a small group of entrepreneurs, the venture goes through different stages. Initially everyone has to wear many hats. In a small company there are only a few processes, everyone knows what anyone else is doing. The level of specialization is still a little vague and every member has to take more ownership of his work. If something is going really well or really bad, it's easy to praise or blame the right person. In other words, in a small operation there is no room for slackers, everyone is put to work, but the success is shared and each member of the team can proudly point to his or her own product of labor and part of the success.

When a company grows you can't do everything on your own anymore. You need to hire people for tasks that you either aren't as good at, have no time for anymore, or need help to meet the growing demand. Instead of having a handful of people in your workshop you might need 20–30 or maybe 100 in a small factory. This also means that these people have to be managed and supervised. Once you are not able to manage the people on your own time anymore, someone else has to be hired just to be a people's manager. That is how middle management was born. There are two ways to make one the middle-manager. You can either pick one from the team and make that person the new leader or you hire someone from outside for that task. If you can still have the time to choose that person yourself, you can determine who you want to hire in terms of personality and experience. Once the business is very big an HR department will be established that will receive hiring guidelines. In a next step they will develop their own life and make their own rules. With each step in growth of a company it is getting more complex, workforce will get more specialized, the number of tasks that each employee has to fulfill will get smaller and with it the individual's ownership of the whole will decrease. With ownership in the above sense is meant the possibility to see one's own input into the whole enterprise, rather than a stake in equity.

Karl Marx (1818–1883) called this the *Entfremdung*, in his theory of alienation. One may have different opinions on Marx' conclusions, but his description of the alienation of the worker is remarkably precise: The worker doesn't own the product of his labor, it doesn't belong to him, but to someone else. The task itself is not a natural task that somehow belongs to the worker himself and therefore feels like an alien being to him. Stamping envelopes for example, or booking meeting rooms. Therefore the task itself cannot satisfy any of the workers' desires, other than providing the means to satisfy other desires, outside of what is being done as work. In absence of the necessity for the workman's compensation, the worker would "run away from it like from the black plague".[14] Although Marx is referring to the classic blue collar worker in a factory, in today's corporate world, white collar workers have similar sentiments with regards to this alienation. Most people I know do not consider themselves anything close to being a Marxist, including myself. However, I have met countless people who use the term work-life-balance in this exact meaning: You do a job that you don't like very much in order to pay for the things you do like. And upon asking them what they'd do in case they won the lottery, they'd all quit. Personal and emotional aspects can add to the alienation and demotivation. Maybe you were finally assigned to the job you always wanted only to realize that the grass wasn't much greener; maybe you do not get the needed resources to do your job or you experience a micro-managing boss that drives you insane.

No money can compensate for a job you hate.

Love for a job comes through the sense of ownership and the feeling of pride for the results of your work. Finding a job that gives you that sense of accomplishment and the ability to use and expand all your skills, in a highly specialized labor market, is the main challenge for a successful career.

In large corporations you can notice that the ones who have real responsibility and accountability for a particular product or service are usually the ones who actually work and who are also more satisfied with their job. For example a product line manager who overviews all sports car sales for a car-maker or the marketing manager who is in charge of all electric appliances for a particular territory or an engineer who is testing and approving wireless devices. Whenever the job is tangible and their work counts and they have decision power over their own job, people are happier. As soon as you make people simple order takers the motivation of employees cannot be held up for a long time, not even with money. Once you surpass that tipping point it's all politics. Politics of the people who want to get promotions and

---

14 MARX, K. (1844)

politics of the people who do no work, but try to portray themselves as busy and important.

Adam Smith's and Karl Marx's observations are complementary. The division of labor, improvement of production methods and access to new markets has brought the biggest economic growth and opportunities ever seen in human history. Simultaneously growth comes at the cost of many people doing only one particular task, being one pinion in the clockwork without being able to take ownership of the product as a whole. Through the Industrial Revolution rural craftsmen became urban factory workers in assembly lines. In analogy, in today's white collar factories many jobs are executing specific tasks day in and day out which leads to the dynamic on the labor market where people are looking for new jobs every day, hoping to find something more interesting, more meaningful or at least better paid.

How can it happen that you are qualified for many tasks, but only get to do a fraction of what you are capable of?

In 2004, when I interviewed in Helsinki in Finland for the job at Digital Chocolate, the company was looking for a sales person who was fluent in German. The fact that I also speak several other languages was almost worrisome for them. During the process the HR manager sent me to a friend of hers to interview me in Spanish. Her friend was also working in HR, but at a different company. The purpose of this interview, as the HR manager later even admitted, wasn't to see whether I am actually fluent in Spanish or not, but to see behind my real motivations. Digital Chocolate was worried I could only use the new job as a platform to get somewhere else. In the interview conducted in Spanish, the interviewer mostly asked me about whether I could see myself living in Barcelona or how I feel about working at a big well-known company. It was a little too obvious to fall for it. But certainly it showed me that they were worried I might not stay long enough. The battles for a career path that I fought with Digital Chocolate later, reinforced the impression that their sole interest was to pick one out of the many skills they needed, rather than hiring me for my potential or a possible long-term career.

It helps to see through the eyes of the HR manager on what they are supposed to screen for rather than trying to sell all you have to offer. You will always hear generic questions like: "Tell me about yourself? Where do you see yourself in 5 years? Why are you interested in this position? How can your past experience help you with the job we are hiring for? Tell me about how you turned around a difficult situation in your old job?" The questions are always the same, so it is quite easy to prepare: Practice your elevator pitch and resume in front of the mirror; have the soundbites ready that tell your story. This usually gets you through round one.

The bait has to taste to the fish, not to the fisherman. Give the HR person something they are enticed to take.

This is derived from a compromise that finding what you are good at or would love to do has to be matched with the reality of what jobs are available. Companies offer you what you already have or seek to hire you for one or two particular skills. If you happen to find the job that you would like to do, the chances that they hire you for it are subject to what your previous tasks have been. And those are compared to other people applying for the same position. You apply for what you would like to do in the future. Companies hire you for what you have done in the past. The constant need to fill positions and comparing the needed skills with resumes presented by candidates is the common practice.

This desire to compare apples to apples is the biggest reason for misallocation of resources.

The origins of these static hiring processes lie in the division of labor and has become part of people's DNA to put everyone into boxes depending on their previous work experience. The division of labor leads to specialization and specialization leads to comparability. If you have too many or too few skills, you don't fit. That's the dilemma.

People who are all-rounders and can do anything often have the hardest time finding a job, because they don't fit any specific requirements. Specialized people often enjoy more job security, but might get stuck in a job they don't like.

If you have been in one position for very long or extremely good at doing your job, chances are your employer will not want you to move on to other tasks. It's for their own sake, they need your job to get done and you fulfill the needed task so well.

When one doesn't get the opportunity to live up to his competencies, people are quickly to blame politics, favoritism, and bad management for it. Most of the time though it has to do with the sheer fact that not all your skills might be needed at that time, or tasks have been divided into so many little pieces and employees are matched to one piece at a time. You are supposed to do *this*, but not *that*, because that's Joe's job.

It can be felt as if *they* would work against you, because they aren't doing enough *for* you. However, maybe there is no demand for everything you have to offer. An even bigger issue is that many companies, instead of taking their employees' concerns serious, they talk about the bright future.

Finding a job is about what a company is hiring for, because they are paying for it. If you want to start at that company, you will have to squeeze yourself into the hole which they have to fill, regardless of all the other talent and expertise you may have.

Economic Sciences call the matching process for open positions "Signaling & Screening":

The labor market can be divided into companies who have job openings and people who are looking for jobs. Jobs seekers are signaling their availability to work and their related skills, forming the demand for jobs, and the hiring companies, which are screening for candidates with the desired skill set for the open positions they need to fill.

Companies are first and foremost skill-takers, not career-enablers. Many claim to look for self-starters and winners, but in reality they're looking for the best person for one particular open position. You are hired for a task based on how well does your past experience match with job requirements and how likely you are to stay in that position for a long time. In the process of signaling & screening, the HR department is the matchmaker that takes orders from hiring managers that need to hire a person with a specific skill set. HR's task is to find someone as close to provided job description as possible, and yet stands out from the crowd. HR's or a professional recruiter's job is not to find *you* a job, but to present a number of good candidates to the person who pays for it.

In a highly specialized world, how could an HR person know if you are a good chemical engineer, a good software programmer or a creative marketing person? The hiring process has become a match-making of job titles, skills and education based on what is signaled and screened.

Boxes are being checked: How many years' experience in a similar task do you have? How many projects of similar nature have you managed? How long have you worked for a similar company? The apples to apples process often leads to the outcome that the one who prepares for an interview well enough and twists his resume to get the most checked boxes has the best chances to land the job. In addition, once you are in front of a hiring person, it is a lot more about emotion, about how convincing a person can be, how likeable, and how trust-worthy. This also leads to hiring people who are extremely good in an interview situation and can sell themselves well. It is difficult for HR to verify if what people claim that they have done previously is a true statement or if they are taking credit for the team one was part of. It often boils down to some kind of amateur-psychology in which the hiring personnel tries to gain enough evidence to prove that a person is a fit or not.

For the applicants this turns into a race for more qualifications and the constant attempt to stand out, to be special.

Many companies claim to hire top talent for a long term career, but most of them fail to deliver on their promise due to the permanent-imme-diate business needs. That is also the main reason why most applicants for job openings have to twist and tweak their resumes with each application, to make it fit into the few requirements HR departments are sampling for. To make a good impression for a hiring person you have to present yourself as a seasoned professional with a lot of experience, better if decorated with some brand names in your Curriculum Vitae. In the interview you will pretend that from all the things you are good at you just happen to love this one particular thing that a company is hiring for the most. You will say that you are excited and happy to find the match to the biggest of all your skills and interests. What a great co-incidence!

Some people get positions that they aren't fit for and others have to settle for one they are overqualified for. Every players' effort to move on in their career is to overcome the initial dealing of the cards and getting ahead of the game.

The first job is often the one that determines our future steps. The need for an income and the motivation to start working is pushing us to take the first offer we get.

The necessity for candidates to signal their skills to potential employers is enough to feed an entire industry behind it: It ranges from the reputation of your higher education institution and its alumni network, specialized higher education in different fields, post graduate programs, MBA's, professional resume writers, career coaches, head hunter, paid job search websites and expensive job seeker consultants. Everything goes around the idea of signaling to an employer that you are the one they are looking for. It costs a lot of time and money to find a job that pays you good money. Seems illogical.

On the flip side, the opportunities of the Internet have made it possible to apply for any job anywhere. Companies receive way more applications that they could possibly read through. They are faced with the challenge of weeding out and finding a good amount of suitable candidates. Usually this is done through referrals and keyword searches in a resume database.

In 2005, during my first year at Digital Chocolate, I asked for more opportunities and different responsibilities. I did like my job, but I had two reasons to look for the next step:

1. I did not want to get stuck in one job and narrow my future career to only similar jobs.

2. I didn't want to continue working hard only that my supervisor could take credit for my success.

The lack of the future outlook and the not-so-bright one in front of me killed my motivation and drive. This type of situation is very common and leads people to put their efforts to the minimum needed to get by.

Upon raising the issue of new endeavors for me in the future, the HR manager said to me: "But you are a money machine!"

What I could do for them was more important, than what they could do for me. To the company that's not personal, to the person concerned it is. Business is never about you, it's about the business. The overall profit of a company is more important than individual successes. Companies, by nature, follow an economic-utilitarian approach.

Utilitarianism is an ethical theory defining overall happiness as the goal of all action. It is a form of consequentialism, meaning that the moral value of an action is only determined by its resulting outcome:

In utilitarianism the ends justify the means.

The main intention of utilitarianism is called the *maximum-happiness-principle*: all actions should be focusing on maximizing the most possible happiness for the largest amount of people. The utilitarian approach was systematically developed by Jeremy Bentham (1747–1832) and John Stuart Mill (1806–1873). First published in the year of the French revolution 1789, Bentham explains in his *Introduction to the Principles of Morals and Legislation*, that the principle of utility is that any action is measured and valued by its tendency to create happiness of that party. Utility, according to Bentham, is what includes the attributes that allow the creation of wellbeing, advantage, luck, or happiness.[15]

The critique on utilitarianism is that it lacks universalism, because in a society or company, overall happiness can be maximized without

---

15 PETER, F. (1996), P. 16

taking the intrapersonal distribution of happiness into account. Bentham defines human action through the intention to avoid pain and thrive for happiness. However, if for example, a factory significantly increases the weekly work hours of the workers without adequate pay increase, happiness of the workers will go down, while profits go up. Under utilitarian principles, as long as the overall profit, hence the total amount of happiness, will outweigh that, this scenario would still be counted as the maximization of happiness. In today's language this is called shareholder-value. Today, utilitarianism serves as a philosophical base to equalize monetary means with happiness. It also supports lobbyists of supply-side economics and are used as a disguise for trickle-down-theories. These claim that the wealth of the few will eventually trickle down to every member in society. The trickle-down economy is a theory for which scientific proof is still outstanding.

The utilitarian principle can also explain why mediocrity can spread through leadership positions. They may simply not have any other skill and suit a company best at a non-productive task. Maybe everyone else has moved on to do what they are best at and the only one left in the room is assigned to build a new team to replace the old one. At this point that person will be the one with the most experience, solely based on time served. Later in this chapter I will give a mathematical proof for this.

The maximization of the happiness of company owners, shareholder value, is making a company itself the mean to an end. Under this assumption an employee is a utility, a mean to an end, that serves the overall goal of a company. No matter how much a company cares about its employees, the overall profit margin and growth outweigh concern for employee well-being. There are companies that are known for treating their employees very well. However, some of them also constantly lay off people. Being treated well by your employer is not equal to absolute job security.

While I was at Dell between 2011 and 2014, we saw several people with a long tenure at the company let go. Difficult to guess if it was representative enough to prove a point, but it was noticeable how many long-term employees were laid off. A 1st semester finance can explain that:

The key decision driver to make a financial investment is the return on investment at a given calculated risk. The higher the risk of an investment, the more interest an investor will ask for in return. In this calculus, a replaceable employee is a neglectable risk. Salaries in return have an influence on profitability. In a simplified economic model of labor and machinery, the machinery has a set price. At a given output the capital gain becomes a function of the labor costs. If one assumes that anyone could do your job, you can be replaced.

This has been the pressure to keep salaries for unskilled workers at a minimum for centuries. In the early 20th century, Henry Ford did the opposite and introduced the 5$ day. Most factory workers used to earn just over 4$ a day. If you work on an assembly line and do mind-numbing work, why not get at least a little more. Ford never had problems to find labor and to keep it with that strategy. In addition this creates a corporate identity.

Today, corporate identity allows companies with popular brands to go in the opposite direction again. They can get away with low salaries: If everyone would love to work for your company, the people who are inside, will do a lot to stay, even accepting a salary that's not matching their skills or their input. And many more are underworked, only for the sake of being at a well-known company. The pressure of being replaceable has always existed, only it's face has changed. And the jobs that were formerly assumed to be safer, because they required higher education, are not safe from that perspective anymore either.

It can be concluded that doing tangible work does not only make you happier at work, it can also make your job safer. If nobody really knows what you do, and you don't really know it either, then why are you working here at all? Hiding in the crowd and trying to get away with the minimum is only mind-numbing and a bad insurance for job security.

High salaries – the goal of most career seekers – can turn into the biggest risk of maintaining an income at all. In a utilitarian environment, with commoditized human capital, price becomes the determining factor. The motivation to work harder to make more money can be jeopardized by the risk that too much salary can make one's commodity price too high. The first question a management consultant would ask a company executive: Isn't there anyone who can do that job for less?

Human capital becomes commoditized with increased division of labor. With the increased specialization and the intent to compare apples to apples, people and salaries become arbitrary and everyone is replaceable. For hiring companies this can be counterproductive, but is widely ignored. To spread the word of replicability of work force disintegrates loyalty. Fear is never a good agent for motivation. Specialization of skill and standardization of screening converts human capital into a commodity that can be procured like any other component that is required to produce output for a company. It will only be distinguished by price. The human part of the proper word of human recources gets diminished through its own process of skill taking and little incentives to promote personal success. The more comparable the work force becomes, the easier it is to hire, yet the less job security an employee has. This can convert itself into a decreased loyalty and productivity of such. At the same time it puts an enormous performance pressure on each individual, knowing and being reminded constantly that one is replaceable. It's neither healthy for the individual nor a sustainable business model. If a company can only afford it, it's worth to cut costs elsewhere and give the people their 5$ day. Productivity and loyalty will be paid off by increased turnovers and make business partners happy for having less frequent changes in point of contact..

Change is opportunity.

The necessity to stay in business leads to the prioritization of the happiness of the owners over the individual employee. Companies constantly have to re-shift their focus and their investments in order to react to a competitive environment and trends in technology, consumer behavior and macroeconomic developments. This competitive pressure on any company is an opportunity for an employee who wants to move on. In a very static business environment you may only be promoted when your supervisors moves on and you are the next one in line.

In a fast changing business environment you have the opportunity to start new things and promote yourself into new challenges. Remember Cervantes' words saying that diligence is the mother of good fortune, and idleness never brought a man to the goal of any of his best wishes.

Reading between the lines of your company's internal announcements, business analyst reports from your industry and conversations with co-workers and executives will help you to foresee where your industry is heading and what the next hottest growth areas are. Through your own impetus you can attempt to be ahead of the curve and focus to become part or even the driving factor of the growth areas.

The importance to drive change yourself is partly forced through the passive behavior of HR departments. Career development is officially always a part of HR, but in reality their job is often reduced to writing career guidelines and processes. HR is there when to hire and to fire, in the meantime they are mostly absent. This behavior leaves career development in the hands of every individual, and gives leeway to the politicians who are able to take credit for other people's work, the networker and the one who always has something to say in meetings. Many people are very good at what they do, but they either despise the politics or they aren't good at it. If there would be true career development driven by HR adhering to their tenets, there wouldn't be as many charlatans around. The indifference for what happens in between hiring cycles favors mediocrity, and the talkers. The ones who are unhappy and make decisions to move on, never voice them due to the unwritten rule that you should not burn bridges. You never say that you leave, because your boss is an abusive yeller or a complete moron or because your company pays a lousy salary and doesn't enable you to do your job. No, you claim to leave for personal reasons and because you have found a great opportunity that you could not pass on. It is like social media on the Internet in which every participant tries to portray a perfect and happy life. And HR can always claim they have never heard anyone complaining. The things that are going wrong are never pointed out, because people are afraid for their job and their reputation. Nobody wants to be the complainer. And the recipients of complaints usually take them personally and become defensive. So let's not talk about it at all. All of a sudden each and every one looks like a worker bee, every company is great, happy happy joy joy.

Some people have an audacity to claim credit for success because of their leadership skills and blame the world's economy for any failures. Kurt Tucholsky (1890–1935), German journalist, satirist and author said that the advantage of being smart is that you can play dumb, the opposite is a little more difficult. Unfortunately, in large corporations even dumb people can play smart and get away with it even if their low IQ is noticed.

Scott Adams (*1957), the creator of *The Dilbert Principle*, said: "Leadership is nature's way of removing morons from the productive flow." [16]

Some people recommend that if you have a problem with your supervisor, you should talk to him or to the HR people to solve any issues. At Digital Chocolate, in 2005, I went by the book and voiced my frustration about the leader of our sales team to the HR manager. I believed he had been chosen as our leader because he knew every trick, because he was a superb salesman who can help anyone in the team close deals and help to learn something new every day. The Dilbert Principle would have been a better explanation for his position in the company. The answer to my complaints was: "We knew he's not a good sales man, we hired him to be a team leader." I would rather call that a team administrator, since it was a far cry from leadership.

I wish I had read the Dilbert Principle before that experience. Maybe I would have taken the whole situation more relaxed. Back then, I still wanted to believe that to be a leader, real skill and intelli-

---

16 ADAMS, S. (1997), P. 310

gence was required. Reality hit me quick and hard. I also thought that if you went to HR and talked to them, they were there to help you. Second naïve thought.

I felt trapped: A useless supervisor and no way out in sight. And the worst was that the company seemed OK with that. Giving in to my complaint, which was the complaint of the entire team, would have been admitting to have hired the wrong person. Within months people started to leave the team and the manager was able to make every incident look like a personal decision that had nothing to do with him. He tried to diffuse the notion of conspiracy by isolating every incidence as the act of an individual. He even demanded from one of my former co-workers who had left, that he shall not talk to anyone in the team anymore. Probably because he was afraid that he'd talk about the real reasons of his exit. We all knew the real reasons and the desperate attempt to rule someone who already left only led to more gossip. Nobody wanted to burn bridges, they were just happy they had left. One may give him respect for outsmarting everyone to get a sweet deal like that. Take the credit for a great team, travel and collect mileage, no work, no sweat and a management that's indifferent. His job was like having a rich dad.

These incidents happen very often in companies. Once the leader is picked, that person is there to stay. And by the rules of job matching, they will also get a new position just like that and ruin the next team's spirit. All while thinking that they are so amazing.

I asked myself why do the hard working and most skilled people not always rise up? Maybe it wasn't the strongest that survives? I found a clue in Evolutionary Theory:

Charles Darwin (1809–1882) noted that "it is not the strongest or the most intelligent who will survive but those who can best manage change."

Some people call this the concept of the *survival of the fittest*, even though being able to adapt to change or to be the strongest are two separate attributes. Martin Shubik (*1926), while at Princeton University had a good explanation in 1953 in his *Readings in Game Theory and*

Political Behavior: "The origins of this term may be traced to simplified interpretations or misinterpretations of Darwinism in attempts to draw social and political analogies from the work in the biological sciences."[17]

Some people say that if you aren't successful it is because you didn't work hard enough or you aren't fit enough. Some people in higher positions feed off of those misinterpretations, and this misconception is supported by standard career advice. A hierarchy is created to delegate decision making to a defined group of people to ensure consistency and responsibility for the functioning of any operation within an organization. This delegation is in the first place a necessity, not a line drawn to arrange skill level into proper order. Theoretically the aim is to align this hierarchy with experience and skill. Unfortunately in practice it represents the biggest failure on the labor market.

Misinterpreting his real statement, the "tautology of the Darwinian Theory would mean: whatever survives is "fit" by definition! Defenders of the notion reply by noting that we can measure fitness (e.g., speed, strength, resistance to disease, aerodynamic stability) independent of survivability, so it becomes an empirical proposition that the fit survive. Indeed, under some conditions it may be simply tales, as game theorist Martin Shubik showed in an ingenious example:"[18]

Alice, Bob, and Carole are having a shootout. On each round, until only one player remains standing, the current shooter can choose one of the other players as target and is allowed one shot. At the start of the game, they draw straws to see who goes first, second, and third, and they take turns repeatedly in that order. A player who is hit is eliminated. Alice is a perfect shot, Bob has 80% accuracy, and Carole has 50% accuracy. We assume that players are not required to aim at an opponent and can simply shoot in the air on their turn, if they so desire.

---

17 SHUBIK, M. (1954), P. 43

18 GINTIS, H. (2009), P. 13

Note that Carole has a 52.2% chance of surviving, whereas Alice has only a 30% chance and Bob has only a 17.8% chance.[19]

The incentive to survive is the motivation to hit the better shooter in the beginning, so that your own chance of surviving is higher. If Alice starts she will shoot Bob, because he's the 2nd best shooter and the most likely to try to hit her. If Carole, the worst at aiming the gun, starts she will try to shoot Alice. If she misses, Bob will try to hit Alice on his first shot as well, which gives Carole another chance afterwards to hit Bob. If Bob misses, Alice will shoot Bob first, not Carole. Shubik concludes that "If all participants act completely individually without any type or form of *esprit de corps*, then the strong will be forced to eliminate the strong in order to maximize their chances to survive."[20]

This behavior is common in a non-cooperative environment, hence the larger the company the more decreased loyalty and intense competition one will find. In a large company you are fighting for positions and reputation, salary and power. You don't feel bad for others who did not get your position or reputation. The larger a company is, the more it becomes a jungle and less co-operative.

In game theory, the model above is considered a non-cooperative game. They are however only mathematical models and do not take certain human interaction into account. In a zero-sum game, where one player's loss is the other players win, like in a chess game or an ice hockey match, we can rule out any form of cooperation. It can be noted though, that "in any situation involving more than two parties, it is impossible to define pure opposition. There is always some element of common interest to some group if the participants are strategically interlinked."[21]

If we imagine Alice, Bob and Carole to be three potential candidates for a promotion and they all try to win it; Bob and Carole might

---

19 See GINTIS, H. (2009), PP. 13–16 for the detailed mathematical calculation of Shubik's model. See also SHUBIK, M. (1954), P. 43–46

20 SHUBIK, M. (1954), P. 45

21 SHUBIK, M. (1954), P. 46

have a strategy, as Sun Tzu described it, to destroy the alliances and the stronghold of Alice in order to be considered. They might work together against Alice, even if the result will be that someone from the outside will be hired. Maybe even someone not as good as Alice, someone more like Bob and Carole themselves. And Alice will walk away with empty hands. They could also be three companies that are competing over a business award or trying to sell products into the same market. Smaller, even competing companies could stick together to gain an advantage against the market leader.

In a manufacturing business this is common practice. Companies combine their orders for general components into larger quantities to increase their purchasing power to gain better pricing. As an example large car-makers could order brakes or tires together with their competitors, knowing that they will compete over other features with each other later.

The non-cooperative game can also be an explanation attempt to describe how some companies or products can survive on a market, even if they aren't the best, but the ones who find the best ways to market themselves. What most people want is not necessarily the best product, but may be the most popular or the newest.

The same game applies to politics. In the United States, the parties hold primaries, in order to select their candidate for the presidential election. Following and observing the debates and campaigns of such primaries you notice a pattern: the weaker candidates often focus most of their attacks on the leader in the polls. Sometimes there are 2–3 candidates who attack the leader together. The attacks against the most popular or most skilled candidate can lead to the laughing third party or the lowest common denominator becoming the presidential nominee.

Game theory puts a mathematical concept behind human interaction and proves easily how mediocrity can thrive and what survives is not necessarily fit by definition.

Often the strong will try to eliminate each other, even though it would be a better tactic to cooperate in order get rid of the weakest first, before dueling each other. Only when the difference in relative strength is very significant, can the strongest actually survive, says Shubik.[22]

Howard Stevenson puts it in very simple words: "A-level managers hire A-level staff, and B-level managers hire C-level staff."[23]

This is perhaps why mediocre managers try to hire a group of people in which the difference in skill compared to the manager is significant. People who are not very skilled, but in a leadership position, often want to make sure that the ones around them are a bunch of yes-men and even lesser skilled than they are. In addition they use other tactics to feel powerful, among other: withholding information, purposely delaying decisions, taking credit for other people's work, blaming their own mistakes on the ones who aren't in a position to stand up for themselves, and treating people differently depending on their level of hierarchy. It can get as simple as not greeting people below you or never join colleagues for lunch that belong to that group. Basically they are trying anything to make sure everyone sees who is the boss.

This leads to a business culture where the average is celebrated and it should be no surprise if business is not thriving and loyalty shrinking. The larger the corporation, the larger the competition, the more you have to watch how you present yourself. It can be good to let some people think you are not as smart as you are, so they spend their time on gossipping about someone else. One has to be alert and plan when and how to voice opinions or demands for changes, new roles and responsibilities, promotions and pay raises. If you only try to do everything right there might be people competing with you, just because they see you as a threat. Being the best or better than your manager can bring its own challenges, because others can be incentivized to put obstacles in your way. It's a good virtue to try to be the best. What requires some tactical planning is when and how to market it effectively.

---

22 SHUBIK, M. (1954), P. 45

23 SINOWAY, E. (2012) P. 130

A Bavarian proverb says that "the dumbest farmers always have the biggest potatoes". There is nothing you can do about it. Some people in our lives can drive us nuts. We have to learn to deal with them and learn not to get distracted by their audacious behavior. It wastes your energy and distracts from focusing on your own strategy. There are better and more sustainable ways to make a career than to take credit for other people's work. To be smart is not always a sufficient condition to get somewhere. Some people say that if you can't beat them, joint them. To me this is similar to selling my soul to the devil. Others resign and give up which is the spirit of a coward. The middle way, and to me the only viable option, is understanding the system and adapting your strategy accordingly rather than trying to emulate the charlatans' behavior. Kant said in his categorical imperative: "Act only according to that maxim whereby you can, at the same time, will that it should become a universal law." Already as children we were taught Kant's teaching with the words that you should not do to others that you don't want them to do to you. Some people get into positions they should not be in, yet knowing how such things occur, it allows us to to be more indifferent about it. I spent many years complaining about supervisors that should have been fired instead of micro-managing me, which only fed into growing frustration. It's a waste of energy to complain. The healthier way is to see them like any other challenge that needs to be overcome on the way to success. A good friend always said to me: "Take the rocks that are in your way and use them to build a house."

The German writer Adolf Knigge (1752–1796) said that you shouldn't complain to people who cannot help you solve your problem. In corporate language one would say you should only "propose change" to someone who is able to make a decision that you benefit from. The hierarchy and reporting structure of a company make it very difficult to change anything, because you do not have a place to voice your concern in a way that it would lead to anything. Everything is split into too many pieces. It's hard to find anyone who cares enough to deal with it. Others are concerned with their own issues.

The only ones who would fight on your behalf are the ones that could benefit from doing so. They are the allies to look for. For many aspects in your job you thrive by working together with the right people focusing on doing the right things. One thing though seems a mission impossible: how to get rid of a difficult boss.

It is very difficult to complain or do anything about a supervisor whose behavior is affecting your ability to work, or your stress level and health. You would have to go to his manager and complain to that person about having hired the wrong one or at least demand monitoring his behavior. That can be taken personal, and your boss might have told his boss all kinds of fairy tales that will make you look like a fool if you show up with your complaint. A lot of people are able to behave completely different depending on what social or hierarchical level they are talking to. Most likely you will get rejected and the issue might get to your boss. You should discuss this directly with your manager, they will say. Then you'll be in a position where you have to explain yourself. Your boss may want to talk to you about the problems. Maybe you think that the problem can only be resolved if he is removed. You can't tell your boss he should go home and come back to work five times smarter, less angry, less of a micromanager, basically come back not being himself. What would you actually say? There are ways to deal with a difficult manager, yet you always have to consider what your objective is. Mediocre people in leading positions have an ability of considering themselves as pretty smart, and they also react very sensitive to critique, as if some sub-conscience tells them "you're caught". In practice you don't have a lot of options with a terrible manager, besides either putting up with the person or leaving. It's important to learn how to deal with and overcome working with difficult co-workers and supervisors. I will discuss some methods later in this book.

Some people believe that hard work alone can lead to success, and being the best would bring you to the top. Big corporation HR policies and career advisory assumes just that and therefore words career guidance accordingly into the improve-skills-to-impress-managers doctrine. The mainstream literature that targets almost entirely executives and wannabe executives always uses the top-down view from an organization, where the management has to make the employees understand and embrace, get engaged and focused, work has to be delegated and teams have to be motivated. The hierarchical view is based on the assumption that increased skills are required to get to the top and by that definition on the top of the hierarchy you will also only find top skilled personnel. Theoretically this approach helps with the standardization of human capital, however it is far away from reality. People will always work at their best capacities if they feel a sense of entitlement, ownership over the results of their work and pride. Most people aren't lazy and gullible to need guidance and tough leadership, they need empowerment to do what they are best at. If you don't scrutinize people's work to begin with, there will be no need to motivate people.

Declaring everyone found below you on the hierarchy as less skilled by definition is a great way to maintain leadership. It is reserving the right to ownership on some secret skill of management only you possess.

At Dell I had a colleague of mine once who tried to leave his role and interviewing over several months to get into another team. In the first week in his new role, his new team was made redundant. So he had interviewed himself out of a job. Maybe he tried to run away from his current role and wasn't paying close attention to the whereabouts he was going. In large companies one has to read internal and external announcements carefully. Usually if a company announces changes and investments into the future it means a slow shift in priorities. Often you can put one and one together forecasting on who will get under the wheels with the new strategy.

In a world where job security is a foreign word, climbing the ladder has become something like the survival instinct of the jungle. It is not an insurance against getting laid off, but while it lasts you get more money and can possibly put more savings aside. Networking is also easier in a higher position, because other business partners and customers often want to talk to you, the person in charge. There are many benefits to be in a higher position in a company: more salary, more influence on your own future and a better network are just a few of them. This network will help you if you have to start looking for a job or to start your own business within the same industry, maybe even as a competitor to your former employer, just like I did when I became an entrepreneur.

Bob Dylan (*1941) sang a long time ago that the times they were a changing. In the old days people were working for the same company throughout their entire life. Nowadays it can be seen as a one-sided experience. Working for too long at one place can give you the stigma of not knowing any other thing. Even if you were committed to stay at a place forever, the commitment probably wouldn't be mutual. A company always reserves the right to get rid of you if it is economically necessary. Companies and employees alike have to adapt to a world of less commitment, both ways. A company that wants its employees to commit long-term has to be a lot more convincing than the usual. Top talent is not naïve to be following a the-future-is-bright story for long.

It can be the quicker way up to get promotions through job changes. One has to practice a good balance of staying long enough at a job in order not to be seen as a jumper and staying short enough in order to advance and get new opportunities before getting stuck. In addition it's important to make steps forward not sideward. Running away from one company to end up with more of the same is not progress. Sometimes one has to stay put, learn not to take everything too serious and emotional, and wait it out for the right moment to make a move. This takes practice.

Our parents' generation faced different challenges. In today's labor market you compete in your hometown with people applying for the same jobs from abroad. It's more common to fly in applicants for an interview. Recruiters fly around the globe to meet possible new hires.

In late 2010 while living in New York I landed a job at Dell in Texas over several local candidates. I needed a job and I did not feel bad for the ones that didn't get it. I had also been #2 or #3 in job interviews when the same happened to me. And I bet they didn't feel bad for me either.

Increased mobility from employees, and willingness of employers to hire people from elsewhere and pay for relocation is leading to an ever more competitive labor market. As more people are willing to move for a good opportunity and often enough want to move for experience, it also demands increased willingness for mobility to stay competitive. Your home market gets crowded. The necessity for a paycheck in combination with career progress may require you to move elsewhere.

Moving is for some people a chore and it's difficult to leave your social life behind, but if it lets you maintain a certain quality of life or continue on a career path, it's worth considering. Some people are more home-bound than others, yet even if you have a really hard time leaving your soil, the experience you may gain elsewhere can be worth gold. If you decide to return one day and then you may be much better off in your home-town, than if you had never left. It happened to me and to many people I know.

Your current or most recent job is the most determining factor for your abilities to move on to a new job later. Working too long in a job that you are overqualified for can seriously hurt your long-term career path, because you will be judged by what you do at present. Trying to explain that you can do much better is difficult and probably won't resonate in the presence of a plethora of competitors. It can be worse: you might not even be considered for a job interview and get a chance to justify yourself.

It can be counterproductive on the long run to take the first job opportunity that opens up if it is below your qualifications or something you seriously do *not* want to do. If it is financially possible to get by one may consider to pass on a job or two that is not worth risking the long term career path. It will be easier to pretend that you took a sabbatical than trying to explain why you did a job below your skill- and pay grade.

The myth of an open ears policy in large corporations is just as insubstantial as the HR support for career progress.

"We listen to our customers" is one of most abused slogans in the corporate world. When I lived in Texas, in 2012, I entered a store to buy a car seat for my then unborn first son. There wasn't any on the shelves so one of the employees went to get one from the back. I kept waiting for quite some time, the customer service lady started to get impatient too and kept calling the responsible person over the radio. As her colleague finally came walking towards us with the car seat box she asked him what had taken him so long? He responded that he had to do something for the supervisor and he had wanted that to be done right away. She gave him a look of being upset about how he could make the customer wait. I stepped into that conversation and said: "Don't worry. Your company says that your customer comes first, but if your supervisor wants something that doesn't really matter. That's fine; I work for one of those companies, too. I know the drill." Everyone laughed, I paid for the car seat and left.

Other management booby traps to look out for are things like:
"Employees are our most valuable good",
"I have an open door policy",
"We encourage you to question the status quo",
"We reward risk takers",
"We don't shoot the messenger",
"You can make more money under the new incentive plan",
"I haven't heard any rumors".

These are empty notions that might have had a meaning at some point in time, but have been over used and are among the typical flowery textbook phrases of HR policies of public enlightenment. When you try to hold someone accountable for the phrase mongering above you will find a helping HR person just like you'll find a needle in the hay. These types of policies are often decided in a committee after a well-guided panel discussion and then publicly announced like the biggest achievement of business history. A company culture cannot be decided, it has to be lived by example and embraced by everyone.

Sun Tzu said: "He will win whose army is animated by the same spirit throughout all its ranks." A company that lives by those standards has no need to create a committee to come up with the 10 management commandments.

As long as every team member is excited about the common goal in the same way as he is about his personal tasks, the team will always be able to win. As soon as competition within the team arises over positions, reputation, ego, fame or compensation, the team spirit will suffer and with it the ability to win.

The cardinal error that one may make is to openly criticize. Kurt Tucholsky said: "The one who points out the dirt is considered more dangerous than the one who makes the dirt." In general one can assume that the messenger always gets shot and the one who questions the status quo is burnt at the stake.

Some people never question anything to begin with, especially not hierarchies. Change is for some people too much effort and creates anxiety even before the start. Some people are resigned with the world and say that nothing can be changed anyway. Therefore they prefer adapting to the world as is, accepting anything as a given. One cannot assume that everyone else is as driven for innovation and change as oneself. This is why the half-life of yes-men in a company is usually longer than the motivated ones'.

Being adaptable is a strong skill. To adapt oneself to *anything* is a step to a conformist-monolithic picture of a society in which innovation and creativity shrivel. The golden mean is never to give-in trying to change things without becoming a martyr over it either.

To improve processes and decisions in a company an individual has to start working on improvements on his own impulse by seeking private conversations with those who have power to change things. The best intentions to improve the way things are done can turn against you, simply because others take it personal and some people have grown to like the status quo. So be careful and pick your allies wisely.

Business isn't as rational as people pretend it to be. We are all humans, and therefore often decide emotionally, based on our own world view and experience, and only afterwards try to justify our decisions rationally. Even discussions about facts and causalities are often irrational and emotional.

People may go from one opinion to another triggered by an emotion of excitement or happiness, fear or threat. Colleagues who are on your side can turn against you if they feel that you are in the minority, regardless of facts or their initial stance. Don't expect from others to have the same courage as you. People who used to be allied enemies of your supervisor might not back you if you bring up the topic in public. It will only bring you into trouble if you are a lateral thinker in the midst of rigid hierarchies and an un-even distribution of power. In a casino one should only gamble as much he's willing to lose before placing a bet. Odds are what they are: just odds. The ones who encourage you to openly question the status quo are often the ones who want change, but fear to voice it. Only if you are successful people will come out of hiding and claim to be your supporter or mentor and how much they always knew you had potential. If you fail they'll call you a fool for running alone into the open field.

Watch out for people's intentions. Most people have the someone-should-do-something-about-it attitude hoping someone else voices what they think and bring change for them. I would not voice an opinion to get praise, but only if the content actually resonates with others.

The debate culture within a company is a good indicator of the happiness of its employees and the potential success of a company. The less people feel comfortable to raise their voices, the more mediocrity will spread, innovation gets to a standstill and most employees will see work as a necessary evil in order to pay for ones' bills. B-managers will blow their own horn out of the belief that they are such good leaders since all team members continuously agree with them. The larger an organization grows and the more hierarchy is introduced, the less culture around brainstorming ideas or changing processes will survive.

You would never go into an open battle against an army that is better equipped and stronger than yours. In a direct confrontation with higher-ups you will be most likely to lose. Any manager can always end a discussion by saying "you're wrong". The judge's hammer has hit. There is nothing you can do, whether you find it fair or not. That includes anything that can be felt as an open confrontation, even if you do not intend it as such. You have to learn to stay cool and not take everything too personal. Grow an elephant's skin, be sensitive, but without feelings.

Many things are taken personal even if they say "it's just business". That's why people who say "yes" a lot survive the corporate jungle better. Taking orders is easier than driving progress. You don't have to think.

When I started in the sales team at Digital Chocolate in 2004 we had our hands on every part of the company. Our ideas mattered. At the time, we believed there wasn't any amount of money a large corporation could pay us that would compare to the fun we had, the rewards we earned for our success and all the things we learned.

Scarcity of funds and people can lead to a lot of creativity and people going above and beyond for success.

As competition grew tighter and even more cost-constraints kicked in, the company switched from trying things out to focusing on what sells. More senior people were hired from outside and the creativity behind making games was scrutinized by the time in which they had to be produced until even the content became dictated. This is a typical transition that many companies go through as they grow. Outside people were hired to run Sales & Marketing, our opinion didn't count much anymore. Decisions were made elsewhere. We could give input on what the market demands were, but it was mostly ignored by the leaders running their own agenda. Initially we had rolled up our sleeves and worked late hours, now we were pure order takers. And just did the minimum.

The risk-taking gets a company from a growth phase to a mature phase after which you cannot risk to risk too much anymore. When a company grows, so does the payroll. The number of people involved is getting bigger and it gets increasingly difficult to make decisions during company happy hour. It is a necessity of a business to organize itself and streamline production, control costs, centralize decisions and make them binding to everyone else in the organization. The best moment to join a startup is therefore, when you enter before a major growth spurt happens and you can help expand the company *below* you. Yet, if you want to be in a start-up early enough you'll probably have to take the risk of failing as well.

There are many great jobs in dynamic companies, but there are at least as many boring jobs as well. And you can also have the only exciting job in a usually rather boring company. It's not all gold that is shining. And there is an economic reason to that. If a company has grown big, the dynamics change to continuity under high pressure. While smaller companies have to answer the market's demand with flexibility and agility, bigger companies have to be consistent and reliable.

The timing on when to join and at what level is important to determine your personal growth opportunities. Watch out for traps. Most companies will tell you in the hiring process about how great the company is. That isn't necessarily telling the whole truth, but by asking the right questions you can scope out the role of the position pretty well:

- What are the people and teams you interact with?
- How many departments are there and how do they interact?
- How does this role matter to the success of other people in particular and the entire business in general?
- Who is interested in your work, meaning up to which level will your reports go?
- Will the CEO know your name?
- How many team colleagues will you have and what's their job?
- How long have the other people in the team worked there?
- How long has the team leader been in the company?
- How and where are decisions made?
- Is the team's task the bread and butter business or is it a new unit that is doing something different than the companies' core business?

- Does it allow you to be creative in the job or will you be a pure process-order-taker?
- How does the job fit into the company's long term strategy?
- Is there any travel involved?
- Will the team grow further?
- Can you build your own team in the future?

The constant push and pull in order to get your career forward shows the double capacity in which we are bound to our company. A good comparison is how Rousseau describes in his *Social Contract* a State with the people being the Sovereign:

"Each of us puts his person and all his power in common under the supreme direction of the general will, and, in our corporate capacity, we receive each member as an indivisible part of the whole."[24]

In analogy the same applies to the corporate world. Companies are formed by people and the company has power over us. Humans have a tendency to put themselves into hierarchies, move up and prove their abilities to others. And we obey out of necessity. This formula shows us that the act of association comprises a mutual undertaking between a corporation and the individual. In a company we always stand in an inclusive interconnection with other people that influence our actions and whose actions are influenced by us. The path we walk on our career is interdependent with the goals that others pursue. All of this interaction happens within the body of organized hierarchy and processes.

The major difference is probably that in a political body of a country I can get rid of my leaders and call for incapable leaders to be replaced.

In a democracy, my political rights are bigger than in a company. If I strongly disagree with the leadership of my company and voice my opinion, it can cost me my paycheck. You are hired for your skills, not for your opinion. In that way you are similar to a mercenary who will

---

24 ROUSSEAU, J.-J. (1762), Chapter VI

serve in the army of the highest bidder. You just work for them, but do not get involved in the reason of their battles.

In order to survive within a company you have to adapt to a certain degree to its culture. A minimum amount of corporate identity is necessary, so that you actually care for the company. You cannot effectively question and change the status quo. If for the love of God you cannot and do not want to become like all the others in your company, then you experience an inflection point. Stop complaining and hoping that one day you could change all of that. Once a company culture has spread it cannot be changed easily. It has to be implemented and lived by from the start, otherwise it's very hard to change unless you are in charge. To get to the highest podium of company hierarchy though, you will have to be part of the culture. Otherwise you'll never make it. If that causes a mental dilemma for you, you know that it's time to move on. Maybe you just don't belong there. It's neither *their* or *your* fault. It's a good thing to realize, then you don't waste your time and energy that you could be spending somewhere else, where you feel like part of something and spend positive energy.

I can conclude that in an environment in which politics lead to more success than talent and hard work alone, we need to find different ways to manage our careers. The division of labor creates a specialized work-force and hiring practices of resume match-making. It also creates a work force of many order takers where people become numb and conform; they just do what they are being told. They become pigeon-holed.

Learning how companies work and accepting that there is no conspiracy against you, it's just what they do, is a good start. Taking a cool head when analyzing co-workers' behavior and realizing that their behavior has a pattern and nothing to do with you is the second step.

If you can make a difference, try to make that difference. If your opinion may count, make yourself heard. But don't become a martyr over being right. You have to be entitled to be right in a company, science has never been sufficient proof for believers. Understanding how corporations have emerged and why they functions as they do, make it easier to deal with it. If people don't do what you hope that they'd do for you then it's often because either they can't or they have no incentive to fight on your behalf. In order to make the system work for you, the first thing is to understand how the clockwork is running.

The fittest will not always survive and skill and hard work cannot be the sole reason how people make their way up on a ladder. So there must be another path.

More important than climbing any career ladder is to find meaningful work that doesn't alienate. Tangible jobs are less likely to get cut in harsh economic turbulences. We should neither complain about the politicians who finagle their way through the system, but rather learn to deal with them as obstacles on our way, nor should we look for condolence in a fairy-tale about a balance between work and life. Work is part of life, not a counterweight to life.

Understanding the way how corporations came about and function is to learn the rules of career chess. This chapter was about the role that one plays within a corporate world and which tools one has to maneuver it. This was covering the *work* part. In the next step I will take a deeper look at *life*.

Within the jungle of challenges and opportunities that one has to go through, we shall not forget that a successful career is to have meaningful work in which the money earned is a nice prize for doing something you love. Before getting into the strategy and tactics on how to make your way, I want to look into the why. What is my role as a human in society.

Why is it important to do meaningful work in life?

2 HOMO FABER FORTUNAE SUAE

"Happiness is the meaning and the purpose of life,
the whole aim and end of human existence."

ARISTOTLE (4TH CENTURY B.C.)

Happiness doesn't come around the corner to catch you by surprise. It's when opportunity meets preparation.

My father always says: "Luck is 90% hard work."

The pursuit of happiness is as it says a *pursuit*. It's more than a dream, an ambition or aspiration, it is a quest or a chase: an *act* to striving to gain something. The Romans said:

"Homo faber fortunae suae".

In the English translation it means that "every man is the architect of his own fortune". Literally "homo faber" stands for the creating human, therefore the "blacksmith" or just "smith"; a craftsman who works with tools on material to shape it. Fortuna has a figurative meaning. Fortuna is the Roman goddess of luck and destiny. It would be wrong to take "fortune" literally and setting it equal to monetary values as in the saying "he made a fortune". This proverb means that everyone is the creator of his own destiny. To translate fortuna with money means to set way for the wrong incentives on the quest for happiness. Money and destiny are two separate things that can come hand in hand, but one is not required for the other. Certainly, nobody will complain about making too much money, but it ought not replace

41

the actual pursuit in life. The past 250 years of economic growth have led to more choices of consumption than people ever had in human history. In parallel this evolved a Zeitgeist that if we are able to consume more, we must be happier. And it's what TV commercials suggest by the minute: buy this and you'll be a happier person. Essentially it creates a vicious cycle making people want to just do anything as long as they can make money, and lots of it. Only to consume more. Then rinse and repeat.

In the previous chapter I looked at the role of an individual within corporate boundaries; at work. In this chapter I will take a closer look to the role of an in individual in society; in life. The similarities will show that work and life aren't two separate things, but part of the same.

How to live a free life in a corporate world? That is the question that is driving me. It starts with the simple question: Should we conform, go by the book and do what *one has to do* in order to succeed or should we oppose obligations of society and live free spirited? The answer to this is the *golden mean* as Aristotle called it in his Nicomach-aen Ethics in the 4th century B.C. The right mean *(mesotes)* is between excess and insufficiency. Aristotle names courage as an example, the extremes of which can be foolhardiness if manifested as excess, and cowardice in the opposite direction. Cowardice is unwanted, but unreasoning bravery is foolish, too.[25]

All people are different and make different experiences. In theory this should lead to an individual way to define happiness and success. People then draw their unique conclusions on how to get there. Social pressure then, leads to a homogenized and universal view on success. There is big pressure especially on young people on how to get by in this world. In school you have to learn ever more, you compete about jobs with a lot more people than a few decades ago, status and money, reputation and ego, success and recognition, there are many things that are expected in order to be regarded as one who

---

25 ARISTOTLE (4TH CENTURY B.C.), 2ND BOOK

made it. On TV you see people making fools out of themselves to become famous, reality TV shows about the lives of obnoxious people, whatever it takes it seems. Everyone's blogging, posting on YouTube, Facebook, LinkedIn, Twitter, Pinterest, you name it. Celebrity culture and quick money, fame and financial freedom are stigmas of our time. People are carelessly posting their private life and the intimacy of their children on the Internet hoping that others give them immediate *thumbs up* only to repeat the process again a few moments later. Read a post and like it quickly move on to the next post to add a comment, and then all over again. Everything has to be easy and quick and especially TV and mobile Internet continuously influences us on how to live. It's a society suffering from short-term memory loss where last minute's news are old news, where it is hard to be consistent and perseverant to achieve something, even if it takes years in the making. People judge you quickly if it doesn't work out right away. Everything gets dumbed down to fit into a tweet, so people can have their opinions on everything and everyone quickly and easily. Eleanor Roosevelt (1884–1962) must have foreseen this society when she said: "Great minds discuss ideas, average ones discuss events, and small minds discuss people."

Julius Caesar (100–44 B.C.) reigned the Roman Empire under the motto "panem et circenses" – bread and circus games. It was the idea that as long as the people have enough to eat and are being entertained, they won't use their own mind and demand changes to society or politics. Multimedia, or better said, total media, has brought that to an extreme. Today people want lots of panem to get lots of circenses.

It is more than just entertainment. It's an addiction that steers people's mind to care for things that are irrelevant. It seems that people only discuss people and events anymore, because ideas do not fit in 140 characters. Looking at what types of TV shows there are or what's trending on the Internet gives an enlightened mind a lighting strike of a headache. It has come to a perversion of Caesar's motto: dependency of bread to satisfy the addiction to circus games. A wise man once said: "Father, forgive them; for they do not know what they are doing."[26]

Years ago technology was expensive, not everyone could afford it. Today there are more than 2 billion smartphones used worldwide. For one it's the access to the entire knowledge of the world, to the other it's the easy way to entertain oneself. Technology therefore isn't dividing the world into rich and poor anymore, but into smart and dumb.

Not too long ago, during the summer time, I sat outside in a café for lunch. Two young women came, they met for a joint lunch. After a lively "hello so nice to see you" and ordering some cocktails, both took out their phones and played with them without having a conversation. I finished my food and was day dreaming along as I saw two birds on a branch. One was tickling the other with its beak. Two little love birds. As I watched this, the waitress came and asked if I needed something else and I didn't really hear her at first. As if she had woken me up I abruptly said: "Oh, sorry, what? I was just watching these two birds there. They are really cute." She said: "Oh, I love birds. Look at those two." The ladies at the table next to me, with their crookbacked position, simultaneously lifted their head. One of them looked at me and then at her friend and made a facial expression that could have been translated with "what a weirdo." Then they both continued to stare at their phones. I had lunch by myself, but it was certainly more enjoyable than theirs. It was real.

People with headphones walking in the streets, on busses staring at their phone screens, others are chatting and texting while driving. It's not the Internet of Things, but the Internet of everything. Or everything is the Internet. People start to get anxiety and panic attacks when the Internet is out. It's worse than a power outage or a water leak. If you go for a walk after dusk you will see blue lights from the TV screens everywhere. Sometimes it appears that people don't do anything else, but go to work, buy their groceries and after eating dinner they put the TV on. And in the meantime people use their smart-

26 HOLY BIBLE, LUKE 23:34

phones to kill time and to fill any possible gap between activities. This is a self-imposed perversion of Caesar's politics.

It doesn't surprise that this behavior adds to the competitiveness and mental pressure: who makes more money? Who got there quicker? Whose house is bigger, car is faster, wife is prettier, and whose children are smarter? And by keeping ourselves busy in studying, working and enjoying the after-work life of professionals, too often we forget to take a break and ask ourselves what is making us happy? Do we take pictures for our own memory or to just to post them immediately to a mass of people who doesn't care about them longer than 5 seconds? Do we buy something for its usefulness or for the short term entertainment? Maybe the bragging rights? What do we enjoy more: laying on the beach or the amount of comments on our feet-at-the-beach picture?

Do we always have to buy something new instead of repairing the old? Can't we be alone anymore?

The same applies to work. Do we look for success for its own value, or because we feel that we need that in order not to be seen as a hippy or loser? There are ways on how to climb the ladder, land good jobs, make more money, but in order to be happy, it has to be for the right reasons. If you cannot take pride about what you do, in absence of other people's opinion, it is pointless to attempt career development.

The chase for more success will never end and never satisfy you if you don't do it for the right motivation and if you don't do it for yourself. There will never be enough. Take a breath and think about the right reasons of your actions.

Leo Tolstoy (1828–1910) said: "Everyone thinks about changing the world, but no one thinks about changing himself." You get advice from anyone about how to lead your life from the cradle to grave. For some people getting involved in other people's lives is a way not to deal with their own. They tell you what you should do and what's good for you.

Ultimately you are the one who has to live your life. No-one else can do that for you. You can just follow what everyone expects from you or advises you to do, and what pleases others or you go into *clausura* – to retreat to a quiet place – and do what has been right since the dawn of time:

"A man of wisdom and noble character makes up his own mind."[27]

During my time at Digital Chocolate between 2004–2007, the company had about 300 employees in several office locations around the globe: California, Spain, Finland, India, and New York. The latter one was me. Everyone else worked in an office, I worked remotely. I worked just as much as everyone else in the company. But I could sit in my pajamas all day if I felt like it, I went to practice Taekwondo on my lunch break, and I fell out of my apartment into happy hour in the Big Apple. That was great. Taking the time zones into account, I worked from 8 a.m. in the morning till 6 p.m. in the evening every day, but I mixed my hobbies in between. While my colleagues in California would drive an hour to work to be at 9 a.m. in their office, at 9 a.m. my time I had already been working an hour, right after breakfast I was already *at work*. One hour gained. I took 2.5h lunch breaks to ride my bicycle from the Meatpacking District to the Upper West Side of Manhattan to practice martial arts; almost every day. Some people would say "oh, what a life? You have it easy!" I think about it this way: 1 hour to work, 30min lunch break, one hour to drive home. My longer lunch break made up for the time that I didn't waste in traffic. I got fresh air, a work-out and had non-work related social interaction. It increased my quality of life tremendously without affecting my obligations towards my employer: Job done, money earned, life lived. I call this the intelligent hippy.

What is an intelligent hippy?

The intelligent hippy is the middle in between a hippy and a yuppie:

A *hippy* decides to live free, speak his mind, do what he pleases, lives and lets live, travels to learn and experience freedom, and does what makes him happy, while not giving too much importance to social approval. Live into the day and not worry.

The *yuppie*, young urban professional, wants to be a dependable person who is striving for appreciation through society and a lives according to the standards of the upper-middle class. Often working

---

27 SCHIKANEDER, E. / MOZART, W. A. (1791)

long hours, then spending free time in expensive cafés or cocktail bars, buying nice things, living in a representative home and driving a nice car. He wears clothes that add to his successful sex-appeal. While the hippy usually questions almost anything in a society, the yuppie hardly questions anything, as long as he can live a good life he has no reason to.

There is nothing to say against people who work hard to make a lot of money or people who decide not to do so at all; I don't see either option to be very desirable for my life though. One of the most famous wisdoms of the Oracle of Delphi sums this up as:

"Nothing too much."

How to live a free life and make money is the mean between the conformist and the non-conformist. It's to be free *and* independent.

By working like a horse I might make tons of money, but it comes with a trade off with free time, my health and it might not even be anything I enjoy doing. Working in a job and console myself by buying nice things doesn't lead to a happy life. Being a hippy is simply not a financially appealing lifestyle. Being broke while studying or even occasionally being between jobs throughout your life, makes you appreciate the little things more and friendships grow together closer. Choosing it as a lifestyle is not an option for most people. Plus, I like nice things and little gadgets.

Winston Churchill (1874–1965) said:

"Life is too short to drink cheap wine."

So what if you don't want to live like a broke artist, but on the other hand you don't feel like conforming to every rule either? The third way is to do to work that is meaningful to you and spend money on things that enable you to do things that *you* enjoy. Money earned through work you enjoy is of higher value than money as a compensation for pain. You'll never have to force yourself to do a job you love, it will be your own free will to go to work.

Live free and make money at the same time.

This is the result of a compromise that you cannot make money without working hard for it, but you cannot live freely if you don't free your mind at first. Free your mind from obligations that don't exist in form of a law, but only because we believe that there is a certain way that everyone has to act and live by.

One everlasting question about freedom is: Do you want to be free from something, or do you want to be free to do something?

Most people misinterpret freedom with financial independence. These can correlate, but they are not a conditional requirement to one another. "The wealthiest person is a pauper at times compared to the man with a satisfied mind," Johnny Cash (1932–2003) sang. You can be rich, but just a poor man with a lot of money. Or you can be free, but not have money at all. The third way is to take the spirit of a hippy and combine it with the drive of a yuppie. It is the golden mean in a society with all its rules, obligations and expectations.

When I started working at Dell I had an interesting experience: Whenever I told people that I worked at Dell, the immediate answer was "oh, cool!" There were 100.000 employees at Dell, plus contractors, at the time I started in 2011. Just saying to be part of something big and well-known is often enough for people to say "cool". Hardly anyone asked what I was doing for Dell or didn't pay much attention when I explained it.

In the opposite, when I worked at Digital Chocolate selling mobile games, people asked when I was planning to get a real job. Playing is not serious, therefore how can your job be serious? All of us like to play, but the ones who provide us with games aren't having real jobs? Outside of the games-industry, it is often seen like that. As if work wasn't supposed to be fun. Most people just cannot escape from their mental work-life treadmill.

Many people get comfort not having to justify why they do what they do. Hiding in the crowd in a big corporation is one way to do so. Even their grandmother will be able to say: "…oh, and he works at so-and-so."

Solely thinking of your employer as part of your social media profile that gives you a hip reputation is not going to help to be happy or successful. The job itself needs an intrinsic value that makes you happy. Maybe you work for a company whose products and services are used by millions of people every day, like Google or Samsung. Yet if you experience a micro-managing boss and your job is a tedious boring routine, then it is worth nothing more than the title on your resume for your new job hunt. At that point it can only serve as a tool to run away from your presence.

Confucius (4th century B.C.) said: "Choose a job you love, and you will never have to work a day in your life." Do what you love, love what you do. That is easier said than done. It requires two conditions to be met:

1. You know what you love.
2. You get the opportunity to do just that for a living.

Most people trip into a career rather than choosing it. We are barely adults when we have to choose which profession we want to pursue. The decision drivers are a mix of what our parents do for work, what they think a good job would be, what our friends pick to study or work, what our hobbies are and how our world view is from the perspective of a 16–20 year old. This is additionally driven by desire for social approval: quick success and prestige, money and an easy life, power and reputation.

Confucius' advice to choose a job you love, often stays behind the pressure to make money. How can I perform in a job I hate? To be the best at something you need a passion for it. Most people just get any job and try to roll it from there, but then never do, because they become too comfortable. They hold on to excuses like their title, the fanciness of the company's products or they list reasons that speak for their job and why this would be a bad moment to change. I say once you feel that going to work is a chore, it is a clear sign that something needs to be changed. Even if it takes you a year or two to get where you want. The I'm-happy-with-what-I-have attitude is generally positive, but knowing that you could be better off if you did something causes a latent unhappiness.

If you are able to do what you love, you will go above and beyond the expectations of your job, because doing what you love is the sledgehammer that crushes the punch-clock mentality. You feel that the input you give to work is a part of you, and therefore the results are meaningful.

I grew up in Frankfurt in Germany. The Turkish Döner-Kebap is one of the most popular street foods that people eat in Germany, besides Bratwurst. In my favorite Döner-shop, named Köyly, they put garlic-sauce on your sandwich as they hand it to you, but the owner never pours the spicy sauce on it. He shows you the bowl with the spicy sauce and says:

"Do it yourself, and complain about it yourself".

If you make your own meal too spicy, you have no-one else to blame, but yourself. I prefer to spice up my life the way I want, rather than having someone else doing it for me. I want no-one to tell me how spicy I should have it or protect me from over-spicing it.

This includes other people's opinion about me based on the things I have. Material things are static, but happiness is dynamic. Therefore *having* things only make sense if they fulfill an instrumental function that you enjoy. Unless you like to go boating and fishing there is no point of having a boat. Unless you like to cook there is no point of having a nice kitchen.

Life is about relation between human beings, everything else is only providing a different setting to that. I'd rather share a bottle of moonshine with a good friend around a bonfire than drinking champagne by myself in a castle. This is why so many people follow the commonly assumed path to happiness and yet stay unhappy all their lives. Most people just break the pursuit of happiness down to the amount of money they need to earn throughout their lives.

We work to finance our lives and try to stay alive as long as we can, but we never ask ourselves what for are we alive? Life becomes worthy to live once we start *living it up*: we have to dance and sing, drink and laugh with friends, discuss and learn, fall in love and make love, do things sometimes that aren't supposed to be good for you, do all the things that other people call getting in trouble, walk around in the rain without an umbrella, jump in a puddle and get dirty, sing under the shower, make goofy faces at the mirror, and laugh out loud that the belly hurts. Make jokes, laugh about ourselves, do the things that make us human.

In today's world we have more opportunities and legal rights to do the things that the post-war generation had to rebel against. However, the conservative moral police seem to have returned on a self-imposed political-correct lifestyle coaching crusade. Many people religiously oblige themselves to the perfect life, and do everything and only what is supposed to be good for them: watch out for…don't do that…you are not supposed to…but aren't you going to…you don't want to do…it's better not to…this is not good for you…don't eat too much of…do not drink more than… And often those people are more concerned about how *others* live. I think one should lead a mentally and physically healthy life-style, but the rule-mania of all the things we should or should not do is capable of transforming into the body of a medieval monk-style self-castigation; without any need.

They used to call it day-dreaming, now they call it attention deficit disorder. They used to call it impatience, now they call it restless leg syndrome. If we'd take a pill every day to form anyone into the well-behaved quiet person, a pill against this syndrome, a pill against that syndrome, we'll end up with a clone-like society who is incapable of drifting away with its thoughts and is ever present to a truth that the outside wants to indoctrinate us with.

It creates just the opposite of being a healthy, and free human being. In other words, if I make my own Döner sandwich too spicy I am the one who has to deal with the after burn the next morning. This type of rigid society may be one reason why so many people seek freedom in the Internet in virtual realities. I don't escape, I choose freedom in reality. It's the happier choice.

Wine, love and music can do a lot more magic to your health and happy life than a thousand years of pharmaceutical research and therapies can ever do. Francis of Assisi (1181–1226) said: "Health is an attitude, not a condition, it prospers with the joy of life."

The Oracle of Delphi said: "Know thyself".

If you know yourself, you will also know who to talk to and ask for advice. Having the right friends and mentors around oneself is a good way to get to know to yourself. Learning from others is an important factor in our lives. First we learn from the people who raise us, and then we learn from our teachers, later we learn from our mentors. To learn from someone else, doesn't mean that we have to copy everything they do or take over their opinions, but rather get inspiration and guidance. If you only follow into the footsteps of other people, you will not leave any marks. Confucius described it well:

"Learning without thought is labor lost; thought without learning is perilous." If something is taught to you, it is imperative to reflect about it, rather than leaving it to pure immersion. To omit that duty is between ignorance and gullibility.

People act in the way that situations occur to them. To stay with the example of spicy sauce, spiciness depends on the taste of the beholder. In some cultures people eat so much spicy food that their taste buds are numbed to the heat and they are able to eat much more of it, because it doesn't feel spicy anymore. The advice to do or better let something be largely depends on the perspective of the advisor. Only after a due diligence of the source of advice its usefulness can be determined. "Don't put too much spicy sauce on it" can also mean: "I don't like to eat too spicy and this sauce in particular is very spicy. I watch out how much I use and therefore *you* should act the same way I do." Some people can handle more heat than others. People who are risk-averse will always recommend you not to take any chances. And vice-versa. Advice comes mostly from the eye of the beholder. The best mentors are therefore the ones who can see things from your perspective, while staying an observer. In the end you are the one who makes the decisions and lives with the consequences. Therefore one should always gather as much information, experience and opinions as possible and then make up ones' own mind.

A friend is like another self, the Romans said: Amico est alter ego. To understand yourself and others can become the most powerful tool on your pursuit of happiness. What do you want and what do they want? A good friend is not only the one that you have the best time with, but someone who can help you making up your mind with your own words. Someone that can hold a mirror up for you to recognize the crossroads you are on. They may be able to see an inflection point in your life that you haven't noticed, because you are too busy. Pick your advisors wisely. Your best friend is not always the best for all advice, there might be different people for different aspects in life, like love, family, work, fun, sadness, and excitement. Finding the right advisors is important. A good mentor won't tell you how *he* would do it if he were *you*. A mentor helps you to see yourself from a distance and help you to sort your thoughts and derive the right actions.

According to Greek mythology, Mentor was a friend of Odysseus. Odysseus who went to fight in the Trojan War had placed Mentor in charge of his belonging and of raising his son Telemachus.[28] Mentor was sharing his wisdom and experience with Telemachus. He was the person who encouraged Telemachus to be brave, not to be diffident. Telemachus should indulge his father's courage, like he had been when he accomplished his works.[29] Hence the term mentor, someone who can guide you to find your own strengths and help you on your way through life. Mentor doesn't demand from Telemachus to follow his father's, Odysseus', footsteps, but rather that he should internalize his spirit. The idea of a mentor is someone of a coach who can understand your feelings and your dreams, who is able to guide you towards discovery and use of your biggest strengths, set you straight when you are on the wrong way or even walk parts of your life's journey with you.

The two characters in Samuel Becket's (1906–1969) famous play "Waiting for Godot" (1952) find themselves in an endless wait for

---

28 HOMER (8–7TH CENTURY B.C.), 2.225
29 HOMER (8–7TH CENTURY B.C.), 2.270

someone called Godot. Waiting in vain, Estragon and Wladimir, never find out who Godot actually is and whether he will ever arrive. They get caught in idleness and indecisiveness over it. Throughout the play, they have a recurring conversation:

Estragon: "Come, let's go."

Wladimir: "No, we can't"

"Why not?"

"We are waiting for Godot."

"Ah."

Idleness and laziness, fear and cowardice, comfort and excuses, lead to accepting one's fait and the world as is. Hoping for happiness to pass by one day will make happiness appear alongside with Godot. Praying for the better is just as useful as buying a lot of things in the hope for a happier life by owning a lot of stuff. With this attitude life will pass by with your default future running towards you on high-speed. And happiness won't be knocking. Instead, happiness is born out of an activity of the soul.

Immanuel Kant said that "laziness and cowardice are the reasons why such a large part of mankind gladly remain minors all their lives, long after nature has freed them from external guidance. They are the reasons why it is so easy for others to set themselves up as guardians. It is so comfortable to be a minor. If I have a book that thinks for me, a pastor who acts as my conscience, a physician who prescribes my diet, and so on--then I have no need to exert myself. I have no need to think, if only I can pay; others will take care of that disagreeable business for me."[30] If everyone else behaves in this manner it becomes even easier to be part of the complacent crowd. "If 50 million people say a foolish thing, it is still a foolish thing." Anatole France (1844–1924), French author and Nobel Prize winner for literature said.

Early in 2015 in Boston, our second winter in New England, the city had one of its worst winters that locals could remember. There was so much snow, we didn't know where to put it. One day I spent

---

30 KANT, I. (1784)

almost two hours to shovel my car and the sidewalk free of it. When I was done with the job, all I felt like doing was to watch something on TV and have a cold beer. I felt good about my job and about myself and didn't want anything else, but just hang out. As I sat there quite content it came to my mind why it may be harder for some people to further educate themselves than it is for others:

For people that do exhaustive physical labor, it is hard to or they just lack interest in educating themselves after work or use their brains otherwise. They are just too tired. They are therefore also no example for their children who often grow up without thirstiness for knowledge and education. And there are people that once attended higher education, but haven't ever since worried about continuing to learn. It might have been just a matter of getting a degree to secure a higher income and no need for physical labor. Now you have a job and make money, why bother? Why read a book? Why discuss important issues of politics and society? Mark Twain said that "a man who doesn't read has no advantage over a man who cannot read." What is the difference between someone who hasn't learned how to use his own mind to the one who can, but doesn't? I can understand why working class people do not have the energy for intellectual practice after their job is done, but I have little sympathy for people who sit in an office all day hating their jobs and worrying about their lives, only to come home to watch TV. They have no-one else to blame.

With the advancement of the division of labor, the number of tasks workers have to fulfill are limited to a few and the same process is followed over and over again. It can be mind-numbing. Adam Smith says that the everyday tasks of a person inevitably form their ability of comprehension. This prevents anyone from having to use their own reasoning for anything. It is natural for people to unlearn to use ones' mind. The intellectual or mental idleness leads to one to be as simpleminded "as a human being can only be."[31] In other words, if people do not have to use their own reasoning they also lose the abili-

---

31 SMITH, A. (1776), BOOK V, CHAPTER I

ty to do so. A job that makes you complacent can enhance that. To be underworked can be as depressing and stressful as a burnout. If your job is a monotonous routine that calcifies your mind you are at high risk to give in to the misbelief that "that's just how life is."

It is so much easier to accept the status quo and blame others than to be actively working on change. You can sit back and feed yourself with the common excuses that are well accepted by the public, including being too tired, too busy, too this and too that. Kant describes how challenging it is to get out of such a state: "Thus it is very difficult for the individual to work himself out of the nonage which has become almost second nature to him...there are only a few men who walk firmly, and who have emerged from nonage by cultivating their own minds." One can get so used to a routine that it's becoming increasingly difficult to unchain the mind from it.

Kant recapitulates: "Enlightenment is man's emergence from his self-imposed immaturity. Immaturity is the inability to use one's own understanding without another's guidance. This immaturity is self-imposed if its cause lies not in lack of understanding but in indecision and lack of courage to use one's own mind without another's guidance. Dare to know! (Sapere aude.) "Have the courage to use your own understanding," is therefore the motto of the enlightenment."[32]

Happiness is borne out of activity. A good way to visualize this are childhood memories: Most people who say they had a lovely childhood base it on memories that were created through activity, not passivity. Things they did with their family and friends. No-one will remember childhood, because they had the most amount of toys, but because they had best friends to play with.

Children who were active with their parents on childhood vacations and at home alike are more likely to think back smiling than the ones who wore branded clothing as a 5 year old, but never went fishing with their father or crafted something with their mother. Why is what made us happy as kids so quickly forgotten when we become

---

32 KANT, I. (1784)

adults? I will never forget how my father freed a bird that got caught in our fishing net or how I degutted my first fish at the age of maybe four or five. Or how I cut my finger to the bone doing wood carvings with the first knife I was allowed to buy with my pocket money. My grandfather hand-made wooden arrow and bow for my brother and me, to play Robin Hood in the woods in Finland. Today people buy their kids colorful plastic toys that play sounds when you press some buttons. Activity, not passive entertainment, is what brought joy and learning as a child and stays in our long term memories and abilities, as opposed to the memories of plastic.

Finnish people have a saying: "tekevä loma on lomempi" – an active vacation is a better vacation.

I read a study in a magazine a few years ago, in which the perceived time was subject of a field research project. People were interviewed how they perceived hours of waiting after they sat for hours in a doctor's office or doing nothing at an airport when flights were delayed. The interesting results were that while people were waiting it felt to them like time would not move at all, but once the wait was over, there was almost no memory left about it. In a nutshell the overall answer was that it "wasn't so bad to wait." The conclusions drawn were that idleness and inactivity is not remembered. The past time implodes in the memory. This also explains why people who take a week of vacation usually perceive the beginning as long and then all of a sudden the time flies by. At the start of a vacation you try to orient yourself, find places to go and eat, get settled, try everything out. Once the area is explored and one sits lazy by the pool, nothing really happens anymore. In the memory this part of inactivity is felt as time went by faster, even though in the moment it might not have.

A life that follows a boring routine filled with mindless activities in my free time and at work, will also be a short story if someone was to ask me about what I did. Since time becomes relative one hour doesn't equal an hour, its true length depends on how its spent. In the conclusion it means that the one who lives an active life, als lives a longer life, regardless of how many years one spends breathing.

Experience comes through experience, not age.

Time served is not equal to gained wisdom. Doing the same thing all the time is not progress, it's treading water. Then you just grow old. Only illogical thinking people believe that age would be a sufficient condition for experience. It is not. This logic would mean that at the end of our lives we'd all be equally experienced and only our current location on the timeline describes our abilities.

Only the active human, the Homo Faber, will shape his life into something beautiful. Like Goethe let's his protégé, Faust, say in the study: "The spirit aids! From anxious scruples freed, I write, "In the beginning was the Deed!""[33] Go and do is the credo. Form nothing comes nothing.

Neither money alone can make you happy, nor a nice sounding title in a well-known company. The answer though is not to run away from it either. Too many people think in simple-minded ways of friend and foe, black and white, with me or against me, heaven and hell, communist or capitalist, angel or devil, fat or athletic. It is an easy way to make oneself comfortable with the world, but the reality has many shades of gray. Life is not a dual choice test with the options of either doing what everyone does or escaping. If you are neither rich by birth nor feel like selling hand-made things at the beach and live with seven room-mates, slaving away your life is not the only option. The game for you is not over just there.

Don't fall for the work-life-balance myth. There is only balance. You may just pursue the wrong goal or maybe you don't pursue anything. Maybe you find yourself following the common work-hard-to-make-money treadmill and wonder why it doesn't satisfy entirely. If using the brain more than a hamster one will realize the treadmill eventually.

Many people who have a hard time getting out of bed to do a job they deeply dislike while, being visibly affected with unhappiness, too often fall into believing in the legend of a work-life-balance. The thesis is: The more time I spend on doing things that are bad, the better

---

33 GOETHE, J. W. VON (1808), PART I, NIGHT

will be the time that is good. Life-work-balance believers assume that more money for free time is a good thing and work would be a bad thing, but it leads to earning money. And since money is needed for everything to be happy, one has to give in and do that bad thing called work to get a lot of that good thing called life. It does sound like medieval self-castigation and the search of heavenly condolence, rather than actual reasoning.

The definition already makes a pre-emptive assumption that work is not part of life. As if life was all the good things and work all the bad things, and non-life. Dead maybe? Some people do indeed have that walking-dead expression on their faces as they enter their work space. Been there, done that. There are different ways of earning money and money cannot satisfy if you haven't defined it's instrumental character you plan to use it as.

If work and life would balance each other out, it was a zero-sum game, with the overall happiness summed up to nothing at the end. In a mathematical formula considering work as minus one and play time as plus one, the outcome of zero and would equal your total happiness. And if you work more for more money you may put pain at minus two and play time at plus two. The sum of it would still be nothing.

Work-Life-Balance believers commit a so-called *cum hoc ergo propter hoc* error, a correlation falsely made based on the wrong assumptions and the neglect to consider all facts. Work shouldn't be the sum of all things you regret doing and the salary the compensation for it. Because you hate your job and you love your free time it doesn't have to mean that these are opposites. You just have the wrong job.

Work and life stand in a positive correlation to each other, one is part of the other, they aren't counterbalances to on another.

It is difficult to perform at work, if you aren't happy in your life, but if you aren't excited about work, then you bring that attitude home. They are two sides of the same coin. They stand in a positive co-relation with one indicator moving in one direction, the other one moves with it into the same. Or simply: the more-the more and the less-the less.

We can't change the whole world, but we can learn to understand how it runs and make it work for ourselves. To be happy at work in particular and life in general we have to identify the source of our personal happiness. That is different to taking an ex-ante approach assuming that work is the sum of all evil that we have to give in to in order to get the desired outcome of more quality play time.

We all have to eat, drink, sleep, and go to the toilet. Jamie Oliver (* 1975), the British TV-chef and healthy-eating-activist said in an interview once: "If you have to eat three times a day, for the rest of your life, why not be good about it?" We have to live self-conscious and deliberate. Be aware of what we do, and not just exist.

Anyone has probably seen on TV what a time lapse scene looks like: Scenes of streets, pedestrian walk ways or nature fast forwarded. You see people walking to a pedestrian light, stopping as cars go by, then crossing the street when the light turns green. All in high speed it looks like people run on the sidewalks, quickly stop, and when the light turns green they run, just before it turns red again and cars rush through the streets. Lots of quick stop and go. And the sun will go up and down in the background as the scene repeats itself. When I worked at Savox Communications in Finland from 2007–2009, before relocating for a second time to New York, I had to take a bus every morning at 7:51 a.m. to get to work. After only a few days I was able to recognize most people at the bus stop. It was the same crowd of people with the same routine every morning. Only the weather and the temperature would change. During the summer months it was light at that morning hour, in the winter it was still dark. Every morning I stood at the bus stop observing the scene sometimes wondering if it was is going to be like this for the rest of my life? If I wasn't going to do anything about it, my life would go by in a time lapse by taking this bus every morning at 7:51.

Work shouldn't be just one more routine that one does. You can eat to be nourished or you can eat for many other reasons, like being healthy, following an exercise plan, enjoy good meals with friends and family. Going mindlessly to work as an evil necessity or watching stupid games shows stuffing junk food into your mouth are not much of a difference in a mental stage. If I had to take that 7:51 bus for the rest of my life, I thought, I'd better make it worth being there every day at the same time. Bob Dylan said that a man is successful if he gets up in the morning and goes to bed at night "and in between he does what he wants." Dylan won the Nobel prize winner for literature in 2016 at the age of 75 for "having created new poetic expressions within the great American song tradition."[34] What matters here is not that he won a prize, but what he did and what for to be elected for such honor. Bob Dylan probably never set himself a goal to win the Nobel Prize. It was his life's work that got him the prize. In my situation back at the bus station I said to myself: What I do between taking the bus there and back better really matters. It can't be something "that one just has to do".

Between 2011 and 2014, during the three years I was working at Dell in Texas, I had a retrospection of my daily bus stop experience. The scenery had changed, not the call for action. Each and every morning at the same time I walked demotivated to my car, drove on the same highway along the same ugly scenery of cheap motels, strip malls, billboards and eateries to the same exit. I usually felt heavy-hearted and short of breath just before turning the corner towards the Dell campus with its several concrete buildings. With a low-hanging head staring at the asphalt just in front of each step, I walked from the parking lot to the main building, said hello to the front desk person and swiped my security card. With the loud *click* of the unlocking door, my breathing got more exhaustive, because it felt more like the locking of a jail door behind me, rather than the opening of a door to opportunity and a joyful day in the office. As soon as I walked into the door the daylight was a memory of the recent past. As I passed through rows of grey cubicles I would greet people who felt the same, who just forced a smile out to greet you back as if an invisible puppet master would have strings attached to the side of the

---

34 NOBEL PRIZE LAUREATES (2016)

lips to make one smile. Sometimes I liked to think of my colleagues as being my in-mates.

It's the rain that makes us appreciate the sun. What made living in Texas worse was that not even the weather was changing a whole lot. It is just hot and not so hot in Texas. We lived in Georgetown, a small town half an hour drive north of Austin. It was a nice little town, very Old Western. If you'd take the cars out of the main square and put people riding horses there instead, you weren't able know what century it was. Besides that it was pretty boring. And between May and November you are doomed to stay inside after 10 a.m. in the morning, because it's way too hot to be outside. Without clear seasons it felt like every day was like any other. It didn't make a difference. Work and free time were like treading water. For the most part I opened the windows in the mornings and said to myself: "It's just another bloody sunny day." Often I felt like a dead man walking.

My career had started different. I ended up in Texas through many unforeseen circumstances and only due to my desperation I started to remember the old days and situations that made me ready to move on. As I wondered about how I actually landed in Texas, I remembered starting my first real job after University:

On November 1ˢᵗ 2004 I had my first day at work at Digital Chocolate's Helsinki office. It was a large building with various smaller companies renting office space. Digital Chocolate's offices were on the higher floors and from the window of the room where the sales team sat you could see a nicely kept cemetery. Finnish cemeteries are traditionally in the forest and are very pretty. So is this city cemetery with its many lines of trees and beautiful, well-kept tombstones. On my first day, I looked out of the window to the cemetery where also my grandfather, Matti Hirvonen, is buried.

"Nice view of the cemetery," I said.

"That is so we can see where the journey is going." Petteri Vainikka, later co-founder of Rovio, answered.

In Texas, then, I often recalled that conversation. Every day this important question came back to my mind: what do I want to do with the time that is given to me in life? I know it's not this, I said to myself. People who had near death experiences always say that they appreciate life and enjoy it a lot more. Do we all need to fear death before we get it? Just push through as if it wouldn't matter as long as you can pay for things? When our soul continues after our bodies have gone, it will not care about how many people liked your status on social media. Death is, as Mozart described it, our best companion. Its presence makes us appreciate our life.

During the Roman Empire, when the leader of an army or the emperor himself returned victorious from a battle or war, he was allowed to march into Rome in triumph and be cheered on by the crowds. Behind him on the chariot stood a priest or servant, holding up a laurel wreath over his head repeating the words to him: "Memento moriendum esse" – remember that you have to die. Shortened over the centuries through monks' monastery Latin, the phrase turned into *memento mori*. Even in the moment of glory and triumph, the highest leaders were reminding themselves that everything eventually vanishes. With the retaking of Greek & Latin studies during the Renaissance, also the appreciation that our time on this planet is limited returned and with it that that leading a happy human-centric life was what we should be striving for. Hence the motto of the Renaissance: memento mori.

Can we have time to be philosophical about life when we are so busy trying to make a living? Why is it important? The question is rather: Can we afford *not* to think about what to do with our lives? A good visualization of use and limits of time is an ancient craftsman tool, the 24-inch gauge. It was an instrument that the stonemasons, the architects, used to measure and lay out their work when they built the Holy Temple of King Salomon during the 10th century B.C.. This tool can have a symbolic, spiritual meaning as well. As the architect of your own destiny, building the temple of happiness and humanity, this 24-inch gauge inheres another meaning: It symbolizes the 24 hours of the day. Just like the 24-inch gauge can be folded into three parts, the hours of a day can be equally divided into three:

Eight hours in which we are at work, another eight hours in which we follow our likes and household duties. And finally eight hours to rest. That said, one third of your life will be spent at work, which is half of your awake time. If time wouldn't matter because we'd all live forever, maybe it wasn't important. However, to stick with biblical history, the Holy Bible demands to "teach us to count our days that we may gain a wise heart."[35]

Assuming that you take between 2–4 out of 52 weeks of vacation per year, you will spend around 2000 hours per year at work in addition to the time thinking and talking about work with friends, family and colleagues. Can you afford to just do anything for thousands of hours each year? Can you just accept it as a given, that this is how the world goes round? Is it better to just come to terms with one's fate, resign and put up with it? Or choose life and get out of idleness and do something about it?

During the middle ages time was perceived only in relation to the almighty God. Thinking and acting piously was a spell of eternity. The bells of the monasteries rang when the sun dial pointed to prayer time. The Renaissance, between the 14th and 17th century, brought among many other cultural changes a rebirth of ancient studies of freedom and beauty. And with it a change to the perception of time. The new class of merchants, that had started out in Florence, Italy, had to think in keeping business agreements and deadlines. Economic activity and prosperity flourished during that time. Time was not about praying anymore: time was money. In the year 1325 AD, Florence has gotten its first tower clock with an even dial and in the following century in almost every town of Italy the bells were ringing every hour during the 24 hours of each day. Time became something important. 15th century Italian architect, mathematician and writer Leon Battista Alberti (1404–1472) said that time was one of the three most precious possessions of humans – next to the body and the soul.[36] Many artists of the

---

35 HOLY BIBLE, PSALM 90, VERSE 12

36 TRAUB, R. (2013)

Renaissance created their work based on that revived Zeitgeist. The art of "Vanitas" emerged, the artistic attempt to grapple with limited time and everything eventually *vanishing*. None of this has anything to do with a death-cult or blasphemy rituals. In the opposite: it was to remind us to cheer for being alive and to appreciate how beautiful life can be.

The Tower of the Town Hall in Leipzig, Germany titles: "mors certa hora incerta" – death is certain, the time is uncertain. Hence the saying that death and taxes are the two only things that are certain in life. Paying taxes on a salary that you earn in a job you hate is a lose-lose situation. If the reward for a life-long slaving is to be buried with your golden watch into the ground, what's the point of being alive to begin with?

How were the times when *Uncle Tom's Cabin* (1852) was written by Harriet Beecher Stowe (1811–1896)?

In the United States in times before the Civil War and the liberation of the slaves, even slaves had it good or bad depending on who they were working for. Maybe some of them where bragging about where they were working? One would say that he works at the Smith Plantation, another at the Jones Plantation. If slavery was assumed by most as a given that cannot be changed by one owns effort then it's understandable that at least you wanted to be working at a well-known plantation that is very beautiful, owned by someone richer than the neighbors', and of course where the slaves are treated better than elsewhere. As I was walking up and down the aisles at Dell, that thought came to me sometimes. Was it a difference if I was working at the Dell plantation or the IBM plantation? The cubicles might not be grey, but brown or blue there? On paper I wasn't owned by Dell, like a slave in the old days, nor could I have been sold, whipped, beaten or killed. But my financial obligations were tying me to the job. It felt like I had sold myself to them. It felt like slavery, without ever having experience the horrors of real slavery. It can feel like that, when you do work against your free will, but only for a financial obligation.

How a company and a job feels to an individual is entirely subjective. For some people their job at Dell was the best they ever had, for others it was just a chore. And for most people it was something they never thought about. I put a lot of thought into why I never really liked working at Dell. I came to the conclusion that it had very little to do with Dell at all. My colleagues were really nice, some of them became good friends of mine. The three supervisors I had in the three years were all really nice and easy to work with and I still keep in touch. I never had any problem whatsoever with any of them. The pay was good, the healthcare and retirement benefits weren't bad either. I could work from home when I needed to or felt like it, I got vacation time whenever I asked for it. The team, Global Strategic Alliances and Global Partner Management, I was part of was very close to the executives and it felt like we had at least to a limited extent, influence on the success of the company. So what was the problem?

I recalled an advice that I received during an internship that I had done a decade earlier at Mercedes Benz. Once during lunch, as we talked about the job hunt after graduating, my supervisor, Richard Mummenhoff, said: "Never apply for a job where you don't care about the products the company is selling." That sentence popped into my head when I thought about my work at Dell. I came to realize that I didn't really care for the products and services that the company offers. Dell sells everything IT from the data center to the end-user: Storage for big data, cloud computing infrastructures, laptops & desktops, gaming PC's, high performance computers. For anyone interested in IT a good place to be. It was just not for me. I learned a lot on how everything in IT works from the technology to the distribution, but I never grew any excitement about it. It strengthened my belief that in order to have a successful career in any company you need to find an industry that you are interested in, not just any big name company.

The second reason was that I didn't see any perspective for a long term career in an organization of that size. Adam Smith said: "The first thing you have to know is yourself. A man who knows himself can step outside himself and watch his own reactions like an observer."

By stepping out of the eternity of my cubicle looking up the aisle of a possible career path the first thing I noticed is that with promotion and pay raises, one thing would never change: The cubicle. A Director still sat in the same size cubicle as anyone on a manager level or below. The Executive Directors had a cubicle twice the size of the rest and the VP's had one that was double of that. If I worked very hard, networked, said "yes" a lot, and did anything possible to advance in my career, after 10–15 years I would find myself in a cubicle four times the size of the one I had started with. A good title, a big salary, more power, now people saying "yes" to all of *my* ideas, and yet I would still sit in a grey cubicle under artificial light.

To compensate for that misery I could use my hard earned money to buy myself a nicer car. That would not change the scenery on my way to work though. I could possibly buy a nice and big house, but if it's so hot that you can't go outside for most of the year, even that would feel like a jail like the clicking sound of the office door. It would be a nicer and bigger jail, just like the new cubicle.

The third reason I didn't like it at Dell was the time outside of work: I was never really happy living in Texas. The weather was too hot to be outside most of the year, for an outdoor enthusiast that was horrible. We were living in a small town, for an urban child like me that put the nail onto my mental coffin. There are fun things to do in Texas and I tried to get everything out of it, including horseback riding and enjoying Texas wild flowers, Rodeo and live music, good BBQ and craft breweries, little town festivals in the Texas hill country and the view at the wineries that remind you of Tuscany. But after all, these are only a handful of things and they started to become repetitive time-killers. When every day in life feels like any other day, it's time to give it a serious thought. Happiness and balance in life looks different. It was clear to me that I could neither work forever in a large IT corporation or live in a hot climate while living in a small town.

My experience at Dell was typical for any large corporation, it just happened to be Dell. Some people know very well how to maneuver such companies and eventually get quite far in their career. I had no intentions for the above reasons. In my mind I dreamed of starting my own business rather than staying in a corporate career. Today I have to say that it was a good experience. Now that I don't have to be there anymore, and the pain has eased, it's easy to recount the good memories and experience. I learned how big companies are functioning, who is making the decisions and what are your chances to do business with a large company if you are a smaller supplier trying to get a foot in the door. This is my the main learning experience. Eventually I was able to use the knowledge on how to deal with large corporations for my own business, and not for my need to survive within. During the time at Dell, as much as I despised being there, I still tried to perform and to learn whatever possible, just for that feeling that it may be useful one day. I also couldn't afford to lose the job, since I needed the money. In the end I was in the exact situation that one should avoid.

That killed all my drive and motivation. I dreaded going to work due to my state of mind and philosophical approach to life. None of that was *their fault*, they were just the easiest to blame. At times the sum of all behavior in a company towards you can feel like a conspiracy against you. Especially when you aren't moving forward or you don't like your job it's very quick and easy to blame the company for it. But maybe it doesn't have anything to do with the company itself. Maybe you are just at the wrong place. Just like I was at the wrong place. I just didn't belong there. One could certainly ask why I went their then. Quite simple: I needed a paycheck, I knew I needed a good sounding job to continue my career path, not just any job at a gas station or coffee shop, and I underestimated the hot weather and its effect on what I love to do most, being outside.

In 2014, after three years it all came together. My wife had gotten a job offer from Boston at the same time as Dell offered voluntary separation packages as part of a work force reduction program. My wife was my partner in crime to help me on my jailbreak and Dell gave me the cash I needed to pay my bills while I started my own business.

"Everything has been figured out except how to live." Jean-Paul Sartre (1905–1980) said. There are many people that don't know what they want in life. This is quite normal, but too few give it a real thought.

Philosophy has it's fundament in the determination and structure of life, the world and knowledge. We have all the time in the world to think about marketing strategies, investigate human genomes, fly to space, build gadgets, and spent hours on posting profane things on the Internet, but thinking about what to do in life seems for most people as out-of-touch with real needs. Circus games are just more fun.

Some people may be afraid to think about life, because the result could be that they have to get up and do something about it. Like defining what a meaningful job could look like. Some people rather lean back and find condolence in saying "in this economy one should be happy to have a job," "but now you have a job, just do that for now and later you can see," or "think about the money you are making". These comments have its validity only on the peripheral, because we all need an income. We shouldn't make this requirement the excuse for everything, because it distracts from the possibility to lead a happier life:

1. If you always do what you have always done, you will always get what you have always got.
2. If you never do what you always wanted to do, you will surely end up doing something that you never wanted to do.

Passively wasting your time in idleness with your brain on stand-by, accepting the world as is and do just anything to get by is not a path to happiness. But what exactly could be the right way to go then?

The ancient Greek believed, that the active being, the Homo Faber, is the one that is making a difference for himself and is ultimately able to live a happy life. Up till today nothing of that has lost any of its wisdom and beauty. Aristotle said that all humans are striving for happiness, in Greek *eudaimonia*. What happiness means can be argued about. For some it is visible like money and power, for others it's to plant flowers on a balcony, save an endangered species or to teach generations of children the ABC. For one it's this, for another something else. And it might depend on the circumstances, like health is to the sick or prosperity to the poor.

Aristotle defines happiness as to be *living well*. Living well should not be misunderstood with what we commonly understand as someone that is *well off*, like having a house, a car and a big salary. Living well is a non-static attitude or activity. The good life is led by constant proficiency of living a life of practical reason and to live it consistently. Happiness is not a constant state of affairs, but a being-able-to-be-happy-with-oneself. The happy person would never do anything that is against moral integrity, but lives according to good manners and being a good person.

Aristotle said that all human action is always based on the decision to strive for something good. The goal is the *good*. The determination of a goal is the intentional structure of an action. To be a human being is to be an operative subject, a subject that is in action, doing things. The operating of the soul and the action resulting from practical reasoning, is what makes us human.

Examples for practical reasoning are that building a house goes back to architecture and philosophy goes back to understanding. Aristotle calls this kind of specific goal the creation (*ergon*). In general we can distinguish between three types of goals:

1. Actions that are not being performed for their intrinsic value, but because they aim to achieve a certain final condition. The action and the outcome are separate from each other. The reason for the action is not the action itself, but the outcome. For example you wouldn't carry bricks and mortar around for the sake of carrying them around, but to build a house. The action gets its affirmation due to the desired outcome. This is the case if we work to make a living without liking the work itself.

2. Actions that are performed because of their own intrinsic value. The action itself is also the creation or the goal. Examples are playing music, reading a poem, or mourning about the loss of a loved one. Such mental actions do not have another meaning outside of their performance. If you mourn or play an instrument, it is about mourning or music, not about a

product our outcome of it. When you stop playing the instrument, the music also ends.

3. The third type of action is the type that is performed for its intrinsic and instrumental character. Eating, playing sports or working, belonging to that group. Preparing and eating good food create joy and satisfy appetite, playing soccer with friends is fun and is good for your health, and fulfilling work is enjoyable and secures your livelihood.

The things we do for their intrinsic value are the ones that serve happiness the best. Otherwise all our actions would be meaningless: If we'd do everything in order to achieve something else, but never for the performed action itself, then the reason for our actions would always lie with the desired outcome, not with our current action.

We should strive to create a harmonic unity among the things that we do for their own intrinsic meaning, such as exercising, playing an instrument, reading, mourning, and thinking, and the instrumental character of actions. Otherwise our lives would be missing the essential unison which makes us say YES! to our lives. The pursuit of happiness is to find out what meaningful work means to you and the quest to be able to do just that.

Aristotle said that humans distinguish themselves from all other living creatures through the capability of active thinking, using your own reasoning and plan to live according to virtues that lead a happy life. Plants are also alive and breath, like humans. To be an observing creature is not enough to be human, since animals observe and live actively as well. Animals' life is instinctively driven by two main factors:

1. Surviving (eating and not get eaten).
2. Survival of their race (reproduction).

Unique to humans is that we are capable to use our own reasoning to plan our life and live according to our plan (some people just don't do it).

71

We also acknowledge that our life is finite; therefore we know that everything will come to an end.

Aristotle does admit that not only the exertion of the soul, but other outer and physical goods do play a role, including heritage, prosperity, friendship, honor, descendants, destiny, health, beauty, physical strength. Therefore Aristotle also believes that to a certain extent other things influence our happiness. However these are born out of the activity of the soul: Valuing outer physical goods come through the capability of valuing them. Friendship e.g. cannot be monetized, yet it has an enormous value to us and plays an important role for leading a good life.

The life of humans is driven by rational oversight. According to Aristotle, the final stage of life is neither a static moment, nor has it any instrumental character. Therefore leading a good life, full of virtues incl. bravery, temperance, generosity, munificence, honor, truthfulness, wit, natural justice, prudence, and of course friendship, have to be the real goal for happiness.

For Aristotle the *good* that we strive for is the one thing that we want for its own value, and not in order to be the enabler for something else. Things that are of material value and can be exchanged for other things are measurable to each other. Striving for monetary wealth cannot be the final goal of life, since money has *only* an instrumental character.

Money is a medium, a tool to pay for things that we need or may make us happy, but it is not a replacement for happiness. Money measures everything, the surplus and the paucity, also how many shoes are equivalent to a house or food. Through an unwritten agreement among people, money has therefore become the substitute for desideratum.[37]

Simple people always have an opinion ready like "just get any job" or believing that "work is not fun". How different to an animal are we when all we do is do just *any* job (survive like animals) and come home and watch TV (breath air and observe)? Doing anything just to survive, in a philosophical meaning, sets you at the same stages of an animal.

---

37 ARISTOTLE (4TH CENTURY B.C.), 5TH BOOK

There is no way back. Once you start thinking about your life and the world as is you cannot return to a simplified and profane world view anymore. I certainly can't lie to myself and give in, knowing that it's against being human and against the economics of the labor market.

So what should we do? How I can we find out what we want?

It doesn't require dedicated time. It doesn't require to set an hour aside every week to sit down and think about life. All that is needed is the ability to actively observe and reflect, reflect upon your own life within your personal circumstances. That happens, while you wait for a bus, when you go for a walk, as you wait for someone to bring you a cup of coffee in a Café, while a colleague talks too long in a meeting, as you take the elevator, or when you chop onions. You can eat an egg for breakfast, and as you are strengthening yourself for the day, you may ask yourself if the egg was first, or maybe it was the chicken after all? Our brain can process an unlimited amount of information in split seconds. When someone says to me: "You have too much time" I like to remind them that my day has 24 hours just like theirs. The question is only how much you seize of it and how many hours do you exist and feed of your pre-defined opinions and half-wit life advisory? What do you do with the time that is given to you?

The pockets of time that one has every day to open one's eyes are infinite. Maybe we are just too busy being entertained. With small children we see that boredom turns into creativity. When you don't give in to begging to watch TV or play on your phone, they will soon start to think about stuff to do. We should maintain that child in ourselves, take our lives offline, be less entertained by things, especially electronics, Internet and TV. You'll be surprised of all the things that one comes up with, when we aren't passively lounging our lives away.

Goethe, after spending a good amount of travel time in Italy from 1786–1788, said traveling was like a game, there was always winning and losing within, mostly from an unexpected angle. One receives some times more or even less than one hoped for. For people "of my nature a journey is priceless, it revives, corrects, instructs and teaches." Traveling is a process of learning about countless things. Not only does it educate you about different places and people, but most of all about yourself. With travel I mean self-determined active travel, plan and execute the trip on your own, pick a place and explore, instead of passive travel like cruising on a luxury ship, a beach resort or amusement park. When you travel, you think about home and what you usually do there. You compare it to other things that you see throughout your travels. It can enforce your thought that what you do at home is good, or it might urge you to change something. Seeing your life from a distance is like having that good friend who is your alter ego and helps you to get to know yourself. I try to travel as much as I can, which doesn't mean I buy a plane ticket and jet around the world. I try to get out of my neighborhood once a week, out of my town once a month. You don't have to go far, just don't follow your usual routine once in a while. It will do wonders. I like to be a tourist in my own town, go to see places that travelers would come and see. It can be fun to go into a touristy restaurant to meet people who visit your city. Or it is nice to just get away for the day into a nearby town, try out a new winery, visit a medieval castle or monastery, hike a small mountain, or cycle along a river. The importance is to do something outside the usual routine. Stepping out of yourself and see yourself from a distance.

The same fear that keeps people from doing what they always wanted to do is that others could judge them for it. They call it a gap in your resume. Like taking a year off to backpack around the world, or staying at home with your children for a few years as they grow up. People hesitate to do what makes them happy, because they worry too much about what others think. Privately and professionally. They worry that something might be counterproductive to what is considered a "good" resume. It is counterproductive for your long term career to take a job beneath your qualities, but it's far from that if you branch out for a while. Your resume is needed for the job hunt, so it shouldn't be underestimated. But you will put a strait jacket on yourself if anything you plan on doing is subject to the question of whether it helps your resume or not. In that moment your life is determined by what others think of your life, self-determination & freedom ends right there.

If something is supposed to be good or bad for your resume then that would require that someone is entitled to judge about what's good and what is not. Why would you leave it to others to judge about whether your life until today was good or bad? I'm not hiding behind the piece of paper that my resume is written on and hope that the reader will lower the paper and look at me saying "well done, I'm impressed". Sometimes our own beliefs are the actual obstacles that we are creating for ourselves. A resume is a brief summary of your skills and experience, it's what most of the world calls a Curriculum Vitae. The Latin word of curriculum can also be translated as syllabus, course of instruction. Universities use the term curriculum on their summaries of what is included in a subject of studies. It is an ex-ante term, the plan of studies before you enter. Though, it does also have an ex-post character, because it tells about the skills you are expected to have once you graduate. Curriculum vitae can therefore mean: subject of studies of your life. That is why many get so nervous. They think about how it can look to others if they do this or that. It is important to take that into account before quitting a job in order to travel the world. What it should not do is that every action we do is based on the fear about what others say about it. To live a free life means not to be afraid. Fear is an agent for people who want to control others. Don't be afraid. Live your life and then write your resume. You can always make anything look nice and shiny in the aftermath. Even your resume is just a marketing tool, not a proof of a successful life. Work for your life, not for your resume.

While I was working at Dell, the company merged the Small- and Medium Business (SMB) department together with the Public and Large Enterprise (PLE) department and formed one single commercial business unit. I had been part of PLE and was used to a certain process to conduct the business. As an analytical self-thinking person, I questioned some of the new processes on their usefulness. Not because I don't like change, but because I don't like stupid. I asked

75

various colleagues why we would have new processes that were more complicated and less useful than before. The common answer was: "we do it, because that's the way SMB used to do it." That wasn't an explanation of the usefulness, but only that the process came from elsewhere. I made it a little experiment and found that most people were reciting that exact sentence. Not a similar explanation, no: the exact same words! My field trial dummies were therefore either all dumb and extremely gullible or they were resigned and didn't want to deal with such questions knowing that they can't be changed. It was a question to end any conversation: "It is what it is." Either way it is a frustrating situation for people who want to make things better. Regardless of the reasons why people just keep doing what they are doing, none of them had any excitement about it either way. Why else would someone just accept any change unquestioned just like that? They may be simply gullible or became indifferent and resigned, or they just prefer to not get involved, because they can get away with three hour work weeks and not bother; none of which is a desirable state of mind for a person with aspirations.

Socrates (470–399 B.C.) said that the only true wisdom is "knowing you know nothing". His purpose was not to tell everyone they'd be stupid, but to engage people to question presumed knowledge on its truth and roots. This is called a *Socratic conversation*. You cannot lie to yourself, you can only ignore the truth. Eventually you will have to continue pursuing your dream and there is no valid reason why one should ever give up.

Reasoning is what makes us human: "Cogito Ergo Sum – I think, therefore I am", said René Decartes (1596–1650). And Kant demands you do have the courage to use your own reasoning: "Sapere Aude!"

Among Kant's major works are the Critique of Pure Reason (1781 and 1787) and the Critique of Practical Reason (1788). If it was possible to summarize in a sentence each what these immense works are about then one can say that the first one is about "what can we know" and the following about "what do I have to do?" Kant's call to have the courage to use your own reasoning and his categorical imperative therefore goes much further than treating others as you want to be treated yourself. Imperatives cannot stay hypothetical: If you *can* use your own reasoning, then you also *have to*. To do the opposite can simply be considered ignorance. I have never really understood what is going on in an ignorant mind, but it must be full of a constant discomfort and fear that someone might stick a needle into the bubble you live in. Or is it really possible to just not care at all?

To find ourselves and to make up our own minds, we also have to assure diversity of the sources of information and support we use. Technology, especially the Internet allows one to get all the world's information on the touch of a button. Using it without thought though, can lead to an auto-gentrification of our lives and our world views.

One of the many benefits of the Internet is that we can find groups of people that have the same interests as we do and meet others who think alike and may have the same hobbies and interests. Even in the most foreign places in the world you will be able to make new friends quickly that way. Having specific interests is more fun if you find others to share your passion with. It also means that we are more surrounded by people who think alike. That provides comfort and security. If you use the Internet to find people or information that you can translate into real activities with real people in a real life it has an enormous benefit, because you can find more information in a much faster time than ever before.

The flipside is that many people mingle only with their own kind. While that is fun, it doesn't always help to step out of oneself. To spend your life among likeminded people alienates you from the ones who are different. Especially in political debates it is noticeable that the stronger a group feels, backed up by large group of supporters on the Internet, the more it hinders dialogue and aggravates the division between people with different opinions. The same applies to getting your information only from one source, which would be similar to have censored media.

The challenge in stepping out of yourself arises when people live their lives virtually and gain all their knowledge, experience and world view from one source: The way we gain information through the

Internet is following ever more the principle of similarity. Algorithms of search engines and cookies that are set to follow your browsing habits and screening of the content of your web-based e-mail are used to profiling you. The strategy that search engines and other web service providers follow by doing so is to find results that you care for quicker. It is meant as a service to make it easier for you to find what you like. The business side is that the more you can profile people the easier it is to place targeted advertising and sell that placement to companies that want to sell you something. If you email a friend that you liked last weekend's bicycle race you will probably see an advertisement for recreation and outdoor products on your web browser soon. If you tell your friends that you are going to travel to Italy next spring it won't take long until you see offers for flights and hotels popping up. On social media the sites are programmed to show you mostly the news feeds of people that you interact with a lot. All of this creates the so-called "filter bubble". Search results are not based on what Kant's Critique of Pure Reason follows, the question on what *can* we know. Instead it only shows us what we *want* to know. In the same way as the Internet helps us to find information and share our interests with others, it puts us a silo mentality. Through our behavior on the Internet we start to indoctrinate ourselves with our world views. We are creating our own truths and the more we will search online for results, thanks to search engine algorithms, we will find just that. Anyone searching with different words for a specific topic on the Internet will soon end up finding the same results, no matter how often you changed the wording. This can lead to the misbelief that there are no other options out there. To live too much online, and too little offline can get you stuck in your situation. The way to see your life from a distance is not to browse for people who have the same problems, but to get your mind to open for other things that may not have anything to do with your current challenges. This is the way to get unstuck.

To maintain friendships and relations only with like-minded people and gaining all our knowledge from a single source bears the risk within to manifest a world view that can be far from reality and is making it difficult to step out of ourselves. Many social media sites are set up to use little text, mostly pictures, encourage to approve and share, yet not to disagree and discuss. The users who have grown comfortable to get a daily dose of compliments to their profane life are quickly hurt when they hear other than positive feedback on their cat video or mom blog they just posted.

The way how people make decisions in their lives is correlated on how situations occur to them. According to Goethe a man is the sum of his experience. People all over the world do the same things, but everything people do is seen through their own eyes, based on their own education, traditions and beliefs, myths and urban legends, opportunities and experience, and access to education and travel. Everything that happens in the world occurs different to each one of us. Anything we do makes complete sense to us, but it doesn't necessary do to others. And by seeing the world as it occurs to us, we also make our decisions based on our worldview. It becomes what we consider the truth. By doing so, we create a default future running towards us, our lives seem to be pre-written based on the assumptions we have about it. The way to change our future is by realizing the actual world we are in and changing our life into a future-based present, away from walking through a life with a pre-defined path. Away from thinking *this is the way it is and we can't change it.* If we see our lives only through our personal tunnel vision we also tend to think that everyone else is having a tunnel vision too, and whatever others do must be either for or against us. It creates a friend and foe thinking that kills the ability to reflect and synthesize. Other people's acting has usually to do with themselves, not with you. To see the world through a tunnel can make you assume that being affected by other people's action is because they wanted to affect you. Even if it was unintentionally. To put yourself into the shoes of others is the best way to understand and influence their actions, and to understand the alternatives the other ones have. It can also help you to get a better picture on how others see you. The way we think of ourselves is not always a mirror of what others think of us. Because most people want to believe in the truth of their own bubble it can give you enormous power. Whenever people follow a specific pattern you can predict and influence their behavior. It is because people grow comfortable to like themselves, especially if social media approves that message daily.

One good way to visualize life's patterns in a simplified way is food and eating habits. I like examples around preparing food and eating habits since it is an essential necessity for survival that every living being has in common, only with regional nuances to the way food is obtained, prepared and eaten. In the Western World we often eat a soup as an appetizer before dinner because it gets you into eating and enjoying the flavors of a meal and gives you more appetite. In China you eat the soup after you have eaten your main dish, because the fluid fills the rest of the holes in your belly. Why would you fill yourself with a bowl of fluid if you still have the main dishes to come? Which one makes more sense? That really depends. Food is a great example to show that things occur different to everyone. On the whole planet people eat the same things: meat, flour, eggs, vegetables, fish, chicken, rice, pasta/noodles, milk, etc. Yet everywhere in the world food tastes different and the habits differ even more. An Englishman would eat a sausage for breakfast; a German would eat it the earliest for lunch (with the exception of Weisswurst in Bavaria). Why would you eat a sausage for breakfast? Why wouldn't you? Eating habits are, besides language, one of the best ways of getting to know to a culture. What people eat, how they prepare it, how they behave at the table, the manners. Is it a drive-through culture with disposable plates or the two-hour-lunch ritual? Do they eat with their hands, or do they use knife and fork, or chopsticks? Do the people share from main plates on the table or does everyone get its individual meal? Do people talk with food in their mouth, spit on the floor, burp at the table, look into each other's eyes when they toast with a beverage? All of this tells you a lot about a culture and how serious they are about anything. The way you cultivate the basic human necessities is also a projection on how you treat anything else in life. Within your own society though, this always seems normal.

Behind any social media profile there are always the true worries of a person. To oneself your worry is weighing on you like the sword of Damocles, but to others your issue might be profane or too ambitious.[38] It all depends on the level of confidence, experience and attitude. Some people aren't ambitious to ever think beyond their daily routine. Others don't want to be ambitious because they have other priorities in life. Accept it and don't bother them with your issues. Find your mentor(s) to talk about what your challenges in life are and have a good time with everyone else. You have to learn to not think about it sometimes and enjoy being with people who don't always want to talk about big dreams. It makes life too stressful anyway.

Learn to become a renaissance man, or -woman. Leon Battista Alberti, the 15th century Florentine architect created the term of the "L'Uomo Universale" the universal man, also called the "renaissance man". It describes a person who can develop his capabilities and talents to the fullest extent. Alberti believed that "a man can do all things if he will". Renaissance Humanism "considered man being the center of the universe, limitless in his capacities for development, and led to the notion that men should try to embrace all knowledge and develop their own capacities as fully as possible."[39] Alberti, like Leonardo da Vinci or Michelangelo, was someone that we call a polymath: Architect, painter, classicist, poet, scientist and mathematician. Those men that became famous during the Renaissance time were gifted people and not everyone has the talent to sculpt David out of a single block

---

38 Damocles was a courtier of Dionysius the Elder, tyrant of Syracuse in Sicily in the 4th century B.C.. Damocles is famous for the legend of the "Sword of Damocles". Damocles, so the story tells, was jealous of the extravagant lifestyle and the power and wealth of the tyrant. Dionysius therefore decided to teach Damocles a lesson by inviting him to a sumptuous banquet. He seated Damocles underneath a sword that was only hanging from the ceiling on a single thread of horsehair. Damocles wasn't able to enjoy the feast and ask for permission to retreat. He had learned the lesson that power and wealth do not safeguard you from dangers. Sometimes they can be the cause of it. To have a sword of Damocles hanging over your head means to be in a constant threat or danger of something. See ENCYCLOPAEDIA BRITANNICA, DAMOCLES

39 ENCYCLOPAEDIA BRITANNICA, RENAISSANCE MAN

of marble or paint the ceiling of the Sistine Chapel. However, one can apply that attitude and thirst for knowledge to his own life. The attitude to improve on a multidisciplinary level is the way to challenge yourself, find your talents, and to keep on going. If you focus on one thing only you will experience very emotional downsides when this one thing is not working out the way you wanted. To become interested in many disciplines broadens the mind and hedges against falling into deep mental holes. It enables to see life from different angles and pinpoint your talents and interests more precisely.

Aiming to become a polymath should not be mistaken with multi-tasking in the meaning of doing many things at the same time. It's about doing one thing at a time, with focus and passion, and then to take breaks in between. This can help to get your outcome faster, even though it feels like it takes longer. One of my Taekwondo teachers, Grand Master Suk Jun Kim, said that at a certain age practicing every day might not improve your skills as much anymore as it used to. You need time to let things settle, think about what you are doing and after a day of break you retake the practice. The same applies to most things in life. Not everything gets better, because you work every day on it. To focus shall not mean to be single-minded. To focus is to concentrate on one thing without distraction in the moment of exercise. I tend to follow 2–3 things at the same time and I read many books at the same time. In University I also had different subjects to study for, what's the difference? The topics should be different in nature though. Studying Spanish and Italian at the same time can lead to major confusion, since they are very similar languages. To study home-brewing and Japanese at the same time do not interfere with each other. By this method you can constantly work on something in parallel without wearing yourself out, getting distracted or bored. I can work for a few months on certain kick or punch techniques in my Taekwondo practice, try to improve a recipe for homemade sausages, work on this book, study Chinese characters, or start building a company. This aims to improve my skills in a wide array of aspects of life. I don't do all of these every day, but switch them around. That way every day I learn something new, I practice something that I want to improve, yet none of them are getting boring or wear me out. However, I still keep going all the time on all ends. Like a renaissance man, I try to be an expert at many things, not just at one. That is how you progress as a person and they will ultimately complement each other: Good health, brain training, satisfaction from being able to prepare your own food, a job that is fulfilling and pays for my livelihood. Each activity has its own intrinsic value, they are worth doing on its own. And they also lead to balance, satisfaction, confidence, and joy of life.

By switching up the hobbies you also prevent yourself from living in a bubble, because in each one there are very different types of people involved that keep you from thinking everyone in the world is the same and wants the same. You keep yourself from only learning to use a hammer and seeing a nail in every problem. It helps you to dive into a different world each time and by a wide range of hobbies you see yourself and your abilities always from a different point of view.

Your professional life will also benefit from accumulating a wealth of knowledge and expertise in different disciplines. Lunch with a business partner, dinner with international customers, a small talk with the CEO at the cafeteria, or a networking event at a trade show. If you are able to talk about many interesting aspects of life, understand food, language, culture, politics, arts, technology, history, manners and you are inside and out a healthy person, you will be able to build long-lasting relations with literally anyone in the world. The one who only talks business is boring, it's the guy who walks around with a hammer looking for nails. It is great to learn something new every day, and it's just as great to be able to participate in any conversation you might get caught up in.

While living in Argentina as an exchange student from 2001 to 2002 I became good friends with a local from Córdoba, named Javicho. He had graduated in Architecture, had a beautiful girl-friend, had a job, a lot of friends, and everyone loved him in his town. He had a job and everything looked like a good life by the book. He would not have had any reason to complain about his life, anyone from the outside would say. He has a very good heart and he is a deeply spiritual person as well. He started a tiny non-profit for malnourished children in the "villas", the ghettos of Cordoba. He organized folk-music evenings where he and his friends had live bands performing, and offered food and drinks, and all the money went to feed 24 poor children between two and five years of age, who would otherwise face malnutrition. Later he spent a year traveling in Spain and upon his return he decided that he wanted to become a priest. It wasn't that he went from Argentina to Spain and saw the light and wanted to become a priest. He told me that he had contemplated with that thought for a long time and he wanted to get away from his routine, to get a clear mind about it. We spent a lot of time talking about his decision before and during his time of studying to become a priest. As his closer friends and family heard the news, it was the beginning of the summer, we were all sitting on the back patio of his family's home. Javicho didn't make a big announcement, but he went to each one of his siblings, his mother and father and his friends, one by one. He wanted that each of them understand his decision based on the relation that he had with each individual. I was impressed by that approach, because even though a family might live together for years, everyone has a different personality. And the world views are different. Even though it's the same world and the same family, it always occurs different to us. For a father, the view of his family is the view of a father. For a child, the view is that of a child. Making good food for dinner may for the child be a joy of eating good food, for the parents the relief that their child is eating enough.

Javicho was about to start a 10 year program to become a priest with the first year being the toughest. Going into the jungle of Paraguay, isolated from the world. With lots of books and opportunities to exercise, but no telephone, Internet or TV. A year of finding yourself. Usually the year when most people would quit, I heard them say. His mother was upset and she kept asking us, what we thought about it and what we could do to make him stay. She kept repeating that he had great friends and that everyone loved him and he had a job and his life was so happy, why the need to do this? She was sad and proud at the same time, like any mother would be. She knew how hard the program mentally was, what good a person Javicho is, and she was proud that he would take something like that upon him. But she was upset that he was going to leave and we didn't know when and how we would see him again. As people were staring into the air I said: "Listen, I think the reason why everyone here is upset is because of ourselves. We all love Javicho, because his presence is always a time of joy, no matter if it's in good times or in bad times. If you would want to have one friend in your life, then it would be him. And the reason why we might be sad has nothing to do with him, but with us. If he leaves then he leaves, because he believes that it's best for him. Trying to find reasons why he should not do this has nothing to do with him and what's good for him, but all with us, that we don't want to lose him from our vicinity. And if we really love him like we all do, we should stop being sad about losing him in our presence, but be happy for him that he at least is one who found what he wanted to do and wants to go through with it. It is totally irrelevant if we understand or want to understand the reasons behind his decision."

When we decide any course of action in our lives we will always have people around us who suggest us otherwise or might not affirm the same beliefs we have. The interesting thing that Javicho has done is that he took his time to make up his mind and when he finally made a decision it was firm and final. Then he informed everyone close to him. People always think about how the action of another will affect them. If a person that you love is going away then the first reaction is often that you want them to stay. That has to do with you, not with the other one. If you ever decide to do something that is not among the typical, it can be a wise decision not to tell anyone about your plans. It is nice to be affirmed in your thoughts, but talking to too many people can also gather a crowd of people that thinks that you can't do such a thing and just waits for you to fail. That will bring a lot or pressure on you. Another reason is that we look for affirmation, not for doubts. We don't want to hear that our idea is not a good one. Basically we are hoping the others help us make a decision by seeking their support for it, not their warning. Social media has brought this to an extreme: people are only looking for approval for their actions, but react hurt when they earn criticism. It is nice to get approval, but in general you should either be open to criticism and look for people who can give you constructive feedback or otherwise keep it for yourself and make the decision in absence of other people's opinion. A decision for or against anything is the right decision if you weigh in all knowledge and experience that you have at that time to make the decision. It has to be independent on the likelihood of social approval and even the likelihood of failing or succeeding. You don't make decisions in order for others to like them, but in order to move on in your own life.

At work and in free time, the personal talk will always get you further. Big announcements are often used by the speaker to get attention to himself, but to find understanding people and their support, the private conversation gives a lot more room to explain one's reasoning and derived actions.

Javicho told me about what had changed his life, and it inspired me to do the same. He had sat down and wrote down 100 things that he wants to do in his life. Basically a bucket list. That exercise can take several weeks. He wrote everything down that came to his mind, from simple things, to others that take years in preparation. Making a bucket list helped him to get structure and meaning to his life. It was also a result from being away from home and seeing his life from a distance.

If there are 100 things you want to do and you know you only have so many years left to do them, then should you better get going: The rest of your life starts now. It can take quite some time, effort and perseverance to complete a long bucket list. But you'll start to organize your life better, and your time management improves tremendously. Some things are really simple and others not. On my own bucket list I checked off things like "I want to learn how to make sushi" and "I want to learn to play the harmonica". The first one I learned to do, the second one I didn't. But I tried and realized it was not one of my talents. Now it's off the table and no-one has to listen to me playing the harmonica ever again. I wanted to become a black belt in Taekwondo.

It took years in training to get there and a life-time to keep it. A bucket list isn't always about taking flight lessons or climbing to the base camp of Mount Everest.

A bucket list starts with things you always wanted to do, but you just never did, regardless how long you have until you kick the bucket. A lot of the items on your bucket list are quite simple, you'll be surprised. When you tell others about things that can be found on your list you will hear a lot of "oh but that is easy to do." Yet many people don't even do that, it just seems to easy. They can do those things on someday-island. If it's too easy, they don't bother. But here is the key: it doesn't have to be difficult every time, but it can be very joyful. So just go out and check the boxes off your list. While you do that you will discover new interests and talents about yourself. Your list will turn into a working and living document and might get altered quite a bit. You will put a lot of meaning to your life, because you are constantly active. And you will be very happy about yourself. Life will be more exciting.

How many people live a life that is pleasing others and do anything to get social approval rather than just following their heart? Writing a bucket list is something where many people nod and agree that it would be something good to do. But actually sitting down to do it is different. Writing on paper and having it black and white in front of you can be an eye opener that you might want to change something in your life. By trying hard to get to 100 things you always wanted to do you might even find out what are the things that you really like in life, they might differ from what you thought that you like. You can discover your own personality and may find interests and talents that can also steer you towards a completely new career path as well.

Fyodor Dostoyevsky (1821–1881) said: "The one who lies to himself and listens to his own lie, will ultimately reach a point that he cannot distinguish any truth anymore, neither his nor any around him."

I have seen people who were a long time successful in terms of their number of promotions. They have always found a way to use politics of a company to their advantage and after a while it became their reality. The white lies, the exaggerations, taking credit for other people's work and always looking for their own benefit turned into that lie which Dostoevsky said became their own truth. When that type of person gets laid off they don't understand the world anymore. It will be an Alice in Wonderland experience. They believed that up is up and down is down, and left and right are where they are. And they wake up one day and realize it's actually all different. To know yourself also includes to know when you are talking yourself into something, because you want it to be the truth. You will be able to see your own limits better and stay humble.

To make a plan and going for it requires to locate yourself on the map of opportunities, to see which way you are facing in order to go forward. Step out of yourself and to get to know to thyself. Traveling, doing things outside of your routine, discussing with your friends, find good mentors, and doing things you love are a great way to do so. Making a bucket list is another.

The role of the individual human in society and the role of the individual in a corporation meet very often. Some people work the same way as they do their free time, others act or force themselves to maintain a certain reputation. Whatever the motivation of the others are, one thing to keep in mind is that they are all humans that want to be happy one way or the other. The rational business talk is only a cover on top of it.

They are all humans. Trying to understand other people's logic, world view and rhetoric make the realities of corporations more bearable. The more versatile you develop as a person, the more you also gain the instrumental benefit to becoming very adaptable to each and everyone's style and personality you meet. It enables you to become more personable, you are more likeable, and therefore you will also like the others better, too. That helps you to find support for your personal goals.

Whatever we do always makes perfect sense to us, yet not necessarily others. It's also how others see you. Your behavior might not make any sense to others. If you want to like others and be liked, try to understand other people and accept their way of doing things. That is neither becoming a yes-man nor a cold-calculating politician. It is a way to get along with other people, to stay sane and at the same time become a nice and likeable person in the mind of the others.

Simply said: No-one will ever do you a favor or help you with anything just because you are smarter or work harder. People help you if they like you.

Mark Twain said the one who always spoke the truth wouldn't have to remember anything. Adapting to other people's character has to become your second skin if you want others to like you. That is neither having hidden thoughts, saying only what they want to hear nor the attempt to mislead people: It's a way to adopt to people's way of life and thinking and to speak in a language that they can understand and relate to.

Everyone has the option to make a difference for him or herself. Many people just choose not to. They accept life and society as is, assume that this is just what one has to do. And because most people do it must be the right thing. Some people choose not to use their own reasoning, they have grown comfortable to be indifferent and lazy. It's easier to find excuses than getting to action. However, happiness is a dynamic state of mind. It is the ability to say "yes!" to life and to live it up in a way that makes us happy and not in the way people expect it from us. The Homo Faber is the one who turns the rough piece of metal into a useful tool. You can't pay anyone to do that for you and you cannot wait for happiness to knock on your door. It only comes out of the activity of the soul, the intrinsic value of what we do. For work and career it means that we have to find out who we are, know ourselves, and then derive a plan of action and go for it. There are explanations or complaints about others who have it so easy, but that is irrelevant. Do not use other people's lives and their actions as an excuse for inaction. We have to step outside of ourselves for a moment and take money out of the equation. If you find out what you really want then you will also be able to make a living with it. And appreciating that our time in life is limited also makes it much more exciting to spend it with something that we love, rather than living up to social approval. Your default future is already written. That's where you are heading towards if you keep your life as you are now. You are the only one who can change that direction.

Your personal freedom ends where the other person's freedom begins. There are rules that we have to obey to and rules that are unwritten. The pursuit of happiness is a long and never-ending endeavor. You try things, some fail, some don't, you learn from them, move on to new challenges. Happiness is the path and goal at the same time. It is to maneuver around the obstacles and the limitations that we face.

The economies of the labor market are dysfunctional. Not always the best will prevail, but the ones who best learn to adapt to change. Signaling and screening is everywhere. On the labor market just as much as in almost any aspect of society. Understanding how the world goes round, diagnose what is out there is a pre-requisite to plan for success. Following a plan for success, however, has to be based on the right reasons. Money should be a tool and a nice side effect of the high level goal, the pursuit of happiness. Knowing yourself and what activities at work and in your free time make you happy, what environment you are living in, who the people around you are and what is it that you do on a daily basis play a fundamental role for that. Stepping out of yourself and seeing your own life from a distance is a way to recognize inflection points, moments in which you realize that it is time to steer your life into a different direction. Like any goal in life, everything can be broken down from a big picture into small, scalable steps. Confucius said: 千里之行 始于足下 – A journey of a thousand miles begin with the first step.[40]

---

40 The original word 里 equals 500m. The correct translation would be a trip (之行) of a thousand Li (千里) starts (始) at the bottom of your foot (于足下). It is therefore irrelevant if we are using miles, kilometers or Li, the meaning is that every long journey starts with the first step.

3 THE GAME PLAN

"Life is a chess game."

MIGUEL DE CERVANTES (1584–1616)

Live free and make money at the same time, how can we plan that? John Lennon (1940–1980) noted well that life happens when you are busy making plans. When you try to stick to rigidly to a plan you aren't open to seize or deal with sudden inflection points, yet if you have no plan you may just walk cluelessy through life. As in everything the golden mean is to make a plan, not lose sight of your goal, yet to be able to maneuver around sudden obstacles or seizing unexpected advantages. It may have been a result of growing up in Germany where people love to have rules and well-thought plans that get executed to the last detail and on the other hand I spent many years in South America, where life seemed a constant improvisation and living into the day. In combination these two cultural attitudes make a healthy mix of not stressing too much and yet getting things done.

The first time I made an actual career plan was in 2007. I was laid off after a year and a half in São Paulo and New York. For Digital Chocolate I had built new business and had driven revenue in key accounts in Europe, North- and South America. I had opened new sales channels for the company, I was a pioneer for new markets. And some point we had loosely started to consider the opportunity about going to Japan to do the same. And that wasn't even my own suggestion, but came from the leadership. Economics came in between. Costs had to be cut massively. I returned to Finland to continue life's journey.

It was yet another inflection point: It felt like I had to start over, though with newly gained experience I was far more confident in the job hunt than right out of University. After my ex-pat tenures in the Americas some people only said: "Look, now you got laid off." Would it have been the safer option to sit tight and do my job in Helsinki, trying to get along with a useless manager? At least I would have had an income? Should I have taken off and gone to Rovio to do something similar, but at least in a new environment? It really depends on your attitude. Living a year and a half in different cultures and major cities, and experiencing a different life-style, was priceless. A life experience that no-one can take away from me. Your car can break, your house can burn to the ground. The life you lived carries on in your memory, and builds the foundation for your future. When you learn something new and you challenge yourself, fall and get up again, you gain self-esteem, and you learn to pick your battles, you learn your limits and what your current frontiers are. Only through action, not reaction, this can be gained. The risks you are able to take do change over time, but that should not mean to become complacent and reserved.

I lost a job that I was starting to get tired of, but my experience can't be taken away by anyone. I was forced to do something that I should have started earlier: Look for a new opportunity. The lesson learned wasn't to not to take the chances, but to read the signs when the job starts to be less challenging and simply boring, or the company you are in is going downhill. I had not started to be active about a new job opportunity because I had an easy life in the big apple. I had been holding on to the job without liking it.

Needless to say that it also had to do with human behavior, also known as micromanagement. The boss I had ran the sales department ruminating the same three sentences over and over:

1. "I assume this is not going to cost anything."
2. "Can't you do that over the phone?"

3. "That is not going to happen!"

He was a corporate style naysayer in a startup company. Processes were introduced in a big corporation manner: Everything had to be approved, but hardly anything was approved. One time I received an e-mail from the marketing assistant:

"The new t-shirts are done. Please get your approval and let me know which customer you want it to send it to."

Me: "Please explain, what do I need approval for?"

She: "You need manager approval to send a t-shirt to your customer."

Of course none of my customers has received a t-shirt. I'd rather invite my customer for a drink with my own money, than wasting my time trying to get a lousy t-shirt approved.

It was the reaction of former corporate directors that believed when things go bad, maybe they should introduce a new process and grab more control, get a lot more structured, and automated. Startups usually have a latent lack of resources and a few people move things forward. Converting them into corporate style worker bees building rapport and following processes, you nip things in the bud that make or break a startup: the free flow of ideas and the can-do-spirit.

Following the idea of creating more chief positions and have even lesser Indians, more layers of management were created to play that corporate game further. My boss promoted himself, and for a short time, until my eventual lay-off, mommy's little helper became my micro-manager 2.0. I complained to him that there would be way too many approval processes and that we'd be better off to just go and do things, *especially* given the financial situation of our company. In a properly managed environment budgets and spending are planned and organized, then people are motivated. Here you were put in chains and were expected to run.

"You should see how it goes in big companies, it's all process." He responded.

"Well, isn't that why we aren't working for one, so we don't have to deal with all of that?" I wondered.

That didn't fly, but I just wasn't born to be a yes-man, I can't help it: When people say or do dumb things, I have a hard time keeping my mouth shut. I love my freedom of speech. And to say it with George Orwell (1903–1950): "If liberty means anything at all, it means the right to tell people what they do not want to hear." It is too bad that in many companies this liberty is limited by the people with limited skill and character. It can cost you your job, if the B-manager in front of you is intimidated when you make him realize that his assignment is not a sufficient proof of talent.

An individual on the expedition through a corporate career can feel like a drop in the ocean.

It can feel as if the world only appreciates you for what you can do for it. Intuitively one may be hesitant out of the fear to bite off more than one can chew. However, this is individual as it is universal. Others feel that way, too. It puts you into a position of strength at your starting point. If we expect others to look for some form of personal benefit, we are able to give them something they are enticed to take, as the ancient Chinese general Sun Tzu's advises us to do. Any little thing can make an impact as science proves.

The research field of chaos theory addresses non-linear dynamic systems that heavily rely on the initial conditions and whose outcomes seem to be unpredictable at the start, even though they are subject to deterministic equations. Repetitions of similar experiments can be influenced by a so called butterfly effect, where the outcome of the experiment will be different each time due to the high sensitiveness to minor changes at the start. These can lead to different outcomes.

The way we greet a stranger or our first encounter with a new boss, the things you say on a first date or choosing this job over that, all human interactions follow an analogy to Oscar Wilde's (1854–1900) observation that an acquaintance that starts with a compliment was sure to develop into a true friendship. Or in the opposite the saying that we started on the wrong foot. Our personal attitude towards life has a determining factor for the outcome of it. We meet and interact with other people every day, each new encounter can influence our future. It's a constant state of affairs in the exact Aristotelian meaning.

From a mathematical perspective we conclude that all human interaction is a game. The rules of this game and the ability to play are set by a wide variety of things including the cultural habitus in your society, your education and your life experience, your social status and your inclusion into community, your ability to grasp what is going on from far way and from close up, general beliefs and Urban legends, your attitude towards life and the ability to interact with others.

For any game and its rules a strategy can be developed. Chess is a strategic game, and according to Cervantes, life is a chess game, too. To see life as a chess game could mean that we can develop a strategy to win this game called life.

In a life's chess, set in a corporate world with a given society, the rules are somewhat set. Freeing our minds we learned that rules of society are rules, not dogma that need to be obeyed. To unchain oneself from social pressure converts you from a passive to an active chess player. I'm moving my figures, no-one else. The obvious step that follows is to elaborate a battle strategy.

Chess has been the most popular strategic war game since the 11th century A.D. Similar games had been played by people for much longer. The word *chess* is derived from the Persian word *shah* which means *king*. Chess is therefore considered the *royal game*. In this strategic game, two players are alternating in moving their figures on the board of 64 fields (8x8). Each player starts to play with 16 figures: with a king, a queen, two towers, two bishops, two rooks and eight pawns each player goal is to set the other player's king check mate. To reach that goal the players use different tactics of distracting the opponent, by attacking and withdrawing their figures. Each figure on the board has different strengths and weaknesses and the player has to choose wisely on how to use each figures' abilities effectively. Both players have to adhere to the same rules. You win the game by setting the other player *check mate* by threatening the opponent's king to be attacked without leaving any alternative left to remove that threat. In that case the other player has to cede and accept defeat.

Our battlefield in career chess is the job market and the internal organization of a company. The terrain we are fighting on is made of unequal distribution of information, un-even distribution of power, and one-sided contractual agreements. Usually you are up against superior strength which obliges you to move wisely.

This struggle against something more powerful can cause a teen-age like rebellious attitude, which has proven for centuries to be nature's way of young men and women to emancipate themselves against their elders. It's an exhaustive process for everyone involved, yet if parents can keep teenagers from doing too many crazy things, and teenagers get to experience enough crazy things, the outcome is often an independent person that has both feet on the ground and the necessary self-esteem to go out to the world. To become a yes-man or not starts early in life. A teenager may slam doors, turn the music loud in their room and think: "now we are at war." Now he or she will try to find other ways to undermine authority and impose their own will on their parents. But, what is war then?

"War is a political instrument, a continuation of a political commerce, a carrying out of the same by other means."[41] said Carl von Clausewitz (1780–1831) in his famous work *On War*. Clausewitz said that "war is an act of violence intended to compel our opponent to fulfill our will."[42] It is therefore an extreme tool when diplomacy and negotiations do not lead to the desired outcome. For centuries people often fought wars even before negotiating, just to get a stronger position at the negotiation table.

When you believe in your own capabilities, but talent and hard work do not represent a sufficient condition to reach your career goals, maybe it's time to rethink the methodology. This is an inflection point: If I'm not taking action, I will never get to where I want.

Recognizing the overwhelming starting position gives us guidance how to prepare for the uphill battle with many skirmishes. Sun Tzu

---

41 CLAUSEWITZ, C. VON (1832), Book One, I, 24

42 CLAUSEWITZ, C. VON (1832), Introduction, XIV

recommends to evade your opponent if he is superior in strength. He suggests to "attack him where he is unprepared" and "appear where you are not expected." Given our initial position on the battlefield (hierarchy) it is clear that we have to use guerrilla tactics.

Before going into the battle, let's get ourselves excited and motivated by internalizing important lessons from martial arts, especially from General Sun Tzu and the Japanese Samurai Myamoto Musashi (1584–1645):

1. Never lose sight of your goal.
2. Choose your battlefield wisely.
3. In war, then, let your great object be victory, not lengthy campaigns.
4. He will win who knows when to fight and when not to fight.
5. He will win who knows how to handle both superior and inferior forces.
6. The clever combatant imposes his will on the enemy, but does not allow the enemy's will to be imposed on him.
7. Never let your army rest.
8. Think of what is right and true.
9. Become acquainted with the arts.
10. Practice and cultivate the science.
11. Understand the harm and benefit in everything.
12. Learn to see everything accurately. Become aware of what is not obvious.
13. Even if superficially weak hearted, be inwardly strong hearted, and do not let others see into your mind.
14. Whether you are physically large or small, it is essential to keep your mind free from subjective biases.
15. See that which is far away closely and see that which is nearby from a distance.
16. Show profile and you will be recognized.
17. Never besiege the stronghold of your enemies.
18. The bait has to taste to the fish, not to the fisherman.

19. Act, don't react.
20. Attack the strategy of your opponents.
21. Removing weaknesses is a strategic task.
22. Making good use of strength is a strategic task.
23. Bravery and caution are no opposites.
24. You cannot be everyone's favorite.
25. Be steady on your feet.
26. Do not become distracted.
27. Take from others all they have and use it to your advantage.
28. Know your opponent's character.
29. Never let your enemy see what you are thinking.
30. Keep steady eye on what is moving and try not to blink.

The Latin proverb *Verba Volant Scripta Manent* means that words are flying and the written stays permanent. Since a good plan is half the victory, we need a paper and a pen to build our strategy. You can dream about your life all day long, but when you put it on paper you make your dream firm:

A plan is not a plan, if it is not written down:

Targets have to be measurable.

What has to be achieved and when is it considered achieved?

Targets need a deadline.

A plan that is only in our heads cannot have clear deadlines because we can move them to later dates.

Targets need to be doable.

By doable I mean everything that you can either do yourself or influence that it will get done. What is out of your reach is not considered doable. While most of our plans in life seem to be out of our control at first, the more diligent we work on the aspects that we can influence, the less room we leave to chance.

Goals can be broken down into smaller milestones. In the past 20 years, my goals were usually between a year or two in the future. Broken down into measurable goals with set time frames plans become more attainable and less overwhelming. Often you just have to get the ball rolling and things will start to take shape. Once started, the path gets a lot clearer. Some tasks are successive, others can be handled in parallel.

Sun Tzu urges the object of war to be victory, not lengthy campaigns. In a chess game the only goal is to checkmate the king of your opponent. The rules of chess are simple, yet winning is complex. The focus has to be on removing all obstacles that keep the other side from ceding to your attack.

Setting a career goal is to set a check-mate condition: To create a situation in which all potential no's from the management have been removed, so that the only alternative left for your career step is: yes!

Do not lose sight of that condition. Do not retreat from battle. And with Winston Churchill's words: "never, never, never give in."

Some people tend, too fast, to find arguments why this or that won't work. And especially simple people always have an opinion ready. It is essential to separate the heart and the brain in this exercise. Building a plan is to define with plain and simple words what has to happen. Do not mix feelings about its attainability in it already at the start. For example, part of your strategy could require achieving the sub target to *make my boss like me.* That is very simple to formulate. The fact that you might not like your boss or vice-versa *must not* play a role in the moment of the definition of a goal. The means that lead to that goal might be difficult to attain, but it should not affect the planning process at an early stage. The preparation and execution is what takes a lot of time. Especially when the goals are difficult to achieve. If you start a plan by saying "they will never do that for me" or "he will never like me" then you can get in line with the timid people who believe in destiny. Myamoto Musashi said that *it is imperative to master the principles of the art of war and learn to be unmoved in mind even in the heat of battle." In other words: Stay cool!

Other people's attitude towards common goals, you as a person and your personal goals have major influence on your success. Your personal eye-of-the-tiger spirit is what will drive you. Clausewitz says that *moral forces* in battle have a big influence on the outcome of it. He has experienced the French Revolutionary armies' (1792–1802) *élan* vs. the old order's compulsive recruitment armies. The level of motivation and the *human factor* played a major role then. The same difference in spirit can be seen even today with modern sports. A team that maybe less experienced and less skilled than another may still win a game or tournament if their will to win and their spirit is filled with *élan* – impetus and momentum. Working hard without a real reason is only going to burn you out and never lead to anything. It's like going to fight in a war that is not yours. Working hard to please society is one of those. Once you fight for your own reasons, you will notice that élan that you were missing. You switch from carrying brick and mortar for others to actually building your own house of happiness.

In career chess the idea is to impose your strategy onto the decision makers in a way that they will have no other choice but to cede to your proposal. Winning in career chess is not to kill your boss or blow up the company headquarters. Winning is meant as in winning support for your cause. It is a much more inclusive result at the end as it might sound at first. The opponents aren't really enemies in a martial meaning, but players that have power and different agendas than you have. You are not playing against your employer, yet you are sparring with a lot of forces that have influence over your future. It's almost like each figure on the chess board is played by a different person following its own interest as you are trying to get through to the king. In a corporation it can feel that way. You have to get through many skirmishes in order to get to the person who is in the position to decide in your favor. In career chess one task is to find out who's the king, before attacking him. You might be fighting long battles until your realize that you have been after the queen or the tower. For example you might be asking a team leader for a raise. If the person you report doesn't manage a budget you won't get the raise, if he doesn't feel like fighting on your behalf. You are in the jungle of rigid and illogical decisions, mediocrity, jealousy, and flattery. All the non-rational behaviors are the opponents you will have to beat.

Winning this game is not like winning the FIFA World Cup and in the end you get to hold up the trophy and celebrate. After the game, is before the next game. The same people that you have convinced to do something for you have expectations that you need to live up to. In the future, you still have to deal with the other players. We aren't aiming for knockout, but for winning others over for our cause.

Treating your career development like a game has a couple of immediate advantages. Firstly, it takes the stress out of it: it's a game. And unlike most games you can only win. You do it for yourself, not to please others. It helps not to take everything too serious, to stay flexible; focused but not fixated. Secondly, for every game there is a theory:

Game theory, a discipline within economic sciences, aims to create a mathematical model to strategic interaction of rational players. This allows the analysis of a game and a prediction for its outcome. *Rational* is not what would be considered the logic and best solution from an outside perspective. Rationality, in game theory, are decisions that a player makes based on the rules of the game and the information he has. Information can also include the world views or believes that are influencing the player. While corporate decision making seems irrational, each player follows a pattern based on his own reality and benefit. Just like the figures on a chess board they follow certain patterns consistently. That makes each player rational based on the rules, not by outside standards. Game theory is therefore extremely helpful to understand, explain and predict the behavior of the players within a company. And you are in the middle of it.

Your co-workers and superiors, business partners and customers, are in the first place the professional players in your work environment. Yet, all of them are human beings who are the sum of their experiences. They will see you and your proposals, your actions and reactions based on their own competence and experience, and the expectations which their job is requiring from them.

While your goal may not change, the means that you need to get there will have to. In martial arts you adapt your own fighting style according to the physical size of the opponent and his level of skill. You will try to keep a bigger opponent at distance and strike by reaction to an attack, while you can chase a smaller opponent around the area. Your goal is still to win. Therefore we should neither repeat our tactics, nor should we only use a single technique. The same applies for the different characteristics of the players in your career chess game. To build a positive relation with as many people as possible, you have to adjust your interactions with others to their personalities, without becoming a different person yourself.

Companies are formed by people and people are political and emotional creatures that all have a particular cultural and educational background, some are more and some are less intelligent. People often don't understand the world as it is, but as it occurs to them. It is difficult to define what outside standards should look like, since even these would be determined based on a method of thinking.

Align your personal strategy to the goals of the company you are in. Any company's dynamics of the competitive environment it is in comes with challenges. The constant changes of a business are your opportunity to steer strategy your way. In stormy waters you help to row and to navigate the boat to prove your abilities. When they trust that you can do it, you can steer the boat your way.

In order to achieve third party support for anything in life, you have to create must-have situations for them. Nice-to-have is not a good formula for success. For example, many startup companies fail, because they may create nice products, but do not manage to monetize. For nice-to-have products you often don't find enough people willing to pay for them. Inside your organization it is similar. They can choose between you and others for a promotion or give or not give you a raise, a new task, relocate you, change your assignment, put you in a different team, or onto a new customer account. The way to get picked is by creating a must-have situation for the decider. In what situation does the decision maker have no other choice but choosing you? When do they want nothing else but to pick you? What's in it for them if they support your proposal?

Based on the above I plan my strategies as follows:

1. Define a goal: Write a mission statement on what you want to achieve, why and by when.
2. Gather facts around your goal: What conditions have to be fulfilled for your goal to eventuate?
3. Create a list of 5 strengths and 10 weaknesses that help or keep you from reaching your goal.
4. Cross out all weaknesses from the list that you cannot influence and focus on the rest.
5. Create sub-strategies to eliminate weaknesses: Getting to yes, by removing the obstacles that could others lead to say no.

   Sun Tzu said that "the clever combatant imposes his will on the enemy, but does not allow the enemy's will to be imposed on him."
6. Define a target image: How do you want to be seen by others. To do so you have to see the battle from the point of view of the opponent. Put yourself into their shoes and see what they see. Musashi calls this to "become the opponent." If you play a role game and put yourself into the situation of the decision maker, what would it take to pick a certain proposed option?
7. Get to yes by executive decision or smooth transition, depending on your personal circumstances.

At times the management cannot or they have no intention of dealing with you at this given moment. Because of that risk, in addition to creating a must-have situation you will also have to create an urgency to make the decision when you need it to be made. You could even call these must-*do* situations.

This methodology is a frameset that keeps in mind that most things in life are circumstantial. It's meant as good guidance to one method that can work.

Clausewitz said that the study of strategy and history is important to find *directions for action*. He added that an analytical study of a subject leads to an exact knowledge, it should "educate the mind of the future leader in war, or rather guide him in his self-instruction, but not accompany him to the field of battle."[43] In the heat of the battle, one has to rely on self-judgment. The above steps are directions and mean that they are not strict rules that have to be followed one by one. They are rather interconnected to each other and interdependent. The idea of this exercise it to get a clear picture on what you want, what keeps you from getting there and how you can go about to drive change. It also helps to focus on what is important, to pick the right battles, get done what matters.

You will never be able to execute a strategy 100% the way you have planned it, but it will guide you on your way and follows fluidity. Yet you have to grasp precisely what is happening around you, by instinct and by intellect. Especially taking human behavior into account it makes any plan very circumstantial and unique. You can never copy how someone else solved a problem.

The moment I was let go from Digital Chocolate it felt that I had reached the limits of a possible career path there. It was a great moment to do something new. Only that the better option would have been to see it coming and prepare for it, rather than being forced out of employment. It threw me back into the uncomfortable position of being outside the labor market and having to explain why I lost my previous position, yet why I'd still be a great person to hire. In the economics of the labor market this is called an insider-outsider problem. The people inside the labor market – the ones with a job – find it easier to change a job, while the outsiders have to struggle to get back in. Time is ticking: The longer it takes, the more difficult it will get.

---

43 CLAUSEWITZ, C. VON (1832), BOOK 2, I, 27

The need of an income makes this position even less comfortable by decreasing the option to be very picky about the next role. To do a job that you are over qualified for can harm your career development significantly. To be underworked for a long time can also cause psychological stress similar to a burnout. This situation needs to be avoided. When work turns into chore, like it did for me, it's a clear sign to start looking for an alternative, which I didn't. I knew I had to, but I didn't do it full-heartedly. Classic symptoms are when you are unconcerned about the results of your work, you may turn to company internal gossip, become cynical and maybe even talk about your company with customers. This may be noticed by others and will change the spirit and can cost you your job on the long run. No matter how much you are getting sick of your job, keep that poker face and don't let others see into your feelings. Hang in there, but recognize this inflection point: It's time to look for something new, before they will make that decision for you. It's what I should have done.

A new opportunity appeared. With my ex-pat experience ending in 2007 I was quite happy to return to my beloved Finland. The moment I had wanted to leave Digital Chocolate the first time, my best option was to get a similar job as the one I had. I never really wanted to leave Finland, but I had always wanted to be an ex-pat, become ever more of a global citizen. I did not want to regret in the future not to have gone abroad when I had the opportunity. The moment I decided to go to Brazil I felt like Elvis Presley (1935–1977) singing *it's now or never, tomorrow will be too late*. At this point in time when I finally left the company, after my experience in the Americas, I was able to present myself with confidence as a go-to-market specialist in an international business environment for high-tech companies. A diplomat who can open doors, build long lasting partnerships, strategic alliances, engage with customers around the world in their local language.

Companies usually offer you the job that you already have, just like Rovio had done. Now, in 2007, my new job at Savox Communication was to roll out a new product worldwide. This underlines that it makes a lot of sense to get yourself a promotion within a company first, before you make a move. Otherwise you make a step to the side, not up. It happened unintended this time, but it proved a point. Before you switch jobs, try to get a promotion first, even if it's just a better title for the same job. You'll be able to trade it for a better job next time you are looking.

It was when opportunity met preparation. In comparison, in 2004 I had lived off 350€ per month for six months before finding my first post-graduate job. This time, three years later, it took me a month to get five job interviews and two written job offers on the table. I accepted a job in an international business development role, as a Sales Director, with Savox Communications. Savox develops and manufactures communication equipment for mission critical and industrial communication, Fire, Emergency and Safety. My new task was to build and execute their global go-to-market strategy for a new Bluetooth speaker-microphone for Push-to-Talk (PTT) that connected to a PTT-application on your mobile phone. Think old school walkie-talkie, but using your phone instead.

When I started it was still a relatively new technology by which mobile operators around the world tried to build new enterprise business, after Nextel had disappeared. It was a tremendous opportunity and exactly what I had hoped to find. I could be a pioneer for a company in a technology that was in its infancy. Lucky me.

I wanted to be the person who conquers new markets, takes responsibility, drives the business, engages in product development and work with partners and customers to develop a product roadmap that drives user experience and innovation. It felt that I could continue my international career where I had left it, only a couple of levels higher. I was on the way to reach the level of my own competence. It felt great.

This new job at Savox would eventually lead me to the idea to build my own business after our paths parted a few years later. But first things first: My mission was to make Savox send me to New York.

There I had met Meredith. We wanted to make it work somehow, even while being apart 6615km by plane between Helsinki and

New York. She had just started a Master Degree program, so at the time it wasn't an option to come with me to Europe. We had a long distance relationship over the ocean and saw each other every two to three months. I travelled globally with my job, including to the USA. I made it a habit to stop in New York on my way in and out of the country on every business trip. In 2009 I returned to the Big Apple and Meredith and I got married at City Hall in Manhattan. Getting through that year and a half was quite a challenge. We had to maintain a healthy relationship and at the same time I knew that I had to make a move happen in a foreseeable future. Failure was not an option. I had all the right reasons to go for it: Love. It makes people do all kinds of things.

In theory it was quite simple: Make them want to relocate me! Clausewitz said: "In strategy everything is very simple, but not on that account very easy."[44] The goal should be simple in the way it's formulated. The way to get there can be complex. The Italian painter, sculptor, architect and poet Michelangelo (1475–1564) said "I saw the angel in the marble and carved until I set him free." In other words he was taking every piece out of the marble that was not angel. That is indeed a very simple and humoristic way of formulating it. The actual work of a sculptor requires talent and practice, but it's the right approach. In the pursuit of happiness you are removing roadblocks. You are removing pieces of marble to set your angel free.

When I moved to New York again in 2009 I came with a promotion and a big pay raise, just like I had planned it from the start. This was my mission: "I want to move to New York within the next two years, in charge of the worldwide business of the entire line of business for wireless products. This will allow me to be with Meredith, secure a good quality of life and make an important step in my personal career."

The personal mission statement has to include three elements:

1. What do I want to achieve?

---

44 CLAUSEWITZ, C. VON (1832), BOOK 3, I

2. Why do I want to achieve it?
3. Until when?

It seems quite obvious and trivial, but only if you give your goal a reason why you wish to attain it, it becomes a real life's quest. The *why* gives you tailwind. Saying that you want to make a career to make a lot of money is not a mission statement. It has to be concrete. Write it down on paper. Define the intrinsic value and instrumental character of achieving your goal. Only then it becomes meaningful. To be with a great woman has intrinsic value; being able to do a job you love as well. Making a career step up increases your salary and widens your future job options. Setting a deadline creates urgency requiring action. I wish, I'd love to, I hope, and if I could only, are day-dreaming pointless prayers on some-day island. Give yourself a realistic and attainable deadline. You may be forced to alter some sub-strategies and timelines along the way, however, setting milestones at the start make your plan firm.

My main goal 2007 was to get another ex-pat assignment to go back to New York in order to be with Meredith.

The Big Apple is an amazing place to be. It is very expensive though and I was only at the beginning of my international career. Out of sight – out of mind. Remote work locations have a lot of benefits for your lifestyle, but you always bear the risk of being made redundant before all others. The changes won't be noticed as much by others in your company, because they are used to not seeing you in person a lot. Going abroad for a company is always an opportunity and a risk at the same time. I had just undergone that experience and here I was going for it again. This time I wanted to be better prepared for the uncertainties.

My goal was to be with Meredith. Learning from the past experience I could not count on always having a job and anyone moving to the United States always puts is job security on the line. In the US you can be fired any day for no reason, which isn't the case in Europe. It is not surprising why so many people are afraid to speak up in US companies. You have too much to lose. The threat of hearing "you're

fired" any time kills creativity and open-debate culture and promotes
yes-menship. On a first look it seems to be helping business, because
they stay financially flexible, but this only works in a short-termed
economy. The insecurity decreases employee loyalty and deteriorates
sustainability and long term growth. Therefore this time I wanted to
be prepared for the likely event that a company's future isn't as bright
as management claims it to be. I needed to climb the ladder within,
in case I was forced to switch jobs again. I left Finland for love, not
for a better life. I was neither a refugee looking for asylum, nor was I
looking to leave my home for a better future. Going abroad had to be
better than staying and the promotion and raise were part of the risk
mitigation in case the career would be interrupted, again.

I gave up a lot of security to be in the U.S. And I gave up the life
that I had grown to love. I felt that I had more to lose this time. I
wanted to make sure there was more in it for me this time than just experience abroad, since I had that already. In Helsinki I had a network
of very good friends and family, I lived in a modern apartment with a
view to the sea and even a private sauna in the bathroom. Especially
because of the long winters, your own sauna is something extremely
valuable. I was at walking distance to the subway very close to Helsinki's city center. I made a good salary and traveled the world, life was
good. I certainly wasn't running away from my life and I have been
missing Finland and my friends ever since I left. A Fin is probably the
best and most loyal friend you can have in your life.

Deciding for something new often requires letting other things
go. Whether you like it or not. Making a tough decision requires the
decider to be part of the consequences, otherwise it's not really tough.
Going to New York meant to leave a life that I loved for a woman
that I love.

In New York you need a lot of money to get by. Just being there is
pricey: cost of living, transportation, health insurance, hobbies, and
leisure time. Everything costs a little more than in most places. Moving to New York again had to give me more than just being able to be
with Meredith. I could be with her elsewhere as well. If it had to be

New York, there had to be something that topped the status quo. It had to be the next step up in life not the final goal. She was my reason to move to the U.S. again, but this wouldn't be enough to justify a promotion. I needed to have other than personal reasons.

"If you can dream it, you can do it," Walt Disney had said. As much as I say that one can be happy without a lot of money and it should not be the goal in life to become rich, being happy with money is still more satisfying than being happy without money. And you don't want to get fooled either: you have to get paid at market price for your skills! My thesis is not against making money, it is against seeing money as representative for success and happiness in life. In my case I certainly wasn't going abroad to be worse off.

Relocation within two years, general manager responsibilities and a nice pay raise is an ambitious goal. Had I told that goal to someone they would have said I'd be dreaming too big, or I was a little too ambitious. Mark Twain taught us to "keep away from people who try to belittle your ambitions. Small people always do that, but really great make you feel that you, too, can become great." It was my goal and the day I took the plane to New York in April of 2009 I had a signed contract with the desired promotion and pay raise in my luggage.

After formulating the goal we need to gather facts around it. Which are the circumstances you are in and what conditions have to be fulfilled in order to achieve the goal. These can be personal, business, politics, or anything else that influence the outcome:

- External environment
- Structure of the market, the society and/or the company
- Trend
- Communication
- Determining factors
- Distribution/Allocation
- Necessities/Desires
- Values
- Behavior

- Technology
- Political-/Market trends
- Laws, Rules & Regulations
- Threats
- Interventions

It doesn't happen often that you can compare apples to apples. Having two job offers at the same time allowed me to take money out of the equation and make my decision based on the intrinsic and instrumental character of each job. The business environment that Savox was in and the position that they had open, appeared to be the better starting position to achieve a promotion, pay-raise and relocation. I had to face the question of whether to go with a global company with a brand name or with an opportunity to build something new with an unknown outcome. It wasn't the question between a safe job and a risky job, but between well-defined job expectations or taking responsibility to shape my job description. I chose adventure.

The decision to go with Savox' offer was based on the chances I saw to relocate to New York. In addition, again merely by accident, I found myself in an old school industry that is undergoing big technology changes. The days of old school walkie-talkies have become numbered as technology change forces the dinosaurs to adapt or die. Only by co-incidence I landed in this industry, but it was about to change my life a few years down the line. Radio-style technology will survive, the technology underneath that professionals use to communicate has changed. The more challenging a job and a business environment is, the higher the chances that you will discover new opportunities at some point.

Even though Savox offered me less salary than the other company, I saw a better opportunity there to walk on an unbeaten path. A new technology and a worldwide business potential. Since customers in the United States had been using Nextel previously, Push-to-Talk with a phone instead of a 2-way-radio, was not new. Less market education was needed, which allows a faster adaption. This seemed like a good opportunity for me to build up a business and make it big enough in the United States to eventually propose a relocation to our largest market.

On paper it looked like the right opportunity, the field of dreams was wide open, but when my job at Savox started I had to actually make it work. Vision is one thing, executing it another.

Albert Einstein said that not everything that counts can be counted, and not everything that can be counted counts.

Some of the facts around the goal that have to be fulfilled are easily measured. Others are not. Since all businesses aim to be rational, the more hard facts you have, the better chances you have to convince others of your plans. Nothing convinces your boss more than a paying customer for example. No company will do something for you, only because you are a nice person. You need to prove your abilities to get something done as well. The hard facts combined with your personality, your work ethics, problem solving skills, and readiness to taking responsibility have to be in a good mix. They will be the prefixes that determine your target image as well: The reputation that you have, what others think of you and make them decide in your favor.

Here is what I had gathered around the goal to gain a positive decision by the Savox management to agree sending me to the United States. In a first look some or all of the following would have to be fulfilled:

- Cost and benefit justification.
- Market and revenue opportunity in North America and globally.
- Benefits of a local presence.
- Partnership with at least one large reseller.
- A large customer.
- A company culture that generally approves of remote work locations.

And more in particular I would have to prove the following abilities:

- Negotiate legal contracts.
- Forecast and budget responsibility for profit & loss.

- Elaborate and manage a product roadmap.
- Management of remote employees (sales, product management, customer service, operations, and logistics)

The fact that the owner of Savox had acquired several small businesses around the world that were overseen by the Savox Management, made me quite optimistic that my future request to work out of New York wouldn't set a precedent, but just add one more global location.

Savox Communications develops and manufactures communication equipment for fire, emergency, safety (FES). Savox' core business are accessories for Land-Mobile-Radios (LMR), also known as walkie-talkies. The line of products I was in charge of were based on mobile phones and wireless networks. My call for action to Savox was to do what is needed to enable the wireless business to grow. Therefore I was going to propose to create its own entity for wireless products in order to be able to act outside of the entrenchments of the grown habits within the company.

Getting into this game I wondered how I could go about to get Savox to say yes. What did I have to do to make Savox send me abroad? I started to analyze the events at Digital Chocolate and to define what pieces could be replicable. I wanted to put it into a system and methodology on how to play the career game.

Similar to any other game, your skills have to be practiced, strategies planned and tactics adjusted depending on each opponent that you face throughout the course of a tournament. Looking into games from a scientific, rather than an athletic point of view the purpose of game theory is to investigate why we can see a specific behavior or pattern in a given interaction. What are the rules that are played by and can we predict and influence the actions of others and hereby the outcome of the game.

Applied game theory finds its way into many aspects of life. Central banks set interest rates influencing the behavior of lenders and creditors. Higher interest can be helpful to prevent inflation, while they bring up the costs for credits. Lower credits can stimulate the economy if companies can get cheaper loans to finance their investments. Bonus- and commissions structures in companies set incentives: "If you reach 100% of your performance goal you get 15% bonus." People who continuously show up late to work, will get a warning, athletes are threatened to be expelled from competition if they are doping, children get out to play after doing their homework, a dog gets a treat after performing a trick, the number of examples were games – in a scientific meaning – are played is endless.

In game theory, games are distinguished through co-incidence, the skill of the player and their strategy. In a strategic game, like chess, a player has to take the reaction or presumed action of his opponent(s) into account.

Decision is when a player has to choose his actions without consideration of the opponents' reaction. An exception to that scenario are situations with many players where the influence of single players is irrelevant, like e.g. on commodity markets or political elections.

Sun Tzu said: "Do not repeat the tactics which have gained you one victory, but let your method be regulated by the infinite variety of circumstances." At Digital Chocolate I had created a credible threat by packing my stuff and walking towards the door to join the competition. Would that be an option? Was that replicable? A credible threat can lead others to choose an option that would otherwise not be their preferred one. It is a term that is used often in game theory, most famously in a strategic game called the prisoner's dilemma:

In this strategic game two criminals have been arrested for a robbery, let's call them Butch Cassidy and the Sundance Kid. The police knows that the two partners in crime have conducted the robbery, but there is not enough evidence to prove it. In case they cannot be proven guilty for a robbery, both will go for 2 years to prison for illegal possession of firearms. If both plead guilty, both of them will go to prison for 3 years. There is a principal witness rule intact and if one is pleading not guilty, but gets convicted by the other, the principal victim will get a mitigation of a sentence to only 1 year while the other prisoner will go to jail for 5 years. Both prisoners are being interrogated separately and do not have any information of the behavior of the other one.

Butch Cassidy			
		Plead guilty	Plead not guilty
The Sundance Kid	Plead guilty	3 years for both	1 year for The Sundance Kid, 5 years for Butch Cassidy
	Plead not guilty	1 year for Butch Cassidy, 5 years for the Sundance Kid	2 years for both

Table: Prisoner's dilemma

The social optimum could be achieved if both plead not guilty, because the amount of years in prison would be 4, which is the lowest combined outcome. However, the social optimum cannot be reached because pleading guilty is a dominant strategy. In the case of a simultaneous move without interaction or coordination the outcome of the prisoners dilemma is that both will go to jail for three years each. Unaware of the other person's decision it is the better option to take three years in jail, rather than risking to be locked up for five. If they were able to agree on a behavior and co-operate to reach the best total outcome they'd both plead not guilty. However, this is not a stable outcome since either of them would then have an incentive not to keep the agreement: Change the plea to guilty and get away with one year, sending the other one for five years behind bars.

A credible threat could function as a game changer. If one or both criminals would be part of a gang or organized crime that punishes their members if they get caught and plead guilty or wouldn't stick to agreed co-operation during interrogation. The threat could be imminent due to the fear they have of getting punished outside of the justice system once they walk free. Force could lead to pick an option that would otherwise not be preferred by a player.

Telling Digital Chocolate that I am going to leave to the competitor was the tactic of a credible threat. I had an actual job offer, I wasn't saying that if I wasn't going to get a change that I would consider leaving. It was a an imminent real threat that created the urgency to make a decision. A game-changing circumstance was that I was going to join the immediate competition and take my good customer relations with me. In any other circumstance they might have just said farewell. The threat was not only to lose an employee, but customer relations. It was unintended; in the situation I didn't see the big picture of my actions. All I wanted to do is leave. That was it. My boss kept pushing me to tell him what could make me stay. I didn't know what to say so the only thing that came to mind was: "Well, we need to conquer the market in South America, if you send me there, then I'll stay." I had never imagined that the company would actually go for it, but they did. Good for me.

My boss didn't really care for me staying in the company, but to save his own face. Previously, whenever I had asked him for a change in my assignments and a career path he didn't bother to give it a thought. Now that I was ready to pack my stuff he fought on my behalf in front of the management. How did that come about? He needed to make *my* career move happen for *him*. He was one of the most indifferent persons in terms of loyalty to a company that I have ever met. He was idle, passive and reactive in his role, taking personal advantage for himself in any possible situation. That made him very disliked among the team. On top of that he was a completely incapable leader and certainly wouldn't get a spot in the thousand most intelligent people I ever met in my life. A pretty disastrous pick from a hiring perspective. He knew how to sell himself well in interviews and he always managed to make himself look good, blame others for mistakes and get away with it.

Within three months half our team had left, because of him, even though they officially never said so. Nobody wanted to burn bridges, they were just happy they were gone. These were the situations when someone stoically reads down his reasons why he is leaving, trying not to make faces, speaking politically correct about the company and life and opportunities and why they had to make the sad and tough decision to leave and move on. And as soon they hand off key cards and computer at the HR department, they will leave the building screaming "yeehah" from the bottom of their lungs, call their best friend in an overwhelmingly good mood and full of adrenalin, ready to go to the next bar and have a few drinks to celebrate. Many people are excited about a new job, solely because it means they can leave their old one.

And that's what I wanted to do: leave! However, if I was going to be the next one, people would start asking questions how it happens that a sales leader looks like he will soon be the only person left in his team. Not to think about what that meant for revenue. Digital Chocolate's decision to pick the wrong leader had destroyed the team spirit. My boss tried anything to deflect that and therefore handing in my resignation was a threat against his position. It was personal to both of us, a marriage of convenience.

Most companies in the games industry are small. Several people had already left to join Rovio in those days and the CEO, Trip Hawkins, wanted to prevent the flood gates from opening. That was the real threat from an eagle's eye, I was just an actor in this play. They needed to show that ambitious people have a career path at their company. My boss needed to cover his own back. Just looking at revenue numbers it was worth having a sales person like me stay with the company rather than leaving. In that particular situation it seemed like a good opportunity for me and the company. If I had been the first one to leave and it wasn't for the competitor, my guess is that they would have let me go without making it a big deal. My back-analysis is therefore that the decision makers supported my career step for their own benefit.

Achieving an ex-pat agreement for Brazil with Digital Chocolate had one important element in it. Even though I unintentionally created a credible threat, I simultaneously opened the door for negotiations. Had I stubbornly thrown my hat and left I'd be working at Rovio. Since I gave in to my manager's pushing to say what I wanted, I left at least an option. Now there were alternatives on the table by offering my manager to choose between letting me go or giving me an ex-pat agreement. At that moment unintended, but important to realize in the aftermath. In terms of game theory this allowed to change the game between Digital Chocolate and me from a zero-sum game to a co-operative game.

The famous chicken game is a zero-sum game. The win of one player is the loss of the other. It always sums up to zero.

In the chicken game two players are driving on the same lane of a street towards each other. The one who is giving up and steers his car to the side avoiding a collision is the *chicken*, the loser. While every player is trying to avoid the collision they also don't want to gain the title of chicken. Important about winning this game is what one player thinks, the other player will do:

- If a player thinks, the other player won't give up, he himself should give up
- If a player thinks, that his opponent will give up at some point, he should continue to drive straight
- The decision can also be made randomly

Because this battle was personal about me and my manager it was a question about him or me. I had a conversation with Ilkka Paananen, the managing director of Europe, today CEO of mobile games giant Supercell. He asked me why I wanted to leave and I told him that there seemed to be two people in the team who want to be the team leader. "One of them already has the job, so I guess I have to leave." I was disappointed with the company for putting this person in front of me. Even though I liked my job, I did not want to spend any extra days working on his team if someone else does not work and takes all the credit. I had zero motivation.

Yet, because my boss insisted on hearing what I wanted and I came up with an option, it turned into a co-operative game.

A classic example for a co-operative game is the "battle of the sexes":

Peter and Mary love each other so much that they would rather do something together than being apart. Peter wants to go to an ice hockey match; Mary wants to go to the opera. If they both go separately to their events none of them will be happy. However if one is able to convince the other to come to their favorite event their level of happiness is at 2. The other one, who had to give in is not as happy, yet better off because at least they get to be together that night. Their happiness is counted with 1.

Mary			
		Icehockey	Opera
Peter	Icehockey	2,1	0,0
	Opera	0,0	1,2

Table: Battle of the sexes

There are two pure-strategy equilibria and one mixed-strategy equilibrium for this game. Peter and Mary will be better off if they stick together. Choosing to co-ordinate with the other player may not bring the maximum outcome for you, but it is better than the alternative and the overall social optimum will be reached. It will be achieved by the best response, so each player will hope for the other one to give in first.

In practice a period of negotiation can undergo different type of games from threats over chicken to co-operation. A co-operative game is the most sustainable in order to maintain a healthy relationship in the future. However, it may be necessary to bang the fist on the table first, before the other side is willing to sit back at the table and find a mutually beneficial agreement. With this tug-of-war one should always be aware of the current situation, the game that one is in and what the possible outcomes can be.

I wanted to leave the company, my bosses needed me to stay for personal reasons. From a high level it was better not to let me go at all. So the compromise was that I stay, but not on the same team. I gained an ex-pat agreement, the company gained more markets and more revenue, my boss saved his face.

Looking back I was able to get around my manager without having to leave the company. I was able to make a big step forward in my career without having to deal with an inept leader or waiting for his position to finally open in the hopes for a promotion. I had created an opportunity for Digital Chocolate, building the South American market for them, and at the same time forced them to a decision by establishing urgency. From my initially defiant position of "I'm leaving no matter what" it turned into something that everyone could live with. It shows that outcomes of negotiations might not be what you expect, yet they can benefit you more than you were thinking and everyone can leave the table and be happy with the result. It is good to have strong positions at times, to make other people make a move. However, you need to live up to the same standards that you expect from the others: Be open for suggestions and flexible for change if the compromise benefits you.

In the recap of the situation it was clear to me that I would not even intent to replicate at Savox what led to my ex-pat agreement with Digital Chocolate. It had been circumstantial. The circumstances are always different. What is replicable is to create a situation in which a decision in your favor is beneficial to the ones who make it happen for you. When the management does something for you, because they want to do it for themselves, you have created a win-win situation. You can't always threat with consequences, because threat is something negative, while in general the intention should be to create something positive. The intention should be to create an opportunity that everyone can benefit from. It is the art not to ask for a promotion directly, but to propose an opportunity and all the things that *you* are willing to do for *them*. I wasn't going to ask for permission to go to the U.S. for Savox, I was going to offer myself as a volunteer to do it for king and country.

The decision at Digital Chocolate was: "We are going to send Max to South America in order to build our business on that continent and grow our company's revenue. Max has a proven success as a sales man and knows our company and products well. Max also speaks Spanish and Portuguese and therefore he is the right person for the challenge."

The way I have achieved that decision was circumstantial, but there were elements that could be replicated: a person connected to an opportunity, justified by his proven abilities, and skills that stand out and allow to explain the decision to the rest of the company.

The circumstances were different, the smallest common denominator of replicable things between the 1st and the 2nd ex-pat agreement was that before all else it was a *decision*. A decision is when of a set of alternatives, one or more aspects will be chosen. Decisively. I had to eliminate most of the possible no's, and then urge a decision. At some point I just had to go for it and attempt to checkmate them. After a year working for Savox I presented the opportunity to the management to build its own entity for the product line I managed. I outlined my plan in a 50 page business plan including profit & loss calculation and a 5-year worldwide financial plan. Afterwards I started to plan the move.

4 POLITICS

"A great person attracts great people
and knows how to hold them together."

JOHANN WOLFGANG VON GOETHE (1749–1832)

It clearly points to a political career when a person knows nothing, yet believes to know everything. This assessment by George Bernard Shaw (1856–1950) is a wide-spread view which seems to gather more evidence on a daily basis than the opposite.

Politics was a part of the game as I planned to move to New York City. My goal wasn't a speech about the bright future, but much rather to create a real case with real evidence, actions behind my words. I wanted Savox to send me there as a new leader in the company, with global responsibility for the wireless product line. The quest was to propose an opportunity for the company, create a must-have situation with a sense of urgency to make a decision. To create a win-win situation it requires not only to do good things, but also to make others aware it. If talent and hard work aren't enough, then the gap will be closed through self-marketing and selling an opportunity. This happens best by creating empathy and filling your words with actions. Politics in a positive way.

In today's corporate language someone who is doing "politics" is considered as the person who tries to take advantage of the dysfunctional corporate labor market to gain more influence and power without having the needed skills for it. They are the talkers and the charlatans who use politics as a self-service industry. We like to call the ones who try to get somewhere without real work the "politicians", yet politics reaches far beyond that group with the negative stigma.

Everyone is a politician. Aristotle said that humans are a *zoon politikon* – a creature that is a social being that is aiming to building a society and that is interacting in a political way to each other in order to achieve such. By this meaning every human interaction is in some way politics. We argue, propose, meet in groups, formulate opinions, try to move society forward with an ideal picture in mind, and some people want to be spearheading a movement and gather supporters for a cause. Even simple things like agreeing with a group of people on what to do for New Year's Eve or where to go for a family reunion is politics.

I have been very active in real politics for many years. Since 1995 I've been a member of the Free Democratic Party of Germany (F.D.P.). I led their youth organization of in Frankfurt from 1998–2001. It is the party of Hans-Dietrich Genscher, the man who was the face of West Germany's foreign policies for decades. He was an important figure in Germany's reunification in 1990 and peace in Europe. In 1998, as a 21 year old, I ran for the *Deutsche Bundestag*, the Congress of Germany. Later I was elected to the City Council in Frankfurt, twice. In those years in politics I haven't seen anything different than you would see in any other organization, institution or company: there were lots of hard working people who weren't always the best to market themselves, and there were others who only wanted to attend fancy events and give speeches. And quite a few people in between. Politics is necessary for the functioning of any human society. What puts politics into a bad light are the talk-much-do-little types of people, not the profession itself. Being unhappy with a certain type of politician can only be the call to action for yourself. If we don't want *them* in politics, then *we* have to join the party, so that there will be more people like you and me and less of them. That simple.

Politicians are not a race or a type of person, they are humans who follow and voice their interests. Do you want to leave it to others to decide over your fate? In that case you have no right to complain about your life. You can only complain if you participate in some form. The minimum would be to go to the polls on election day.

Calling someone a politician is often intended dismissive and condescending to someone else's behavior, while at the same time excluding oneself from belonging to that group of people. Commonly seen as the opposite of that are the people who make a case for themselves by proving their skills, the ones considered the "hard worker" and the "dependable." Regardless of this or that view, everyone is a politician in the Aristotelean sense. And by calling someone else a politician in a condescending way, you are being just that: a politician. In that moment you are mixing your personal opinion about a person with a description that has a negative stigma. The way it's said is intended to devalue and discredit the other person in the hopes of getting approval from the people that you voice your opinion to. This is nothing short of being political. In order to get through the corporate jungle you have to accept that politics happen, and that you are a politician, too. You can be passive or active, outspoken or quiet, either way is a method to demonstrate opinion. And other people will have an opinion about you one way or the other. Since politics is everywhere there is also nothing bad about practicing politics. The key is to become a person of trust by narrowing the gap between ambition and appropriation of reality. This happens by taking charge of your own reputation, the awareness of the reactions and expectations that your words and actions generate. It's entirely up to you. Accepting that we are in the middle of politics, in reference to Kant, it is a call for us to act. Once recognized you can't be a bystander anymore. It's time to take charge, make your own political agenda and execute it at your own speed.

Politics happen and people have self-interests, instead of complaining or trying to be holier than thou, we should define what our own self interests are. This exercise also helps to get by with people who are very difficult to deal with, like a lazy boss or a know-it-all co-worker. Others don't behave a certain way because of you. They always behave like they do, even in your absence. I treat annoying co-workers like unwanted guests at a party. You can't kick them out or pour a drink over their head, but you can respectfully ignore them and focus on the people whose company you enjoy.

I believe that with integrity, loyalty and dependability you will get further in life, and live happier, because you will have true friends. Following self-interest is not opposing to that. It's honesty to oneself and loyalty to one's dreams. It doesn't imply walking over dead bodies. It can be a fine line, yet there is a big difference. You are not egoistic and selfish, because you follow your own interest. Our entire human society works like that. Everyone is following a specific interest and your personal freedom reaches as far to where the freedom of the next begins. It is a continuous, dynamic and ever changing undertaking.

An ideal politician should adhere to Henry Ford who said that you can't build a reputation based on what you are going to do. Good work is what you were hired for. Promotions are not rewards for past work, but expectations for the future. Your past work is there to create trust in your capabilities, that is a prerequisite, not a sufficient condition for a promotion. Therefore the past work is crucial to build trust and reputation, yet it's only the foundation for your future. You have to convince others that you can do more, they have to believe in your capabilities.

To be the most skilled person in the room is not a guarantee for success. You may work hard and be the most talented, without ever reaching your goal. To be unsuccessful doesn't imply you haven't worked hard enough. Maybe you are so good in your job that your employer wants to keep you just where you are. Or maybe someone else was able to make a better case for himself. Maybe your boss thinks you are very happy at your job, because you never say otherwise. To articulate your goals to yourself and others is an important task on your path to success.

The art of self-marketing is the tactical and strategic application of politics and an important part of playing the career game: Do good things and talk about it! Make yourself noticeable. Stand out without trying to get all the attention, promote yourself without becoming ego-centric. Accountable action well balanced with getting other people's attention creates consistently growing credibility. Thorough preparation and action will enable you to present business opportunities that are aligned with your personal goals and skills. Work hard, study your terrain, prepare and set the stage. Steer the decision makers to naturally align with your strategy one step at the time. Management expects you to be active and build report. The better your delivered results and future plans speak for themselves, the easier it will be for others to trust you to move on to higher tasks. This will take more than one good sales pitch. It requires perseverance and determination. And the patience to build everything up to the moment you want them to make a decision.

A better way of describing a non-ego-centric self-marketing is what the French call the *esprit de conduite* – the Art of human interaction. The charm of making oneself admired and liked without causing enviousness. To be noticed, remembered, respected by others, to get along with the preferences, tempers and opinions of others without being false. It is the ability to find the right tone with any group of people, without losing the characteristics of your own personality; without flattery towards others. Some people have a natural talent to get along with other people, others have to practice how to tolerate others, speak pleasantly, to be able to control their own temper, not to be moody, but are generally always of the same cheerful appearance.[45]

Musashi advices to "be careful even in small matters". How are you dressed, are you using a pleasant tone in your language, do you know how to articulate well, can you adapt to your audience, and do you have manners in communication? Do you know the basic rules of knife-knife fork-fork at a dinner table and have manners about how to eat and drink together like civilized people do it? Do you have a firm hand shake, a convincible voice, that's neither submissive nor arrogant? That's an engineering issue that can be learned. Looking good

---

45 KNIGGE, A. (1788), P. 23–24

without hiding behind fashion, self-confident, but not arrogant, polite, but relaxed, mannerly, but not stiff. If you have important meetings or presentations to give, make sure you get a good night sleep before, maybe go for a run, take in some sun. Don't exhaust yourself the day before an important happening, or as Sun Tzu would say, don't climb heights in order to fight.

Success in a career and happiness in life are always correlated to human interactions. How do we treat others, how to make ourselves memorable and the reputation that we have can determine success or failure. In any moment of your life your conduct has effect on how you are treated by others. If you want to convince anyone to vote for you, to promote you, to make you the captain of a sports team, to hire you for a job, they have to believe with all honesty that you are up for the task. If you have all the necessary skills it might yet not be enough if you are not a pleasant person to be around with. Maybe people don't like you, just because of the way they see you. That is something very subjective, some people just don't like you. There will always be someone that doesn't like you. It is very important though not to ruin that image yourself due to negligence of obvious details. The way you are being seen can be influenced by yourself. Confucius said that it takes a whole life to be a good person, and only a single moment to do something you might regret forever.

Some people say that you have to sell the sizzle, not the steak. That tactic only works to get people excited, but you also have to cook good steaks so that people come back to eat. Over time people will notice if you just say things they want to hear and your reputation will be equal to that of a used car-salesman. Investors, managers and other third parties that want to gain benefit from your performance will conduct a due diligence. So be prepared to deliver on your promise. Otherwise your sizzle will just be hot air and no-one will believe in your abilities. The way you appear, act and interact is the way people will remember you.

Many good things that you do and all the appreciation that you show to others can be washed away fast if you don't work on it every day. Using a lot of swear words show a lack of vocabulary and make people doubt your ability to speak correctly. Answering to a text message while someone talks to you in person is disrespectful. Being late to every meeting is putting your ethics and respect in a bad light. There are many little details in our everyday conduct with other people that can stick with others: "Oh that's the guy who speaks with his mouth full." "He's the one who is always late."

You can't please everyone and you don't have to be everyone's friend. The importance is though not to make any childish mistakes where one could know better. The most common is to lean back and say "that's just the way I am" or "I do this with everyone, that's how I roll." This type of street-smartness of a half-wit may work in certain parts of society, yet to achieve higher goals in the world of business I wouldn't recommend it. Bad manners are learned and self-made, not naturally borne instincts that one just has. Through your behavior you create a reputation, no matter if you believe it's your nature or not.

Knigge said that the one who tries to be funny at all times will not be taken serious if he has to say something of importance. In analogy the one who makes fun of everyone won't get a lot of condolence when he is emotional about something. The one who is always negative and destructive to everyone else's suggestions, will have a hard time finding support if he has any ideas of his own. The one who always says "great" and "awesome" to any idea will not be taken as a person with his own opinion. There are many examples as of where manners, language and conduct can make or break the way people see you.

If you want to be a winner, you have to look like a winner. Some people might say that physical appearance and manners aren't as important as the skills and ideas people have. Mark Twain has the right answer: "Clothes make the man. Naked people have little or no influence on society." This is not limited to the textiles that you are dressed in, but also the manners that you exhibit.

Humans are like any animals, we are attracted by others through look and smell, and courtship. These are important senses to humans and if disturbed by the other one's lack of knowledge or interest, it influences our opinion of that person. Fine feathers make fine birds. You have to find a way to blend in and stand out at the same time.

In a business environment the moments when people meet more personally are at the good mornings and good-byes of a work day, on company outings, and during lunch hours. These are good to create impressions by being a pleasant person to be with. During company meetings then your preparation and attention, participation and follow up influence on your reputation as a professional. It is quickly noticeable who is coming prepared and who is just giving the same speech each time.

There are two ways to get third party support for our goals: One is by a formal decision making process, the other is by maneuvering yourself to a new position or new tasks without ever openly asking for entitlement. The progress of your work just naturally leads there and is recognized by others.

To gain a formal approval some form of decision paper has to be presented to the decision makers. Today, a SWOT analysis has become somewhat of a standard in business in presentations to executives. SWOT stands for Strengths, Weaknesses, Opportunities and Threats. A SWOT model is a shining example of how misleading information can be presented and how irrational business decision making can be. If business was rational, it would not use a model that is so far away from science as a SWOT is. This model is merely an internal marketing tool which purpose is to propose an action rather than analyzing a situation. For business presentations, a SWOT analysis has become something of a must-have, for real strategy planning it is far less useful. In 10 out of 10 SWOT presentations you will read "competitors" in the threat section. Usually the most common three threats and weaknesses are pulled out of the sleeve in order to get the audience to focus on opportunity and strength, things that are great and feel good. How useful is a model in which half of the content is already predefined by common business habits?

For your personal strategy, however, we need to put a lot of focus on weaknesses and the things that do *not* work. Just like a good executive we need to focus on what matters, not what feels the best. In a business presentation then, we should always focus on the opportunities and propose solutions. Use a SWOT as an external presentation model when it's convenient. To set the lever for success, in our strategy model we make a simple list of 10 weaknesses and 5 strengths. These will be the base for our internal analysis from which actions will be derived for sub strategies.

Given that companies usually shoot the messenger the key is to present problems as opportunities. Nobody wants to hear about problems, unless the solutions are delivered in the same sentence. It becomes more tricky if problems are structural. Most people don't want to be criticized and take criticism very personal. That applies especially if criticism is coming from the bottom up in a very hierarchal environment. System-inherent challenges that keeps the business from striving are difficult to change. It's good to be aware of those, but if you aren't in the position to influence the change in an organization, it's better to focus on what is under your control.

Self-criticism is an incredible strength. The ability to step outside and reflect, evaluate and criticize. Only when we are able to admit failures and problems are we also able to learn from them and improve things. If you are caught up believing that you as a person, a group of people, a company or a country, because of your past track record all you do is presumably be the best, you walk a perilous path.

To criticize others directly without having the listener taking it personal is a difficult undertaking. Growing up in Germany I am used to pointing straight at an issue and if necessary telling the person who made the mess directly into the face to clean it up. I haven't seen much of that type outside my own cultural hemisphere, unless it was from top-down in a hierarchy. I have often experienced people being irritated and almost hurt by criticism. You made a mess, you should clean it up. There is nothing personal about that, but that's not how most people in the world take it. In most places people praise a person's work and skills first and then suggest in a politically correct manner a few items with room for improvement. These are usually placed in between the lines. This way they try to maintain everyone's face. Fair enough. I still find that a waste of time.

For our personal strategy however we should take no prisoners. We have to be ruthlessly honest to ourselves, reflect and see ourselves from a distance. No between the lines, no wishy-washy. Straight to the point, defining the problem in a way that is absolutely clear what the challenge is. Only then you will also find the correct sub strategy to solve it. If any issue is not clearly defined, the solution finding is up to the eye of the beholder. Politically correct criticism carries too much risk for misunderstandings. Unless it's stated clear which areas need improvement, there will be still too much room to to slack. So just name it!

To be self-critical and allowing others to criticize has its limits. Just like praise from others will only be effective if the right people do so. If anyone praises you for your good work, how will you know that it was actually good? If the one who praises you, does so with anyone, what is it worth? Praise or criticism are third party opinions that can affect us for our future actions. Others may in fact use them to influence us, since they can feel good or bad, motivating or demotivating. They should be hand-picked, just like the mentors you are seeking advice from. Machiavelli said: "There is no way to guard against flattery, but by letting it be seen that you take no offense in hearing the truth: but when everyone is free to tell you the truth respect falls short. Wherefore a prudent Prince should follow a middle course, by choosing certain discrete men from among his subjects, and allowing them alone free leave to speak their minds on any matter on which he asks their opinion, and no other."[46]

That said we have to use a dual approach here. For your goal we have to write down 5 strengths and 10 weaknesses. Only when we present to managers or others, we will use a SWOT, just the way people are used to. In opposite to the day dreaming of the opportunities,

---

46 MACHIAVELLI, N. (1532), CHAPTER 23

we need to focus more on weaknesses than strengths for now. The exercise isn't about how we could benefit. We know what's in it for us, we know how we benefit when we succeed. The quest is to find what's-in-it-for-them so they support it. One of the main reasons people neglect any proposal is not because they don't see the opportunity, but because they weigh the risk. They look for reasons to say no and weigh them against saying yes. Especially if there is money involved, many tend to be hesitant. While we have to maintain and improve our best skills, it's the weaknesses that we hate dealing with. The way we deal with weaknesses will make the difference for our success. Usually we enjoy doing the things we are good at. It's also one of the reasons we are good at them, we enjoy them. Weaknesses can also be there because of laziness, lack of attention or disinterest. That needs to change.

Sun Tzu said never to besiege the stronghold of your enemy. If your opponent also assumes this strategy, they will attempt to divert attention from your strength and attack where you are weak. In nasty law-suits or intense political campaigns this tactic is well present: the other side will try to undermine your credibility by washing a large amount of dirty laundry to divert the attention from your accomplishments. No-one is fool enough to attack you in what you are really good at. If your opponents act accordingly they will attack you were you are inferior in strength.

You can have a list of 20 arguments that speak in your favor, the nay-sayers will still focus on those two weaknesses of yours. Removing weaknesses is a strategic act of strength. Your weaknesses are what exemplify the road blocks that keep others from deciding in your favor. Remove the obstacles and leave no more room for doubt.

Let's take an imaginary SWOT analysis and a list of strengths and weaknesses to illustrate the different approaches:

Strength:	Weakness:
▪ Our company is the un-disputed market leader. ▪ We attract the best engineers. ▪ We have a large customer base.	▪ The patent for our main product line is about to expire.
Opportunity:	**Threat:**
▪ Expand the R&D team to shorten our time-to-market. ▪ Roll out more products faster. ▪ Take advantage of brand recognition.	▪ Competitors are ready to launch generic products as soon as our patent expires. ▪ Market leadership is threatened without new products.

Now let's imagine 5 imaginary strengths and 10 imaginary weaknesses:

Strengths:

1. We have a patented product that outsells any competition.
2. We have 80% customer loyalty and retention.
3. We are recognized as the leader in the industry.
4. Our company attracts the most qualified engineers.
5. Our channel strategy is unmatched.

Weaknesses:

1. We pay a low salary in industry average which creates large employee turnover.

2. While our product has been the best seller in the industry, it starts to get old compared to the technology trends.
3. Our sales staff is not motivated enough because even though we are making big revenues, the bonus system is not incentivizing enough.
4. Our patent protection is about to expire and the competition is ready to sell the same products at a lower price.
5. Our largest OEM[47] customer is negotiating a project with our fiercest competitor.
6. Our operations are on average 2 months behind schedule.
7. Our Research & Development department has too many projects at the same time for the limited existing resources. Innovation is halted by too many projects that are promised to customers.
8. Our marketing department is wasting money on prestigious good looking campaigns instead of doing market research and targeted demand generation.
9. Our Working Capital performance is low because our finance department is paying bills too quick and is slow on accounts receivable.
10. Our leadership is busy appearing important and citing past success stories rather than facing the real challenges of the employees and the company as a whole.

There is a saying, never trust a statistic that you haven't falsified yourself. In the imaginary SWOT-analysis above the real issues of unorganized, inefficient operations and bad enterprise resource management is covered by the simple statement: we need more people! Looking at the weaknesses this would actually only treat symptoms. Initially the presenter has the feel-good information about being market leadership with a great team and it looks like the threat of competitors entering the market can be halted by just adding a few new products under a similar

---

47 OEM = ORIGINAL EQUIPMENT MANUFACTURER

brand name. While that is usually a good strategy, because customers will buy products from a company that they have been satisfied with, the real issues under the surface are covered up. Many companies that we thought would exist forever, have disappeared, because of the inability to adapt. And probably because nobody dared to say what needs to happen for the fear of getting shot.

High turnover of personnel leads to delays due to hiring and training phases, a high-quality product almost sells itself, without the need of having the shining stars of sales people on board. Going into a different phase by launching new products, sales people have to have an incentive to go out and sell. None of these issues are covered in the SWOT above.

It is a typical example on how many corporations deal with problems: they don't.

Maybe the person responsible for the mess is presenting this slide to deflect that he's actually the source of the delays in research, development and production? Or he really just wants to make a case for himself, because one person cannot change the entire company culture or bad management. The person is not there to change everything or pick a fight, but with a personal agenda. Creating a larger team can work like unemployment insurance. In rough waters they look like the leaders of a crucial team and as a leader they will still be needed even if the company has to lay people off.

With good presentation skills you can lead the discussion into the direction you want it to go. And you would never present the problems that the company has, unless you can be part of the solution. People don't want to be blamed publicly. Whistleblowers and artists are in general an important part of a functioning democracy, because they act like a mirror to society. In a company the whistleblowers are considered the troublemakers, they only point out problems without working towards improvement. Most management is receptive to issues if you can offer solutions at the same time. If tied to next steps with a clear schedule and responsibilities. Blowing the whistle and runnig isn't very long-lasting.

In company meetings many issues are often covered only on the surface, when it gets to detail there is quickly someone saying: "why don't you two take that issue "offline""; meaning outside of the current meeting. That separate meeting usually doesn't happen then. The risk of problems piling up is slowly feeding into mismanagement. Usually everyone knows what's not working, but nobody dares to say anything, and the impression is growing that the management is indifferent. Partly although since the executives are constantly fed the stories that everything is great. There are only opportunities and therefore they don't see the things that do not work. This creates a bad company culture. Mediocre management also likes to hear only good stories to feed into the self-belief of sheer amazingness.

Sometimes it can be wise to start solving problems in quietude. When your work starts to bare fruits you can present yourself as a problem-solver. Since lasting solutions can take some time it is more effective for your self-marketing to start solving problems and show results when you are close to be done, rather than asking for the assignment to fix the issues which you have detected. It also gives you more time, since today everyone seems to expect anything immediately. In addition to work by assignment bears more risk that a mediocre manager will take the credit. To present your results and make sure you get the credit is when others are present, e.g. your boss's boss, or your entire team. You don't have to make big announcements in every meeting, it can be subtle and will appear less self-centered. The constant dripping wears away the stone. Instead of big announcements you can place comments in a conversational style as you and your boss go for lunch with his manager and others. The elevator or cafeteria pitch. Throw in some good news when people are receptive for good news, like a break time. People are also more likely to remember it than in a meeting where most are mentally absent. That way you kill two birds with one stone. You truly help to make things better and you also gain credit for it. Management only wants to hear about problems if you have solved them or you know exactly how to. Your job is not to tell what goes wrong if you can't do anything about it.

Just like you shouldn't complain to people who cannot help you, you gain more when you point out issues if you can be part of the solution. You don't want to look like a complainer, but like someone that makes your management feel good about themselves for hiring you. It's all a game we are part of.

Strength and weaknesses in strategic planning are of a different nature than in an interview situation where one thinks of attributes like "I am good with numbers" or "I'm impatient". In strategy, strength is something that helps you to reach your goal, weakness is something that can hinder you. Having a strong competitor for example is a weakness, even though it doesn't have anything to do with you. They are strong on their own and that can threaten you and is therefore a weakness in a strategic meaning.

In my quest to convince Savox of my plan mine looked like this:

Strengths:

1.   Max has years of international experience.
2.   Max has built alliances with major industry players.
3.   The management is keen on global expansion.
4.   Max understands the technology and the business environment and is capable of handling all aspects of marketing, sales, legal aspects and finance to build international business.
5.   The North American market has the largest potential.

Weaknesses:

1.   The product is not developed to reliable functionality yet.
2.   There isn't enough market readiness for this type of wireless Bluetooth communication device.
3.   The line of business depends on outside funding.
4.   The product management and operations are not under Max's direct control, therefore he has to compete over resources with other business leaders who serve long term customers.

5. Max's direct boss, unlike the management, has little interest in this technology and opportunity.
6. There are constant changes in the company's strategy. priorities and organizational changes impact the motivation of the employees to focus long term on any project.
7. The engineering department has more tasks than resources.
8. Technical Support for customers is poor.
9. The company owner has to agree to the relocation.
10. Max has little leverage to force a decision.

It was a long list of chicken and egg issues and many open items. The best argument that anyone can have to get decision makers to say yes, is if there is a paying customer. Potential resellers hesitated since they were in doubt about the reliability of the product. We have to note though that I started at Savox in 2007 when the very first iPhone was introduced to the market. The world wasn't used to downloading any apps to their phones, they only just learned that. Back then, pushing a wireless product that required to be paired to an application on your phone required a tedious task of customer education. The solution was in a try and err start-up mode still, we weren't sure what was going to work. There was a lot to be learned, yet the people involved either didn't see that or did not care enough for it. To get someone to pay for the product in that moment was a tough nut to crack. Unlike senior management I didn't possess the right to blame the world's economy for slow sales. The poor support resulted from overworked engineers and other projects at higher priority. The situation forced me to roll up my sleeves and get involved in everything. If there is no-one else who can do it for you, you have to take it into your own hands.

The quest to break that cycle was to create enough excitement with potential customers and resellers at least: Plant a field of dreams like a start-up pitches its business plan to an investor. I also needed to make sure that my demand for an independent line of business would only meet what customers expect, it wasn't just my own idea. So beyond the real challenge, I was able to show a SWOT like this:

Strength:	Weakness:
▪ Strong demand for our product. ▪ Alliances with key players. ▪ Strong understanding of the technology and the market.	▪ Product has not undergone thorough quality assurance. Bugs still have to be fixed. ▪ Weak market readiness. ▪ Line of business is dependent on resources of other areas.
Opportunity:	Threat:
▪ North America is one of the largest market. ▪ A local presence would allow faster market penetration. ▪ Building out the line of products into its own entity ensures efficient operations.	▪ Hesitation to enter the market could leave the opportunity to possible competitors. ▪ Continuing the business as is, threatens expansion due to entrenchment of internal resources.

Analog to my previous comparison of analytics vs. SWOT this uses a similar deceiving approach of *if you don't do this, that will happen*. The real problem, a product that cannot be sold yet, is diminished to a few bugs that need to be fixed which could be the bottleneck for revenues to kick in. While this was indeed the reason, everyone agrees that management doesn't want to hear about problems, but about opportunities. Making a great product would have been the solution, yet since I am not an engineer it was a weakness on my list that I had only limited influence on. In the moment of presentation this major issue therefore had to take a less prominent place. It needed to be all about opportunities, the bright future.

The nature of corporations and hierarchies, the politics and short-term business culture supports this type of self-marketing to achieve decisions. If your direct manager is indifferent or opposed to your ideas, you could not win if you were to try to say the truth without customizing it to your needs. Bending the truth, they say.

We are all politicians, and it's all a game. My approach is not to copy the charlatans, because I lack the audacity to do so. I'm not an escapist either, so I choose to participate in the game which is happening whether or not I like it. This doesn't imply an obligation to become *one of them*. In this world it would be naïve to believe that one can achieve anything without selling a field of dream to at least a minimum amount when your audience is stuck in the common habits of entrenched business culture.

How to deal with strength and weaknesses? Solely focusing on strength isn't enough, eliminating weaknesses leaves less room for possible rejection. It is how you defend your borders. I used to play field hockey for about 10 years. We had practices twice a week, and a game on the weekend. One of my coaches had our team practice one-on-one situations over and over again, and we practiced to pass and play as a team regularly. The coach put into our heads that at all costs we should avoid one-on-one situations and keep passing the ball. He wanted us to play and win as a team, and to avoid losing the ball. But it is inevitable that you will get into situations in which you play against a single player, either with or without the ball. He wanted to make sure that if it happened, we'd be able win the duel.

Too many people avoid taking action on what's not working. It's simply easier to do the fun stuff, talk about things you are good at and dream of a bright future and make strategic big picture plans, leave the details to others; ignore the problems. On top of that the messenger of bad news will always get shot. Why bother? Because eliminating weaknesses is a strength and prepares for the real thing. History has shown that the ones who don't want to change will end up losing what they try to preserve. How many empires have fallen for no other reason than decadence and the belief of being too strong to fail? Remember Charles Darwin summoned that not the strongest survive, but the ones who managed change the best. That applies to people, companies and countries alike.

Your strengths come to play when they either help to eliminate a weakness or at a later stage when you are ready for the attack. Knowing when and how to use a strength is a strength of its own. That is the exercise that we have to practice to play the game. It is essential to improve what needs to be improved to achieve sustainability, and with it the reputation that you are capable of getting things done: the proof that you are not just a talker. Meanwhile we have to be ready to present our case in a good light.

To eliminate our weaknesses we create sub strategies for all items that we have influence on. To do so, we eliminate all weaknesses from our list that we have no control over. We have to study our terrain well and resist the temptation to delete weaknesses from our list that we don't *want* to deal with. A typical situation is when a person that is difficult to deal with has to make a decision in our favor. We may quickly say: *He would never do that!* It may be difficult, yet nothing is impossible if we can influence the outcome.

Common family issues are good examples. Your wife might complain that she needs more space. You can say: *ok, let's move* only to hear how much she hates packing. Your husband might complain that his car is constantly broken, yet he doesn't want a new one, because he is emotionally attached to the one he has. Often we admit having a weakness and may even identify a possible solution, yet, then we have a quick reflex finding an excuse and say "but it won't work". If man can fly to space there is not a whole lot that we *cannot* do. Some people put action behind their wishes; others excuses. "Somebody should do something about it" has never made anything better. Complaining about the status quo and defying solutions based on emotions is just as unproductive. It surprises me how many people spend time thinking about what happened if they did something new or different, but hardly waste any time thinking what would if they stuck to the status quo?

On the job hunt our competitors are unknown to us. This is a weakness that we can delete from our list since it is out of our influence. When we compete as companies over customers we cannot change our competitors' products or strategy, but we adjust our pricing and marketing strategy accordingly. Therefore it is a weakness that can be altered by our own input and stays on our list. Thirdly there are things that we cannot change, but we can be prepared. A farmer cannot change the weather, but he can build an irrigation system to avoid excess water standing in the crops during times of heavy rain, and store it for times of drought.

The exercise of writing down all weaknesses at first serves to understand the big picture and starting position. The elimination of certain elements out of our influence is to focus on what matters and not get distracted. It is the application of Musashi's advice to pay no attention to others, but watching everything they do.

Sub strategies are derived from here in a purely analytical way:

Table: Sub strategies

Weakness	Sub Strategy	Target
We don't have enough money.	We will raise money through donations.	Until July 1st this year we will have raised 50.000$
I don't speak French.	Learn French by taking private classes.	Become conversational in spoken French by March 1st next year.
Our organization is losing money through bad creditors.	Outsource debt collection to a professional credit agency.	Improve on-time payment by 6 months from now.

Weakness	Sub Strategy	Target
My colleagues have a bad impression of me.	Increase reputation by participating meetings more attentive, seeking contact for help and interaction, and take interest in co-workers work and life to change perception.	Increase reputation before the next bonus round.
Our organization has slow operations and logistics.	Implement an Enterprise Resource Management system to plan work more effectively, avoid double work, eliminate unnecessary meetings, and bureaucratic reporting structure.	Implement changes until the end of this quarter and report to the general manager on the completed restructuring.
My dog doesn't listen to me.	Train the dog with a professional dog trainer.	My dog knows how to sit, stay, heel and come until the end of next month.
I am in bad shape.	Go for a 15min walk/run every other day.	By the end of next month I will be able to run 5km in under 25min.
My boss doesn't think I am a good performer.	Find out my boss' priorities and work for and with him on what is important.	Close an important business issue by the end of the quarter and have it well documented for my boss to present to his peers.

The above matrix includes sub strategies of psychological nature, perception of how others see our work, and some that are pure hard work. For our remaining list of weaknesses we will have to define sub strategies of this nature including the action resolving it and the deadline. To add complexity you may detail the sub strategy into a to do list. This way any large problem can be broken down in small pieces that are easier to handle, dividing the labor. Most problems aren't overwhelming anymore after a thorough analysis. For almost any problem there is a solution. It requires to describe the problem precisely and to find exact words for our desired outcome. Defining a problem and accepting it as one is the essential pre-requisite to solving it.

Most challenges in life can be solved by engineering a solution. Emotions are the ones that hinder the execution. It is very simple to define a goal like *learn Japanese*, which by no account means that it's attainment was easy. Much easier it is to find excuses for inaction like "I don't have time" or "this is very difficult". To be successful requires to believe in your own capabilities. If you don't go for it then maybe you don't really want it. As Musashi said: "This takes work. It will seem difficult at first, but everything is difficult at first." Where there is a will, there is also a way. Writing the goal down, defining a sub-strategy and adding a deadline converts hope into a plan of action. Often it just takes the first step and then it will pick up speed, create its own dynamic and things will come together. Soon even big plans become doable and the daily progress is a very rewarding sensation.

Problems are easier solved if we learn how to detach our feelings. Many things would be so much easier if they didn't matter to us. But only what matters becomes important. Engineering a solution to a life's problem will always require emotional intelligence as well.

Elaborating a plan for relocation with Savox I had a long list of sub strategies including riddance from my manger in order to report to someone that cared about my work. I needed to get involved in product management and create an entire business plan including profit and loss plan. If I wanted to be a leader I couldn't wait for the entitlement, but had to start showing that I had what it takes. As a result I was able to improve many aspects of the business, focus my own work on what was important from a company perspective, become an industry expert and a driving factor for company success. Even though I am no longer with Savox, I firmly believe that my work has set the stage for them to get traction in the Push to Talk over IP/LTE business.

The common corporate process of decision making requires the employees to gain approval for proposed actions. In other words you present to your manager what has to be done, so he can tell you to go and do it. If this person has no interest or cannot make a decision you will have to try one level up, until you finally get to the person who is entitled to make a decision. Here you have to be very diligent and careful. Going over a manager's head can be very tricky.

I don't like to waste my time going through each step and prefer knocking on the right person's door immediately. I find it irrelevant if that's the director of something or the CEO. I am hired to do my job and if a decision making process keeps me from doing so I go straight to the source. The good managers I had always appreciated not wasting their time on process, the bad managers I had were upset that I would circumvent them. That will never change. The bad manager usually believes to be smarter than you, and neglects your requests for lame reasons. A smart leader would always give your proposals a thought, discuss them and try to find a common ground, even if the ultimate result is that your idea wasn't as great as you initially thought. When ego, the feeling of being powerful, or lack of skill come into the game, it makes it more challenging and requires finding ways to circumvent your boss.

Either way you might face the problem that you don't make it to the top decision maker, because someone slams the door at you or they just don't want to decide or have other priorities. Sun Tzu's advice to avoid an enemy that is superior in strength is basically a call for guerilla tactics if by other means you cannot reach your goal.

A typical locked situation in a company is when your boss demands results, but the rigidity of the hierarchy and the high division of labor keep you from making any progress, simply because you aren't entitled to decide anything and you are too dependent on your peers. In this corporate jungle you have no other choice but using guerrilla tactics: Build relations with the relevant people, built on friendship and favors, and helping each other out. Most people in critical product development or in charge of an entire product line are key people under a lot of pressure. They are overwhelmed with work and receive pressure from above, and often get too little recognition for their work. Once you start appreciating people's work and get a genuine interest in it, they will be open to also help you out here and there, like in any other friendship. In all my different roles in sales & marketing it has helped me to build a relation with the people who made what I sold. Firstly you understand your product better and can sell it easier and also serve your customers better. Secondly you can soon answer most technical questions yourself, don't waste your colleagues' time and thirdly you can actually provide valid input for improvement. At the same time, by showing interest in other people's work, they get a sense that their work is indeed important.

In a complex hierarchy, people see everyone below them as order takers. On the general employee level, people see each other as partners in crime, often become friends. Sometimes because they have an enemy in common. Friendship is a strong bond. No matter what the official decision making process is in your company, peer to peer agreements are much longer lasting than any top down orders. This can be of your advantage when building your internal alliances.

A certificate in a plastic frame isn't worth anything compared to a genuine non-official "thank you". Rewarding an employee in official company meetings without turning that into increased trust to let them work independently, without micromanagement and control cannot be called a true reward. In this case a certificate may well say "yes-man of the month" instead of "most valuable player". In a similar fashion your peers, your reports and your supervisors appreciate if you go out of your way to make something happen for them. It will soon be noticed who tries to curry favor with someone and who is trying to be a good colleague. Life is a boomerang, you will get back what you give. No-one can expect long-term success if he's self-centered.

What starts out as a professional relation of engineering and marketing, can often turn into a friendship. This way, using the guerilla tactic of human relationship-building, you can bypass any mediocre manager. Maybe that bends the rules of hierarchy, yet you break the rules to move forward, not to get a personal benefit. If you do so within your scope of work, you will not get into trouble, but may actually gain a lot of good reputation for being a go-getter. Guerrilla tactics though also mean that you don't openly declare disobedience, you work behind the scenes and don't badmouth others or make them look bad. Especially not your manager, even if you cannot stand him or her. It will only make the attainment of your goal more difficult. Corporate language has evolved to justify anything: You can always say that you don't take no for an answer, put the customer first and you are ultimately responsible for the results within your area of business. You can't leave that fate to others. It is hard to argue against that. If you bring results, most people won't question the means.

Remember *Verba Volant Scripta Manent* – the words are flying the written stays permanent. Make sure to make everything firm that you want to be firm, but avoid to putting anything in writing that you don't want to have others use against you. If you try to achieve a *bilateral agreement* with a colleague, a prioritization of a project without management approval, then do that over lunch, not over e-mail.

Musashi said, the purpose of any duel is to win, by any means. You are hired to bring results in the first place, not to follow orders. The only people who believe that your purpose is to follow their orders are mediocre managers. I have discussed earlier and proven by math how mediocrity can spread through powerful positions. When you detect such a person you will have to respectfully ignore their opinions in a way that they still believe they are in the driver seat. If the rigidity of an organization hinders you to bring results then prioritize tasks, and weigh your risks. Is it more important to follow orders? Will that save you your job or help to get a promotion? Or is it better to bring the results that they expect from you? Usually it's more efficient to ask for forgiveness than asking for permission. Very often people get in trouble with their manager for under-delivering. And in many of those cases it is because the nature of the hierarchy and the decision making is hindering you from achieving the goals, not your personal attitude. No-one will accept that as an explanation. A corporation will always put you into a strait jacket and expect you to be a boxer.

Respect the Gods and Buddhas, but do not rely on them, Musashi said. Breaking the rules is one way to get where you need to and what is expected from you, if you aren't entitled by hierarchy to decide on what has to get done. Focus on results and go for it, regardless of your level in the hierarchy. The hierarchy on paper and the official process isn't always how to move forward. It certainly doesn't mean do whatever you want, but to create your own org-chart. Look for the support and approvals you need, not the official process. Often your immediate supervisor could only pass your requests on, and if you have a great boss, they are happy if their team members have conversations with senior managers. Only the average manager will try to be a door-keeper between you and upper management. To get visibility from senior managers is important. It will show your attitude to move things forward and narrows the room for others to take credit for your work. And to be considered for any kind of promotion in the future the minimum requirement is that the ones who can promote you know who you are. On the long run this will stick. Respect the hierarchy, but do not let it harm your performance. We have to follow self-interest without being hated or walking over dead bodies. Look for your benefit, without being selfish.

Why focus on weakness, why break the rules to win? The answer is simple: You have to build on what's yours. You have to influence what you can touch and try to be independent of the untouchable. We can find an answer in Machiavelli's masterpiece, the Prince, as he asked the question whether it was better to be loved of feared:

"To the question whether to be loved or feared, I sum up by saying, that since his being loved depends upon his subjects, while his being feared depends upon himself, a wise Prince should build on what is his own, and not what rests with others. Only, as I have said, he must do his utmost to escape hatred." Machiavelli's words can sound like the call for tyranny, but it is borne out of his general mistrust against people. Analyzing the content of his words, taking the political advice to a Prince out of the equation for a moment, we find a more general insight through Machiavelli: If you depend too much on others who can also turn against you for whatever reason, you are putting your destiny into the hands of others. Instead of relying too much on others, we have to focus on what's within our reach. In today's world I understand Machiavelli more as the reminder that you should be self-reliant, without putting it into an either or question.

Machiavelli himself continues that we should wish to be both; but since love and fear can hardly exist together, if we must choose between them, it was safer to be feared than loved.[48] In today's language it could mean that showing a clear profile leads to recognition, yet that you cannot be everyone's friend. It happens that by standing out of the crowd you always experience both: Some admire you for who you are and other fear, respect, dislike or hate you for the same reason.

Whatever you do, do it cautiously, and look at the end, is the meaning of the Latin proverb *Quidquid agis, prudenter agas et respice finem*.

In game theory we look at the outcome of games from the perspective of the final decision maker. This allows us to predict and influence the outcome of games. Decisions are based on previous events, the experience of the decider and his advisors, such as the actions of other people involved and, of course, the expected impact of the decision. With our goal in mind we try to influence the final outcome to our benefit. We rewind from the future desired decision back to the presence and build our strategy accordingly. Like the butterfly effect mentioned earlier, we are going back to the future: How do we act today with the end in mind?

The Savox management were global minded people who had lived elsewhere, done business in many countries and therefore were generally supportive of relocations for the right reasons. This was very

---

48 MACHIAVELLI, N. (1532), CHAPTER 17

helpful and influential for me. If it was justified by business, so my gut feeling told me, it should be possible to get support. I knew that if I'd only remove all things that could keep them from saying "no", the answer "yes" would be the only word left on the decision paper.

I knew that Savox wasn't going to allow me to relocate, just because they liked me. Before all else there had to be a business justification. Firstly I needed to convince the management that I was skilled enough for the task by bringing results and a real plan. Secondly I had to give them enough evidence to justify the decision to others. "He can do it." This was image that needed to be branded into their heads.

The target image is how we want other people to think of us. When other people think of us, certain key words, attributes, and emotions come to their minds. These can be a wide array of things. It is the image they have of us. The task is to create an ideal image, just like in a brand marketing strategy, that we want others to have of us.

Brands are not products.

Brands are built through perceptions, expectations and experiences. Unlike certain products, brands become meaningful over time. You aren't a product that you sell, your products are your attitude, your behavior, your skills, your work ethics, your score on the sympathy level and anything that makes you. Your brand is the sum of these products and how they are perceived over time.

Brands are built through consistency.

It requires consistency in delivering a brand promise that meets the expectations of the customers. One swallow does not make a spring.

Brands are created through persistency.

Brands aren't built overnight. To build a brand, you need to be patiend and don't give up. Continually put out messages and brand experiences that consistently communicate and support the promise of your brand. This creates awareness, loyalty and advocacy.

After defining your mission statement, gathering facts around the goal, list strenghts and weaknesses, elaborating sub strategies to remove your weaknesses, we have to define a target image: The target image is how we want to be seen by the others. This consists of three aspects.

1. Promise: The expectation that others have.
2. Position: Determination of your starting position.
3. Perception: The way others see us.

One thing is what we think of ourselves, the other is how our customers think of us. In a career setting these are the sum of people that have a direct or indirect influence on our success.

Behavior as an example is observable and can be measured and compared. Completing paperwork correctly, saying thanks to a co-worker, arriving at work before 8:00 o' clock, yelling at a colleague, badmouthing others, using foul language, giving detailed work guidance, not attending important meetings, visibly not paying attention in meetings, arriving late to work every day, helping others to use a new computer program, or regularly sharing information with co-workers. All of this shapes an image.

The way we are seen by others influences the way they talk to and about us. It has a direct impact on how they act with respect to us and whether it benefits or harms us. In an ideal constellation you want to be seen in a mutually beneficial way. For example if your manager thinks: *He can help us reaching our sales goals better than his colleagues. If I can help him to get a raise, he will be staying on my team longer which helps me to reach the targets for the whole team. That will make me look good and pay me a bonus at the end of the year.*

Living up to the target image is a steady and continuous task. If you are trying to lose or gain weight, one way to start out is to calculate the calories that a person with your target weight burns naturally on a normal day and adapt your work out and eating habits accordingly. It takes longer than radical diet plans, but it is a much more endurable way to build a path towards your ideal healthy weight and lifestyle. Trying radical changes often lead to bounce-backs that are just as radical. Anyone who wants to run a marathon will have to start early on to practice. Otherwise you cannot seriously expect to get satisfying results. Any long term goal takes determination and perseverance.

Working on your target image can be part of the implicit way to get to a new job. While I discussed to remove weaknesses and play strength to get to a positive decision, we can also create ourselves a new job by slowly and steadily transforming our tasks towards that new job. Instead of just waiting for the promotion, you can start projects that are beyond your current scope. This way you can adapt to your desired future role. If you throw a frog in boiling water it will jump right out. If you put it in cold water and then heat the water, you can boil the poor thing without the frog noticing it. I would never boil a frog, but it's a good analogy. Neglecting the work that you are hired to do gets you into trouble, but working more than expected usually helps. You can work on bigger projects that are related to your current job. You can gather more high level information, work with the departments that you need to and create new opportunities. Then you slowly cook your management soft enough that they see the additional work you are doing is benefitting them. Once you have lived up to your newly self-created responsibility and you are respected for that, you can ask for the corresponding title. Isn't it fair to ask to get the job title for the work I am already doing? It will be hard to argue against that, and at first management will usually not say anything against a better title. That doesn't cost anything yet. However, once you have a better title for a short while you can friendly remind them that more responsibility should also come with more salary. And simultaneously you have already put yourself up for a job higher on the pay grade in case a recruiter reaches out to you or if you start looking yourself. The frog is fully cooked. Bon appetite!

In theory this self-transitioning sounds easy, in practice careful acting is required. Many people are defensive of what *their* job is. Don't step on other people's feet or take away their work (do not besiege the stronghold of your enemy). In these cases close collaboration is wiser. Present yourself as a leader and someone who understands the big picture. In the end, leadership is to have a vision and to put it into action by combining different tasks into joint forces. You can lead without having formal entitlement to it. Once others recognize your efforts, you have already made a name for yourself to be up for higher tasks. Initially it's better to keep it for yourself. Musashi said: "Let your plans be as dark as night then strike like a thunderbolt." There are always policing colleagues who try to instruct you into what *your* job is supposed to be and what *not*. And your manager might not be too happy if he'd found out right away that you also work on bigger long term goals, rather than on short term goals that benefit him. This is usually a time management challenge. Focusing on what's important and skipping non-productive meetings can carve out quite a few extra hours every week. This allows to perform on the job one is hired for and work to scale it to the next level.

The way people see us depends on the eye of the beholder. People pay attention to different aspects. They see us for who we are as a person and our performance on the job. Attitude and method of working is just as important as the amount of work you actually do. The rational image is attributing skills to your person. You want people to know where to look if they are in need of certain skills. The emotional image is how people feel about us. Both aspects are of equal importance. It will be difficult to find supporters, even for the best ideas, if nobody likes you. People have to like you to at least a minimum extent in order to be more open for your suggestions. Feelings are triggered by actions or inactions that influence our senses. If you smile at someone they often smile back, if you are friendly to a stranger they will often be friendly to you.

How to phrase the target image is similar to the phrasing of our mission. In our mission statement we wanted to combine goals with deadlines and reasons for which we wanted to achieve them. Our target image is attributing skills and emotion to us as a person or product and includes a call for action. The target image is not a marketing slogan that would be printed anywhere; it is what we want the others to think of us. That's why it doesn't sound like the tagline in a TV commercial, but in analogy to commercials we try to create a connection between content and brand.

We aim to associate certain attributes with our name. How often do we see TV commercials that are funny, but we don't remember what they were for? Those commercials are a waste of money. Effective advertising creates an image of a product that is clearly related to a brand and calls for action to buy in certain situations.

One great example in recent years were the Snickers commercials. Everyone knows how cranky and nasty people can get when they are really hungry. Hence the word *hangry*. The series of commercials shows sarcastic, nasty and unfriendly people, until a bite of a Snickers turns them back into a pleasant-to-be-with person. "You are not you when you are hungry" says the slogan. Meredith and I still make fun of each other when one of us is hungry or we see people that are being nasty in public. One of us then says: "I think you need a Snickers." This type of messaging turns an everyday life situation into the call to buy a product that can solve that problem immediately. It reminds you that it's a Snickers you want in that situation, even though any chocolate bar can achieve the same quick result in lifting blood sugars. With this kind of commercial, Snickers was able to own the hunger-solving issue. They didn't say that if you are hungry you should eat something. They exaggerated by saying if you are so hungry that you aren't yourself you can quickly solve this if you eat a Snickers. It's a villain-victim-hero framework: The villain is the hunger, the victim the people who have to put up with a hangry person and the hero is the chocolate bar who beats the villain and saves the victims.

A target image of Snickers could have been:

- Snickers is a delicious snack.
- Snickers immediately stills hunger.

- Snickers turns any nasty person into a pleasant one.
- Snickers can be bought anywhere at a very low price.
- Anyone who is lightheaded, cranky or nasty due to major appetite should quickly buy a Snickers and immediately change his mood to the better, satisfy his appetite while eating this delicious chocolate bar.

These are imaginary target images that connect the attributes to the brand and include a call for action. The execution of this target image is perfectly rendered in the Snickers commercial:

1. What's happening?
2. How can you change the situation?
3. Buy this!

The final sentence is a summary of the facts aimed to create an insider outsider image and a call for action: if you consider yourself one of the people who demand x, y and z from a product you have to buy this one. The final phrase of your target image is crucial, because it creates the must-have situation, the closing of the deal.

The above target image phrases are what we want others to think of us. Our actions and the way we present ourselves should imply it, without us having to use those exact words. It is not about bragging, but about a constant drop of water. Executing your sub-strategies is intertwined with the target image. Do good things and make others aware of it. Effective politics is not only part of what you do, it is how others think about what you do. You will always have to perform to prove yourself, but this exercise is important to help with self-marketing. You have to live and breathe that image, consistently.

If you have aligned your goals into an existing management strategy or impose one on the management, it will always serve a dual function: Firstly you focus your work on results that help your target image. Secondly, by doing so, you move a company forward and help the management to decide in your favor. You create a win-win situation.

My personal target image to get Savox to relocate me to the United States was this:

- Max has the experience to lead a business unit including all relevant areas including sales, marketing, operations, legal, product strategy, such as profit & loss calculation.
- Max has already been an ex-pat before and therefore knows how to pioneer a business from scratch in new territories.
- Max has built strategic alliances with all key players that represent 80% of the worldwide market.
- Max speaks several languages fluently and is a tech- and business savvy person.
- Max can build relations with anyone from customers, resellers, industry decision makers, and engineers.
- Anyone who wants to build up a new business in a new market selling a new technology has to hire Max to execute a successful market-entry and secure revenue growth.

I only learned that adding a villain to the victim-hero story after my own experience. I definitely recommend adding a villain, since it will then be more than just problem solving. It creates more urgency. Building a target image is "orchestrating" the emotions and thoughts the other ones have. Creating more dramatic or musical tension will bring even greater relief when the hero appears. Anyone who listens to Ludwig van Beethoven's (1770–1826) symphonies for example, experiences this build up of musical tension and an up and down and a heroic relief when the entire orchestra plays loud and majestic.

As you create your target image you can cross check it against your mission statement from earlier. The ultimate goal was to achieve happiness. If the target image is the person that you want to be, then you have done your homework right. If it turns out to be a purely instrumental image then you don't do it for the right reasons. The target image has an intrinsic and instrumental character at the same time. It helps you to become the person you want to be and you enjoy it as you are getting there.

One swallow doesn't make a summer, Aristotle said. A simple elevator pitch and having one good day of great performance won't create the desired image. Perseverance and determination, constant self-improvement and not losing your goal out of sight will lead your pursuit: Honestly living up to your own target image. The more serious you work on it, the more you will be recognized and appreciated. And the more you feel about yourself and like yourself as well. The target image that you created will be in people's heads without trying to manipulate. By living up to our target image we distinguish ourselves from the so-called politicians. Your success will be fruit of real labor, rather than a constant quick-win-and-run sequence. It will be something you can be proud of. You will deserve your promotion, because you earned it with skill and labor.

If you have to fix anything in your home, make a decision on where to travel on vacation or buy a new car or computer, what do you do? You ask Bob, because he knows about computers. Or you ask Joe about what car to buy, because he's very knowledgeable. You ask Max where to travel, he has seen half the planet.

Anyone who makes decisions in life, likes to have their person of trust to support their decisions. If the person with the power over your future career asks his friend: "what do you think?" you want that person to answer that they believe it was a good idea.

Target groups, opinion leaders and multiplicators play an important role for our success. For anything we want to buy, we gather information regarding quality, price and popularity. Many people buy what everyone else is buying, for example in fashion. If everyone wears a certain brand it must be good or you want to be part of the same trend. Those trends can also change. A hundred years ago almost all men would wear hats, it was a way to hide in the crowd. Today people use hats to stand out of the crowd and some people find it very fashionable. So how do most customers decide on buying a product they don't know much about like a washing machine or a car? They may do some Internet research, read reviews and will most likely ask someone who they deem to be knowledgeable about the product they want to purchase. You will be able to sell a lot more of your products if you get a person of trust convinced that yours is the best. This is the reason why so many celebrities are making money through advertising. If you favorite singer, athlete or actor advertises a certain hair product, car, clothing line or cough medicine, the advertiser hopes that those will represent a person of trust to the viewers and multiply sales.

In a business environment case studies and live demos are often used to promote a product or solution. Videos of customers endorsing products or solutions are also a common way of marketing since it's not frontal advertising, but a product in action endorsed by users. Politicians and political groups maintain relations to unions, foundations, business interests groups, and lobby groups to do the same. Third party endorsements strengthen your message and your cause. Getting a famous person to endorse your campaign for presidency can do a lot to influence politically disinterested persons or undecided ones. We can apply the same in our life by finding the right people and affiliations whose members, network and endorsements can help our cause. And vice-versa you can help others and this way you maintain a long-lasting network.

Here as well: nothing too much. Asking fewer people for endorsement focus on the quality is more effective than having dozens of them. If you aren't a celebrity it is very strange if so many people recommend you. Good recommendations might not get read, simply because there are too many. Being picky about who to ask for a recommendation is important. The people who read endorsements will spend more time looking at the person who endorses you rather than what that person says about you.

Getting to yes! One day your high noon moment may come and you have to present your case and gain approval. For Savox I created an entire business plan, defined the market size and the total accessible market, I scoped the business opportunity, calculated the needed budget, I outlined the competitive environment, technology and marketing alliances. I had built sales channels worldwide with customers waiting. This should be my proof of concept. It was like pitching a startup company at pre-revenue stage to a business angel or venture capitalist, with a complete business plan and a deep knowledge of the technology of the market. It was like trying to get a seed investment. I was neither making stuff up, nor were the managers at Savox fools that would buy just any story. It was a solid plan.

It was in early 2009, when I gained approval for a relocation to New York, including a new title, and a raise in salary. From the moment I had started at Savox, 18 months had passed. It was not only a new job description, but we agreed on a new work contract that included all my new tasks similar to that of a general manager, covering all aspects of the line of business. I had concentrated for a year and a half on that goal, but my previous experience at Digital Chocolate was already the preparation for it. I was able to say I have done this before. The more it showed that what you do today can help or harm you in five or ten years from now and that you have to step out of yourself to consciously and deliberately see where you are and where you want to go.

How to prepare for a pitch?

Every presentation to any audience is slightly different, but there are certain aspects that can be in your toolbox of presenting:

- Your presentations consist of 1/10 introduction, 8/10 content and 1/10 your final word, but the importance of each part is 1/3. The first impression and the last words that should stick are just as important as your content. Memorize and practice.

In your opening internalize the following:

- Get straight to the point: what is it that you are selling? Name it so that people know immediately what you are talking about. What's your product? That can be your skill, your business idea, or whatever you are trying to get the other party to support or buy into.
- If you can, use a story, a metaphor or anecdote to get your audience into your way of thinking. Remember, if your audience

doesn't get hooked within the first minute, they will start checking their emails or social media. What is it that got you here? How did you come up with your idea? Why do you do this? This could be for example: In the United States there are 600 000 patrol officers and 400 000 patrol vehicles of the police, wouldn't it be great if they were using our Push-to-Talk accessories?

- Tell the audience what's happening. A technology trend, a marketing fashion, a change in the organization, the greatest idea that you ever had, what is going on? If your topic here was a newspaper headline or a book title, what would that be? This will be already your intro and shouldn't take more than one minute.

In your middle part of your pitch you have to add content and answer the most immediate questions before they arise:

- What role can you or your company play in what is happening? What is the opportunity?
- Create a must-have story for your buyer. Why is it that your proposal is compelling to your audience and what makes it better to buy your idea than walking away from it?
- What are the alternatives (competitors) and how do you distinguish yourself from them?
- How do you make money with this? Business decision makers, investors, book publishers, art buyers, and movie producers alike will want to know how to market your idea, not only that it's good or fancy. How does your audience benefit from your proposal?
- Sell your idea as an opportunity. What's in it for the others? E.g. you have to explain why giving you the job will benefit the hiring manager, why is entering new markets abroad beneficial to the company?
- What would happen if they don't agree with you? How would you continue without their support? They might ask you that to find out how much they can get for free.

- What is the competitive environment? What do other companies, teams or individuals do? How do they handle the challenges that you described in your plan?
- Explain your goals and what has to happen to get there. What is the cost of revenue? At what cost does the audience get their benefits?
- Play out your strengths.
- If you were able to overcome weaknesses and solve problems for the company, be sure to mention them to prove your capabilities.
- Be realistic about time frames and explain what takes which time, who will execute the tasks and who will control their fulfillment.
- What makes your idea, product, proposal unique? How do you show that it's only you who can do that and not just anyone?

In the final portion you have to tell your audience what it is that you want. They will want to know why you asked for their time. If you want an investment, say how much you need and what you would use it for. If you want a new job assignment, then say that:

- Don't assume people know what you want, say what you need.
- Don't ask for a new assignment: plant your willingness to do something for the company or the investor as an opportunity for them.
- The bait has to taste to the fish, not the fisherman. You know what you will get out of the deal, so focus on what the others will get for it, rather than day dreaming about how nice it would be for you if it would work out.
- Get a commitment: ask for the next steps and time lines. Do not take no for an answer, do not let them tell you that they'll think about it and get back to you. Stay in control, drive the decision making forward without being neither too pushy nor too desperate.

When you finish your pitch, don't just say thank you. Conclude with a thought that you give your audience on your way.

Your last sentence has to get stuck in the people's head so that they will continue to think about it even later. The stickier the better: If you were really hungry and couldn't wait to get a bite, wouldn't it be great to have a Snickers? Make your conclusion a Snickers-pitch.

I could have said: "When you think about expanding this business to one of the largest markets, wouldn't it be great to have a business development pioneer that is willing to relocate to build this for you locally?"

Don't give up, even if it doesn't work out the first time. If you do not get approved, ask for the reasons, work on those and retake the discussion when you are ready. Make sure to have the other side line out what it would take for them to approve your case. It is a way not to take no for an answer. Many people make the mistake that if they weren't successful they just move on instead of asking for the reasons for rejection. Maybe your idea was good, but it wasn't yet ripened out in the minds of the listeners. Venture Capitalists say that very often start-ups that are rejected do not ask for the reasons why. From all the no's that you get in life you can learn to build one big YES.

To pursue a promotion for the sole purpose of career development was a good idea. What made it a great idea was to combine it with a move to New York City and get married with Meredith. This gave me the extra drive and motivation and made the success even sweeter. My career development step was therefore of intrinsic and instrumental nature both professionally and personally.

What is the difference now? Isn't this drive to win exactly what companies and hiring managers are looking for? Yes and no. It is what companies *state* that they look for. But as I have shown, skill alone is not enough. Rising to the level of your own competence requires more than talent and hard work. There is no easy way up. In the world as is, even the most talented and ambitious people have to get through the jungle of politics and hierarchy.

My approach is to play the corporate chess game without making a deal with the devil. Influencing your destiny while being true to yourself, without telling people want they want to hear for short-term success. Believing in your own capabilities and making others aware of them.

The difference to the typical talker in a company is to do good and make people aware of it. The typical politician as people call them, is a person who tries to gain advantage without having any substance. This is why they are so disliked. In addition they focus constantly on shining in a different light than others. There is always a me and you in their language. And they often treat people accordingly in this shortsightedness disregarding that you may meet again in a different constellation. Others may become your boss, your customer or your business partner in the future. We should always treat everyone the same, regardless of social status. We have to create an image of how we want to be seen by anyone, not just the ones who make the decisions right now. Your target image has to match with your real skills. I believe that sooner or later the talkers will get called out. The notorious announcer will only get so far. Don't try to look good based on what's not yours or not true. You don't have to be super nice to the people above you and kick the ones below you to try to get anywhere. You can be the same person to anyone. There are always people who back-stab, try to undermine your credibility, and there are people who want to keep us from growing for their own ego. Simply put: There are people that make your life difficult, sometimes on purpose sometimes unknowingly. However, if you know what you are striving for, nothing can keep you from getting there. If you work on eliminating your weaknesses, using your strengths wisely and live up to your target image having your goal in mind at all times, then you won't leave much room for attack. You build character, and self-esteem. And you grow resistance to social pressure.

In sports, after the game is before the game. You cannot rest on your momentary success. What that meant for my career and the next unintended challenge was about to come soon after moving to New York.

5 BEYOND MACHIAVELLI

*"A prince never lacks legitimate reasons
to break his promise."*

NICCOLO MACHIAVELLI (1469–1527)

I believed that I had figured it all out when I moved to New York City in 2009. I thought I had found the secrets to success. I believed that my own success proved my theory to be right. Only one year after I was let go from Savox. How could that have happened? Maybe I thought I am invincible and I overestimated my own capabilities? I'd say I underestimated the speed by which one can fall when the status quo changes, no matter how strengthening the ascent was. It made it clear that one cannot rest on successful events, but has to keep climbing the ladder of personal challenge. Robert L. Stevenson (1850–1894), author of *Treasure Island,* said that one should not judge each day by the harvest you reap, but by the seeds you plant. As I had found a treasure I noticed to be standing on the quicksand of corporate promises.

In the aftermath, only years later though, it taught me that not everything is about success, but to take failure with a good sense of humor. Failure also has a positive side: it doesn't cause any envy from other people. There is something about that.

The rise and fall of my personal career at Savox was after all the ignition to become an entrepreneur, but I will get to that later. First I need to analyze what happened: How could I work so hard and long to get what I want and lose it rather quickly?

"Fixation is the way to death. Fluidity the way to life." Had I taken heed to Musashi's advice, I may not have lost my job. Getting Savox to send me to New York turned into a Pyrrhus Victory.[49]

As I moved to the big apple for a 2nd round in 2009, this time with Savox instead of Digital Chocolate, I tripped over a large ego and fell deep. I am an idealist and I tend to stick to principles. This led me to gamble more than I could afford to lose, because I wanted to be right. My career seemed to be taking off, Savox and I had big plans. After only six months, with a new boss put in front of me, the status quo changed dramatically; and I realized it too late. All I had fought for, and thought I had won, vanished away. It threw me back in all aspects of my life. Instead of a bright future career, and living the life of a young urban professional in New York City, I was back on the job market trying to get by financially. It was a tough moment to be job-hunting since the world was very slowly recovering from one of the worst recessions in decades, which the US president had called the Great Recession. I needed to mentally recover from it, get up and start over again. All as I had just gotten married.

The back analysis from my first career success led to the elaboration of the plan that I discussed in the previous chapters; on how to impose our strategy on our opponent. The back analysis of my second career success and the subsequent steep fall helped me to learn how to recognize inflection points better and be more alert of changes in the status quo.

The biggest lesson learned: it's never about you.

In theory you can always build a winning strategy. But life is not a punching bag, your opponents will punch back. They have their own strategies and follow their own tactics.

---

49 The expression to win a Pyrrhus victory means that the winner comes out of the war as weak as the defeated. The victory was bought at a high price. King Pyrrhus (318–272 B.C.), according to legend, said after his victory against the Romans at Asculum: "another victory like this and we will be lost."

Fortunately career chess is like any other sport, you can come prepared for it. Your advantage: Most other players do not consciously play this game, but follow their own feelings and act according to the way they the world occurs to them. Through observation and communication, we can find out the intentions of the others and win their support for our ideas.

I had started at Savox November of 2007. 18 months later, I relocated from Helsinki to New York, just like I had planned it from the start. I was promoted from Sales Director to VP of Business Development & Strategic Alliances. We set up and signed a new contract outlining my responsibilities for the global market for wireless products for professional users. Both, the management and I, were excited to give this opportunity the right structure and the needed push to be successful as a business.

The excitement did not last long. The status quo changed. Only six months into my new assignment of building the startup within the company, Savox's owner acquired a company called Iqua and left it to the Savox Management to integrate it into the business. Iqua had been built with venture capital on top of the ego of a former Nokia executive. Burnt through investors' money, a day before closing the doors forever, Iqua was acquired. My line of business was immediately put underneath the Iqua brand, mixing professional communication devices with Bluetooth consumer headsets. The old lack of support was more present than ever and spiced up with indifference from the new the leadership. My new boss wanted to demote me to a sales manager for his consumer products and didn't want to have much to do with mission critical communication. Focused on his own agenda and deliverables towards his new boss, he was very indifferent about my scope of work and responsibility stated in a contract, which he himself had re-signed. Did he not read before signing?

The challenge wasn't the fact alone that my boss wanted to change my assignment on me over night. The Savox management had given him the OK for that without ever seeking a professional conversation with me on how my role may change. I did not get that memo.

They never told me, maybe just assumed I'd figure out my new role on my own? Any management that plans to change an employee's tasks should as a minimum inform the person about it, right? How else would they know? If you just agreed by written contract on a scope of work is it right to cancel the agreement one-sidedly and secretly and wait for the person to figure it out? Well, common sense is not common after all. They made up their mind about what I should be doing, but didn't want to raise the topic with me. Maybe because they knew they were breaking a promise, their word and a contract? Bad conscience made them act like teenagers by trying to avoid a difficult conversation? By not communicating, they drove me into a position that I was caught in by complete surprise. This made for a bad beginning and was the starting point for a bad outcome.

The very first time I met my new boss he started talking about how I am going to sell Bluetooth headsets in North America and I thought that I was in the wrong movie. What he said didn't make any sense to me, since *his* manager had told me that I will now receive *more* support.

"Did they not tell you what my job is?" I asked him. "I am globally selling a professional device that – in conjunction with a mobile phone – should work as a walkie-talkie replacement. I'm not a Territory Manager for consumer products in North America." He was visibly surprised and irritated that I basically told him that he had the wrong expectations on what I was going to do. He wanted to reel me in line with his sales people for his own mission. I was just looking for someone to approve my budget and let me go forward with the business that was assigned to do. The expectations could not have been farther apart. They had told each of us a different story. This happens if you try to be everyone's friend and you lack the backbone to be a leader.

I reacted like people who had become victim of an ambush. They defend by shooting at everything moving in the bushes. My new boss was the messenger of my old one who avoided talking to me. He had promised me something and to my boss the opposite and left it to us to find that out. I had totally been cheated on. This was a difficult situation to have a cool stoic head in. I did not have a cool head. For a company that makes professional communications equipment it was an extremely unprofessional way of communicating.

"In a matter of style, go with the flow. In a matter of principle, stand like a rock," said Thomas Jefferson (1743–1826). I saw myself in the right. I had a written agreement, and even more: a word and a handshake. Insisting on what had been agreed on, I was unwilling to just change my job 180 degrees. That cost me my job. I'm not the one who didn't keep his word, I'm not the one who wasn't keeping his side of the agreement, yet I was the weaker one the open battlefield.

Since my childhood it has been an un-movable principle to me that you always have to keep your promises. The Savox management was breaking their promise and breaching my work contract not through simple negligence, but intentional omission of their responsibilities. Leaving management decisions to an ego-centric choleric who yelled every time you disagreed with him.

Having a difficult conversation about a serious topic with that person was similar to disagreeing with a three-year-old having a temper tantrum. Visualize a person that turns burning red when he hears something critical, immediately takes it personal, stops listening, climbs on the closest rock and screams at the top of the lungs, then jumps up high with both legs in the air banging his fists on his chest. Something like that could figuratively describe my boss's character. A wonderful person to have around.

The fact that he was my boss was making me, carefully said, irritated. I practiced Taekwondo every day during that time. I had so much built up energy from work that my bike ride to class was getting faster every day. I entered the Dojang 30min prior to class every day to kick and punch the heavy bag imagining it would be my manager, hitting where it hurts. I was dreaming of having Voodoo dolls or crossing his path in dark alley one day.

You have to take a bull by its horns and a man by his word.

I have always held people responsible for their actions. I am a wholehearted citizen and I live up to the duties of every man in a democracy. Stand up for what is right. That's what society preaches to you from early childhood on. The fine print that only life teaches you is the amount of trouble it can get you in if you do so. There is an uneven distribution of power and with it the rules are different depending on your position within your society or institution. In practice it's possible to stay out of a lot of trouble by adapting, conforming, adjusting, assimilating, memorizing what to think instead of learning how to think, saying yes a lot, and never question authority. Blind obedience, ignorance and indifference is a way to survive. Only: it's not human. To adapt to anything out of fear or convenience creates a conformist society in which nobody dares to say out loud what he believes in. That would be a very poor world to live in.

Many people nod or applaud when it comes to fluffy sounding speeches about freedom. Few are seen when it counts to voice your opinion and concerns, speak up and when holding others accountable for their action and inactions. Especially if you have to stand up for it alone, without the comfort of a supporting mass in the room or hiding behind an alias on the Internet. For the vast majority of people, self-preservation comes before moral principle and virtuous action. *Somebody-should-do-something-about-it* is the biggest form of participation of people in society. And the same people who are quick in finding excuses for inaction are just as fast in judging others for their actions.

As if Nietzsche was accompanying me, I struggled through life not to get overwhelmed by the tribe, always in the ambition to own myself. There is no doubt that this has got me into trouble more than once. In Kindergarten I argued with the teachers that naptime was a right, not a duty. As an 18 year old, in 1995, I brought up my high school principal against me by calling her evidently out on her indifference over a racist teacher who was able to insult his students and punish them without any reason. I had created a flyer and handed out 500 copies in the school yard under the eyes of the principal.

The principal indirectly threatened to expel me from school, the teacher filed a law suit against me, and fellow students who had opposed the teacher now wanted to make me the scapegoat by asserting that I'd abuse the situation for my personal reputation. Others complained about not following a process, and the method of my publishing. It's a very common way to complain: "I just find the *way* you said that inappropriate." After which no word will be lost about *what* you actually had to say. Reflection with the content doesn't happen. Even if you say you are sorry about how you said it and that you'd still like to discuss the issue, usually it will circle back to how you started it. It is a human reaction of the masses to start or be lured into all-out attacks against the people who point out nuisances. The principal herself abused her position. Her only argument was that any kind of political campaigning on school premises was not permitted. This was enough not to discuss the content at all.

Berthold Brecht (1898–1956) said: "When injustice becomes law, resistance becomes duty." What other options do you have if the highest person in the institution is indifferent about a racist teacher? When the argument is not about the content of my complaint, but about whether I have the right to do political campaigning within the premises of a school, what is left? It is a typical reaction of people in charge when they are caught in misconduct. They argue with the law; and with hierarchy and authority they are able to muzzle others. Throughout history the strong have used their power to create right, only to argue afterwards that their actions are based on the law and solely executed to protect it.

The principal is now long retired and the teacher was suspended from teaching. A victory that came at a high price. Principle and Pyrrhus seem to walk hand in hand very often.

This had only been the beginning of my stubborn ways of calling out the people who create dirt and get away with it. While heading the youth organization of the Free Democratic Party in Frankfurt and serving a term in the City Council, I looked for more public trouble: this time with the then governing minister of the State of Hesse, Roland Koch. In the year 2000, Mr. Koch was caught in the attempt to deceive some of the facts in a party financing scandal including hidden bank accounts, and later admitted to have lied about it. My party, the F.D.P. was in a coalition with Koch's CDU and a heated debate was taking place. The youth organization of my party was spear-heading the anti-Koch movement.

In early 2001, Mr. Koch attended a conference of our organization on which he wanted to convince us that he had done nothing wrong. I gave probably the best speech of my life, unmasking and exposing his false-faced and dissembling way of dealing with the scandal and the people he is supposed to represent. I asked him to renounce his post and move to a lonely island. I enjoyed the longest and loudest standing ovation that I have experienced in my political life. The applause and shouting is still echoing in my memory. What a feeling!

What happened behind the scenes was different. It proved that you cannot be everyone's friend. I received phone calls from influential party members that I should stop campaigning against the governing minister and that I should not risk the coalition. My fellow colleagues from the CDU in the City Council weren't too happy either. Nobody threatened me with anything, but it was a heated debate and many people tried to pressure others to vote their way. Some people became my biggest supporters, others became clear opponents.

When you stand up for what you believe in, not everyone will be on your side. You show profile and you will be recognized, but not everyone will love you. There will actually be a lot of people against you, especially the ones who have something to lose, like a seat in the government or an executive job, their reputation as a principal, or their future career opportunities. When something that is yours gets threatened, people circle the wagons and defend it until the last man standing.

The world is not black and white. You cannot expect people to be against or for you. Only by starting your campaign for or against something you might step on people's feet who were initially indifferent about you. You might unintentionally besiege someone else's stronghold and they will do anything to defend it. There are always people that you did not think of, that come out of the woodwork. Others might take advantage to make a name for themselves by rallying against you. Throughout history it has been a successful strategy to gather supporters through the fear of a common enemy. In the moment you start a crusade you are full of good thoughts and you believe you can claim the moral high ground. However, there are people who have something to lose and they will do whatever it takes to keep you from your plans. And it can get very dirty. I have seen many people, and entire societies self-inducing with propaganda on how important it is to stand up for what is right. Yet when the call is out for individuals to stand up, most people are far by-standers and don't have the courage to stand up for what they believe in. It happens in private and public life, and in politics.

Unlike politics, in the corporate world there are usually only a handful people left who speak their mind. Why stand up for something if you have too much to lose? Someone should do something about it. In a democracy you have checks and balances, rules & regulations and an independent system of justice that people have to adhere to. When politicians abuse their power you can vote them out of office, if business partners breach contractual obligations, you take them to court. What do you do if your boss abuses power and is backed by another power-abuser? It becomes systematic, almost organized. Bad culture is created in a company and spreads like an epidemic that's difficult to eradicate.

When the founder of a company looks for an investor, a common recommendation is to make sure you get along with that person. It will be close to impossible to build a successful business with someone you cannot stand. Unfortunately, when you build the business for another company, you can't pick your leaders. What's left is getting along with them.

"A prince never lacks legitimate reasons to break his promise," Machiavelli said. The Savox Management left me standing in the rain. Nobody wanted to be reminded of existing written agreements. They simply said that the new leader "will take the right decisions for the business." It was like our contract had never existed. Everything I had built for the company and myself started to fall apart over personal feuding over responsibilities, agreements that weren't kept, ego and extremely bad communication. Not much left to get along with in this case.

Initially, when Savox and I had agreed on how to run the business, there was joint excitement and enthusiasm. We believed that this was the right way to do it and everyone was on board. Then the situation changed and I lost my support. I reacted like I always do. I called out made promises, signed agreements, and I held people accountable. After a year of skirmishes I was let go. I had lost.

Learning from mistakes, getting up after falling, is the way to become better. Making mistakes is important if you can process what happened and identify the mistakes you made. That will enable you to derive a method on how to avoid mistakes next time. This process already starts early in childhood: to become a conformist or a free person is a lot about nature and nurture. To be put into the situation that allows to try and err, and the ability to reflect upon it, is what makes one become self-sufficient.

It had started with the challenges that remained unsolved and held the entire business back: A budget for the business unit never happened, dedicated product development was an indication error. Based in New York, in charge of the worldwide market-entry, I hired a person in Spain to help with sales in Europe. On his first day I had to let him go again, because I was told last minute that there was no money. This was when Savox acquired Iqua. It was *tabula rasa*, a complete new start, nothing from before counted. And I was thrown back 18 months.

From a high level view it looked like a good move, to put my line of business unit under a bigger umbrella of an existing company. Iqua used to sell Bluetooth headsets for mobile phones. My line of business was Bluetooth speaker-microphones for professional communication. For someone from the outside this was easy to explain: it was both Bluetooth. If you bothered to look under the surface, you would have seen that these two have just as much in common as English and Chinese. They are both a language, but that's it. A Bluetooth headset for a mobile phone is a commodity. An industrial designer makes something look unique, a marketing person decides about what functionalities signify a differentiator on the market and requires specific features, like a heart rate monitor for athletes, or a noise cancellation feature. A project manager puts the design and requirement specifications together and sends them Far East for production. There is no Research & Development happening and from an engineering perspective it's very low-tech; you are using off-the-shelf technology. Hardly anything has a sustainable competitive advantage, can be patented or is otherwise unique. It's a commodity business that differentiates itself over looks and trends, and brand recognition.

Professional communication over Bluetooth on the other hand, requires custom embedded Bluetooth software, and the testing requirements are totally different; for industrial users or law enforcement, quality does matter a lot. If you listen to music over Bluetooth it doesn't matter if the connection is not working properly here and there. For a policeman in a crowd control situation, facing an angry mob of hooligans, reliability is everything.

The Savox Management had solved the old internal resource problem that wireless products competed with an old school technology of 2-Way-Radios, by replacing it with an organization that didn't have any engineering resources at all. In other words: they made it worse; from that moment the Savox engineers all blocked my requests for work by referring me to Iqua. They owned the products from now on, they said. So instead of sticking to the agreed plan, this was a promise to be dead on arrival. I was told that "now you will get more support". Maybe I have understood "now" when they actually meant "no more"?

Due to Iqua's almost-bankruptcy there were only funds to keep operating, not for investment. The Managing Director at Iqua started every conversation by saying: "when I used to be an executive at Nokia…" He tried to create the comprehension that because he had a big title in the past it would somehow prove his capabilities. He certainly could commit suicide if he jumped off the top of his ego. It's not the only time that I have met a person that was accidentally at a company as it grew, and then pretended it was all because of him.

There was a personified reason why Iqua had never been success-ful. Unfortunately the Savox management from that point on, did not want to deal with me anymore, but kept referring me to my Iqua boss. That was a bummer. A very big personal disappointment to be back-stabbed this way and even more a disappointment that all the work I had done to bring the business this far, including the deal for myself, was falling apart. That was quite devastating.

In a back room meeting, Savox and Iqua had decided that I should be selling Iqua's Bluetooth headsets in the North American market. To me they told the story that Iqua will now be able to help me with my professional devices. A total different story that cannot happen by accident. I flew from the U.S. to Finland for a meeting with my new Iqua colleagues. All of them thought that now I'd be their new North American territory manager, while I thought that they'd all be helping me selling my products worldwide. Neither of the sides knew that and therefore the entire meeting was extremely awkward. It seemed like we totally spoke in parallel worlds. Instead of having a serious conver-sation about the changed business environment, they tried to sneak new tasks up on me and communicated a different story everywhere as if they were afraid of saying out loud what the plans were. The rest was quite confused as to what they wanted us to do.

Despite the fact that we took the existing contract I had with Savox and signed it word for word again with Iqua, my boss scruti-nized everything I was working on and did not want to be reminded of written agreements. Now everything had to go his way. I had a lot of fights with my boss. I tried to block his demands referring to what my job description and responsibilities were and that he couldn't just walk in and change it all on me. The situation was gridlocked.

Uneven distribution of power can reinforce that rules don't apply to everyone in the same way. A Latin proverb calls this: *Quod licet iovi, non licet bovi* – what is legitimate for Jove (Jupiter), is not legitimate for the oxen.

I could be held responsible for sales figures, but I could not hold them responsible for not delivering a product that can be sold. They could blame me for not selling by closing an eye on technical problems. But I could not hold them responsible for ignoring an agreement.

I could have avoided all the conflict and the arguments, by just accepting my fate. But I insisted that rules apply to everyone: Stick to your word, stick to your agreements, and keep your promises. Don't expect from others what they can't expect from you.

I wanted to be right, stand up for what's right and I was laid off.

How can you deal with a difficult situation like this? First of all we have to recognize the uneven distribution of power that you have to fight against. In those situations you have to divert the strength of the opponent and practice to do what is counter intuitive. Get out of the way of a battle of strength. Like my word against yours for example. Your boss is always right, even when he's wrong. *Divide et impera* – divide and conquer – Julius Caesar said. The more you can divert the power of others and keep them from unifying against your rule or uprising, the more relative power you will gain.

Musashi urges you to understand the harm and benefit in anything. This was my mistake. I felt strong enough pushing on the agreement we had. Unfortunately, due to the opposing promises that the Management had made, now they had to pick a side. So they backed him and -stabbed me.

Pointing out who made the mess, standing up for what is right, can get you shot. We have to use a different tactic on how to lean up against superior power.

I derived an analogy from martial arts, a basic rule of self-defense: Yin and Yang counter balance. If someone is hard, be soft, if they are soft, be hard. For example if someone grabs your hand really hard and in return you grab the opponents hand and try to counter with strength, it becomes a muscle battle. The one with the better grip and more power will win. If instead you let loose, which is counter-intuitive, the opponent gets confused and usually lets looser himself.

If an opponent is choking you from behind, instead of defending against the choke you can kick your heel onto the top of his foot. No matter how strong the other person is, that spot is pure bone. Heel beats top of foot. In that moment you can twist and turn their hand, get lose and counter attack with a punch into the throat or groin. When you try to beat a stronger person you have to hit them where none of their weight and muscle has any influence.

Another example is when you get punched in the ribs. Most people would immediately tighten their ribs and hold their breath as a protective reaction. In that moment it becomes a battle of strength: The opponent's fist combined with strength and speed against your ribs. In most cases that will be enough to get them to break. When you get hit you have to exhale to give your ribs room to move. That is not intuitive at first. Your mind has to be more powerful than your body to do that. That takes work, but everything is difficult at first, as Musashi precisely said.

Sun Tzu says that "he will win who knows when to fight and when not to fight." In a war you never send weaker troops into an open field and into a situation where the stronger one will win, only because you want to be right. Therefore a lot of getting through the war game at work is to use guerrilla tactics.

At Savox, I stood up for what's right, but I reckoned without the host. I did not know when to fight and when not to fight. I lost my job over wanting to be right. And with it I had lost what I had wanted: A general manager position with a nice salary in order to enjoy the Big Apple. That had lasted only a year until spring time of 2010 and I was back on the labor market. How devastating. Freshly married I had hoped to start a nice little life together; instead we started out by seeing how we could get by financially. It was difficult not to take this personally.

Next to my useless fight against a hierarchy, in the aftermath I was able to point out two main issues that led to that situation:

Negotiation and communication.

My tactical errors were able to occur because I did not notice that the status quo had changed. There was an inflection point and I had ignored it. It didn't matter on what had been agreed, but on how the person in power that newly entered the game, saw his own default future. From his point of view he did not enter in this new organization to join a larger corporation and to serve the needs of others. From his ego-centric perspective, everyone was there to help *him* to continue *his* business. Despite the fact that he was the main reason it was in a mess and it wasn't even his business anymore. People of that type are incapable of seeing that. Anyone who is not aligned with him, agreements in place or not, is an obstacle to him.

Despite recognizing his character, I didn't conclude for myself, that *I* had to adjust to *him*. Maybe because I had a hard time taking him serious, I didn't see that he was the boss after all. Years later I happened to meet a Venture Capital investor that had been approached in post-Iqua time by him. I asked the investor: "what did you think of him?" "I actually couldn't see that he had a skill for anything." he said. A late satisfaction, useless back then as well as today, but satisfying.

In Machiavelli's Prince we can find a great recommendation for the would-have, should-have and could-have of my situation: "A prince being thus obliged to know well how to act as a beast must imitate the fox and the lion, for the lion cannot protect himself from traps, and the fox cannot defend himself from wolves. One must therefore be a fox to recognize traps, and a lion to frighten wolves." You have to be both clever and fierce. One must be more than one dimensional in his acting. A fox acts human, clever, he learns and can find traps. The lion is a beast and acts by force and power. I tried to be the lion when I had to imitate the fox. Negotiating a compromise between the two different expectations was probably the best we could have done.

A good plan is half the victory. The other half is execution. What seems simple on the paper, like "convince the CEO of my ex-pat agreement" or "gain approval for a million dollar marketing budget", can be very challenging once you have to deliver. Communicating and negotiating with others can be a challenging undertaking. Not everything that makes sense by the rules of math and logic, and your own standards, applies to others. Things you say, and how you say them, have to be evaluated based on the way the receiving party understands and interprets your words.

Because we always have to deal with people, not robots, we should shed a light on topics that can make or break your career:

- negotiation
- communication
- rhetoric
- logic

It's not rocket science, yet it requires *esprit de conduite* to build relations with any type of personality, comprehension and reflection of the rhetoric of others and finesse to pick your battles wisely.

Negotiation is a form of communication, both verbal and non-verbal, in which two or more parties with common, opposing, or shared interests, interact aiming to reach an agreement. Not all negotiations reach agreements, and some negotiations are only used in order to gain time. In general we should assume though, that the target outcome is an agreement. Negotiation is a basic human interaction that can cover anything from what to make for dinner, where to go on a family vacation, salary disputes, international free trade agreements or nuclear proliferation. Negotiation can happen in person, through intermediaries, explicit or implicit.

During our lives we always negotiate with other people, one way or the other. Knowing this we can come prepared: what do we want to reach by an agreement? How do we want to achieve it? What are our own true interests? What are the other parties' interests? What are the alternatives to an agreement?

In general people negotiate in order to satisfy their interests aiming to be better off than they would stand without a negotiation. Interests and positions can be separate things. One thing is my interest, the other is the position I take. For example I might want more vacation time, but I ask for more money. Maybe I know that I am in a good position to ask for additional benefits, and that the finances of the company do not leave room for pay raises. I could bargain to get more time off instead of extra pay. This way my employer walks away from the negotiation table feeling treated fairly and content about satisfying my demands without having to give in entirely using real money. In this case I *assumed* the position to get more money to fulfill my *interest* to get more vacation time.

The other participants act in a similar way, knowingly or unknowingly. A good preparation for negotiations is to find out what the real interests of the others are. In addition we have to see what the possible and impossible alternatives for each party are. The other party might have limitations of how much they are allowed to negotiate. For example a government negotiator may only be able to agree to as much as his country's parliament has entitled him to. Or a procurement manager can only purchase commodities that are within the budget that he has.

What tools does the other side have available to leverage its interests and what concessions can they make? There are often terms that the other side will never be able to agree on, because they are unjustifiable to their own backers. For example unless a union leader reaches a minimum level of pay raise, the members will not approve an agreement with the employer. The one who is asking the other side to agree on the impossible is either unprepared and creates a difficult situation or he is purposely doing so knowing that the other side won't agree. By asking for the impossible you can try to gain time or a better position within the negotiations. You can also cover up that you may have never had intentions to negotiate at all.

When I asked Digital Chocolate to send me to South America I asked for something I believed they would never agree with. I thought they would just let me move on. I had thought it was not a viable alternative for them to send me abroad. I was surprised about what concessions others are willing to make if their own interests are outweighing.

In any negotiations one should watch out for traps and learn to see the real motivations behind the other parties' demands. On the other hand one shouldn't be too quick in assuming the other side would never agree with one's demands. Give the other side something that they are enticed to take. A good tactic is to sell what you are willing to give as if it was a concession and compromise. I know there is a very large untapped market in South America, I'm willing to go there to open it for you, I said to Digital Chocolate. It worked.

In Roberto Benigni's tragic comedy *La vita è bella* (Life is Beautiful) from 1997 the main character Guido has to sell a menu to a picky guest, knowing that the kitchen is closed and the only thing he has is a salmon, a side salad and white wine. However, Guido knows that his guest doesn't want to eat to anything too heavy. Instead of attempting to sell him what he has, he gives options to his guest. People like to choose. What the guest doesn't know is that there is actually nothing to choose from and he is being steered to a decision that will satisfy both parties' interests. Guido manages to sell his guest the only alternative he has as and satisfy his guest:

A gentleman from Rome is here from the Ministry. He wants to eat.

> *The kitchen is closed.*
> *Oh, well, he would have given you a good tip.*
> *The kitchen is open.*
> *Come right in.*
> *Doctor, you're not eating anything?*
> *"The dwarves and Snow White—"*
> *I know the kitchen is closed. Maybe a cold dish.*
> *– It's all delicious. Take your pick. – Something light.*
> *Well, we've got meat, a nice heavy steak...*
> *lamb, kidneys, some greasy breaded liver.*
> *– Otherwise, there's fish. - Fish.*
> *We have... a nice fatty turbot...*
> *eel stuffed with fatty sausage and greased with Grand Marnier...*
> *or some lean salmon--*
> *The salmon, thank you.*
> *– Side dish? – There's a side dish too?*
> *Of course. We have very, very fried mushrooms...*
> *buttered potatoes in Nancry butter with a flaky sauce–*
> *Is there a small, light salad? If not, nothing.*

A light salad? What a pity. The very, very fried mushrooms...
were out of this world. So, a light salad...
a lean salmon and a glass of white wine.
Perfect. As soon as possible.
I'll do my best.[50]

At Iqua my boss's interest was to deliver on his promise towards the new owner, not to keep his word with me. He was under pressure to get the business of Bluetooth Headsets back on track. That is what the owner of Savox had paid for when he acquired Iqua. Selling low tech commodity products, quick wins could be made with good sales & marketing. And usually these short term wins are high in volume. With the few existing resources there wasn't much room to invest further into professional communication devices which I was responsible for. Because I was so fixated on what I had been promised I overlooked the big picture. In a big corporate mentality the quarterly results are more important than long term investments.

Iqua didn't have the funds needed for investment, even if they had wanted to. From a negotiation perspective I had demanded something that, under the new status quo, the other side wasn't able to agree on. From the Savox point of view this was also a way to get out of financial obligations that were implied by our agreement. Now it's up to Iqua's Management they said. Cowardly and insincerely that is.

Maybe I should have made a compromise and accept the new role and possibly worked on the other aspects on the side? For the company's sake. Under different circumstance maybe. But that would require corporate identity. If you have to squeeze yourself into a meeting room, because the space is entirely taken by ego it's hard to adhere to company goals. There you are expected to adore someone else's glorious past, not common goals.

Yet, after all, they weren't going to change my salary or title. Yesmenship would have given me the time to find another job at a higher

---

50 BENIGNI, R. (1997)

level. This would have followed a negotiation model that is called a *problem-solving-approach*. Problem-solvers are trying to emphasize what parties should be agreeing on by independent standards, rather than what they are willing to do. So instead of making commitments and concessions, problem-solving is pushing all formal agreements to the end. This approach is supposed to leave more room to create value through the different interests, allow brain-storming and improve all the options on the table.

Nobody can tell what would have happened if we had followed that route. Today, nothing is left of Iqua. Practically it doesn't exist anymore. That is no surprise to me, but that is no use to me now. Still, from an outside perspective it may have been better to focus less on agreements and more on the best possible solution to create a good outcome for everyone.

The issue with choosing a problem-solving approach was that at that moment of time I didn't know what the independent standards were. The company wanted me to take a different role, but never communicated that to me. Even though they had these new plans of what I could do for the company, they never sat down with me to discuss what's best, and how everyone could benefit. They created new facts and didn't want to be reminded of the past. It didn't come to the option to decide whether it was better to be right or to have a salary, about selling these or those products. I was blindsided and ambushed. And because they never communicated I didn't know they had other plans. By the time I started to understand what the deal was, I had already had so many arguments about every aspect of the business that I had lost any trust. It did not seem fair, because they did not want to concede to what they had promised and the Iqua leader didn't have any interest in it to begin with. I had a very bad bargaining position. There was nothing to bargain, it was a chicken game about who's the boss.

Many negotiations end without agreement, not because objectively the options seem unacceptable, but because they aren't perceived to be fair. That includes how people feel to be treated and if the other side shows respect. On the stage of international diplomacy you sometimes see how parties try to negotiate difficult topics and at the same time publicly denounce the other side constantly. The other party might then, to keep the face, walk away from the negotiation table, until fair treatment and trust are re-established.

One party alone cannot *win* a negotiation. To reach a sustaining agreement between parties, everyone has to leave the table believing that they are better off than before. If there is only a single winner it indicates that one party was able to force positions on the other. That negotiation won't be perceived as fair. If one party feels treated unfair, the issue will come back eventually, especially if the currently *losing* party regains power. A simple look at history is enough to see that people have been fighting wars over interests for millennia. There was always war, followed by peace treaty negotiation. Those usually left one party paying for reparations and officially taking the blame for the war, until they recovered and fought back to turn the tables. According to Clausewitz, war is intended as a political tool to force one's will on the other. Military success is intended to get a better bargaining position at the negotiation table, or the opportunity to dictate what happens next. The intention there is *not* that everyone walks away knowing that they are better off. Often opposing forces in a war refuse to sit down at the negotiation table before their "war goals" have been reached. Only when the status quo changes, they plan to negotiate.

My battle with Iqua wasn't a negotiation, but much rather an uprising against someone else forcing his will on me. Working for a company however, is not like enlisting in the army where you follow orders, even if they are arbitrary. A work relation between a company and an employee is based on a contract that is designed to be mutually beneficial and has to be accepted by both sides. A contract is *"an agreement, entered into voluntarily by two or more parties who promise to exchange money, goods, or services according to a specific schedule. A contract is said to exist when an offer is made and then accepted"*[51] I had a written agreement with

51 Encyclopaedia Britannica, contract

Savox, which we had renewed word for word again under the new Iqua umbrella. And yet, the person on top did not feel bound to it. They had therefore breached the contract and wanted to replace it by compulsory obedience. That is unfair treatment per definition.

My boss and I were playing a game of chicken over it. It was either his way or my way. Negotiations did not happen, because neither of us wanted to accept the terms of the other. And there was no trust.

In addition to fair treatment, the outcome of a negotiation requires commitments from all sides to be legitimate, firm and able to be executed. After back-stabbing me, I didn't believe that anything we would agree on can be trusted for long. At the end there was nothing left that could have fixed this. The trenches were too deep. Either my boss or I had to leave. You can't suggest to fire the person whose company you just bought on day number two, so you just shoot the messenger who suggests it. At the same time you also get rid of your old agreement. How convenient.

Relationship represents another important aspect of negotiations. Importance of relationship between the partners influence negotiations. If your post-negotiation relationship with the other party is irrelevant to you, you can take different positions and have less need to compromise. When selling used items in a garage sale or flea market, you don't expect the customers to return. The used car salesman attitude: Sell your customer whatever you can now, and look for a new customer tomorrow. In comparison, people in the services business make a living off customer retention. Your dry-cleaner or barber, butcher or baker, wants to create a good relations and happy customers that keep coming back for more. They make their living from returning customers and their referrals. In terms of game theory, the relationship is the question between playing chicken or the battle of the sexes. In marriage it is more important to maintain the relation than always getting one's will through. In a chicken game it is important to win. When the maintaining of a relationship is important, most parties adapt a soft form of positional bargaining by taking reasonable positions and are more likely to give concessions. If relationship doesn't matter as much, all you try to do is to get the best price, like bargaining for a rug in a Turkish bazaar.

Our overall goal should be victory. However, the type of game you find yourself playing to reach it depends on your bargaining position, your relationship and your personality in general.

In an uneven distribution of power you will always lose the chicken game. Because even if neither one gives in and moves out of the way, you will be the one sitting in the less safe car, and in a frontal accident, they will hit an airbag and get away with it, you won't. This situation is to be avoided.

I took many of the events very personal, especially since I had worked so hard on building the business thus far. I had built up dozens of sales channels and several important strategic partnerships, which were all waiting for a functioning product. We were steps away from a successful worldwide market entry. Giving up now would also signify a big and needless waste. If you build something and realize it's not going to work, at some point you have to admit that you made a mistake. In this case customers were standing in line for a product. This was not the wrong business idea, it was terrible execution. Why not do it right and get it out there I wondered?

What I did not realize is that I was tilting at windmills, a battle I could not win. And it is not worth playing chicken if you are riding a bicycle against a car. Unfortunately I could not talk myself into accepting that the relationship had to matter to me. Maybe in the moment I thought, because I had a written agreement, my bargaining position would be stronger than it actually was. A softer bargaining approach and the attempt to get along with a power-abusing and yelling manager could have saved me my paycheck. Could have. Given the management culture and the fact that Iqua is no more, gives reasons to doubt that the future would have been bright. But, if you find yourself in a situation where you think that you do not care about the relation with that person you have to deal with, ask yourself what a good mentor would tell you to do? Stay cool, don't pick fights, do your job and stay out of trouble until you find something better.

What was right? Giving in to injustice or standing like a rock? In political philosophy, if you are rich or you don't have anything to lose, it is easy to proclaim to be of higher moral and always standing up for what's right. If you sit on a nuclear weapons arsenal it's easy to play tough. In reality most people have something to lose. This wasn't a political debate or a war into which you send other people and watch it from far. I was in it and I had a lot to lose and I had done what I felt was right. I stood like a rock. But that was of no use to me now. In the truest sense of the word.

Negotiations depend on a variety of factors, from the question of whether interests are common, conflicting, shared, different, to the communication style during negotiations, the feeling of fairness, different options, the alternatives of the others, authority to make commitments, and the credibility of such. Think about what you want to achieve and with which outcome you could live. Study the alternatives of the others in order to get a feel how much room for concessions the other one has. Practice a communication style and proposals that convince each party that the reached agreement is better than the best other alternative in absence of an agreement would have been. Never start negotiations by proposing a compromise. Keep it in mind as a possible goal you are willing to settle for, but play the Bazaar-game for a while. Don't sell your compromise too easy. And finally, negotiation is not just the horse trade on different positions and an outcome that's reached at the negotiation table.

Every communication is some form of negotiation.

Rarely you actually sit at a table together and talk about everything related to a topic like the security council of the United Nations does. Negotiations can happen subtly, explicitly or implicitly, and continuously in the way you communicate with others. There is a give and take and everyone tries to reach his own best outcome. Whatever you do or say is part of that ongoing negotiation. One needs to observe the whole situation also by stepping out of oneself to see what is happening. It will allow you to have a cooler temper, formulate positions better, read better in between the lines of the other party's statements, and most of all it enables you to pick your battles wisely, less impulsive or emotional.

Negotiations are a form of communication. To learn how to negotiate and communicate effectively we can start out by getting acquainted with the seven liberal arts. The Quadrivium – Arithmetic, Geometry, Music and Astronomy – consist of elements that stand in relation to time and space, and fundamentals of science. We can assume that the more you know about any topic in life, the more you'll be able to adapt to any cultural environment. It is the preparation to be capable to talk in an educated way about anything. That is what is studied and practiced well in any diplomatic school. It is how you build friendship and relation based on common interests and topics of conversation; a broad general knowledge and education as the basics of the *esprit du conduite*.

The tactical portion of negotiation is Aristotle's Trivium: the method of thinking. It consists of grammar, logic, and rhetoric.

The Trivium is a concept of learning *how* to think, rather than learning *what* to think. Grammar is there to systematically collect raw data and put it in order of a coherent bases of knowledge. Logic is a methodology, to remove all discrepancies of the existing knowledge to get to a comprehensive understanding of the context. Rhetoric is the methodology, to use the knowledge and understanding and communicate the findings in order to make them applicable in daily life. In simplified modern jargon the Trivium are the input of data, the processing and the output.

Rhetoric and communication are the most powerful tools we have as humans. They help us to phrase our thoughts, convince others and gather support. They are the tool of diplomacy and the best way to find out the intentions of others. They are the essential for negotiation. What is being said, how is it said, what is *not* being said; these are tools one has to learn to maneuver through life's challenges.

To gain approval or rejection for your proposals, opinions and actions often have less to do with the content the proposal itself, but much rather with the world view and the motivations of the others. What are the alternatives of the others and how do they feel treated, play a major role for the outcome of negotiations and difficult conversations.

Rhetoric is what people use to speak, convince, influence, defend or attack, manipulate or steer people's attention to certain issues. Logic comes prior to rhetoric, and within the rhetoric of a person you can tell something about the logic that is followed. Logic is not always logical by independent standards, but based on the processing capacity of each person. Basically the person's experience, education, world view, attitude and intentions.

Things you say will get more attention and interest from others depending on what's important to them. No-one does anything without personal profit. Profit means a personal benefit, like the feeling of happiness, satisfaction, or excitement. A person that volunteers in his free time for the World Wildlife Fund does that because the idea of saving endangered species gives him a feeling of satisfaction. The more he can do to save the planet, the better he feels. That's his profit. Another person likes to be the center of attention and does anything to become a celebrity, regardless of monetary benefits that often come with being famous. Some of them are already rich, they just like the attention and get depressed, if they can't get it. Others like to feel powerful and make sure there is always an opportunity for me-and-you positioning. Some people love to entertain and are very happy to decorate their home and have people over. They are the happiest when their guests are having a good time. There are endless possibilities of what *profit* signifies to an individual.

The profit that one sees, the what-is-in-it-for-me, influences the logic one thinks in. Most important is not to assume everyone wants the same. Some people even like to follow a certain pattern, because they want to believe in *their* truth and imply it to the world.

For the same reason people fall for logical miscomprehensions and believe in very simplistic arguments. Just because it fits into their picture.

To be prepared not to fall for other people's tricks and to explain some people's simple way of thinking, I have gathered some of the most common logical miscomprehensions that occur in everyday conversations:

Ad hominem – When faced with factual statements people often attack the person who made the statement. They try to discredit the person in order to avoid having to counter with logical arguments, that the person might not have. In dirty political campaigns that is often the case.

A plea to authority – people refer to someone who is considered an expert. Hereby one should keep in mind that there is always an expert for either side of an argument. In hierarchies people use authority to end conversation or justify anything they do, because some executive said so. It usually works.

A plea to habits or beliefs – because most people believe something or follow a certain habit it must be the right thing to do. That also includes whatever is popular, or anything that is new must be better than what is old.

Contempt – If a person is not able to reach a certain goal or doesn't have the right arguments to discuss a certain topic they declare the goal or the topic contemptuous or unimportant. This can be the a typical discussion where one wants to be right no matter what, without having logical arguments. As that person realizes that they either don't know enough, they are wrong or just don't get it, they will end the conversation with something like "I don't care" or "that is completely irrelevant anyway".

Wrong causalities – people argue that one event A was caused by another event B, even though both events might have occurred independently. That is often used in order to speak for or against some actions: "Because you did this, that happened." Especially when either blaming or taking credit for something wrong causalities are popular.

Wrong dilemma – Someone shows you only two options even though there might be other ways to solve a problem: "We either do this or that."

Repetitiveness – the more often things are repeated the more they become true. These are the most trickiest to argue against with logic, once people have grown to believe urban legends, they want them to be true.

The spotlight – Only because something gets a lot of attention it doesn't mean that it's necessarily relevant, like reality TV shows.

And finally the dummy is a popular way of getting people riled up and gathered behind you. You assume a position or statement of another person, exaggerate and distort it, in order to then speak against and expose it as the wrong position.

Understanding rhetoric is important in negotiations. It allows to filter useful information from any presentation, conversation, news article or book. You reverse engineer from the rhetoric of a person to the logic and the motivation and intellect of others. Especially the cultural and educational background of the person play an important role to see if what is said is also meant, and vice versa. In an international environment that is important, because many things from one culture and language are difficult to translate into another. And for one people one thing means this, for others it means something else.

Observe people in your company and your surroundings and you'll notice many people who follow logical miscomprehensions: what authority says is right, if everyone loves it, it must be good, and if it's getting attention it must be important. For some people that is religious, it is what they want to believe in and gives them comfort.

If you take a company culture and its people as is, you will get much further by taking advantage of common behavior rather than trying to appeal with logic to every individual. Let's say you have a very self-loving manager who always wants to be in the spot light. Try to find moments where he can shine that benefit you as well. If you have a person that believes everything that executives say, make sure to remember a few key phrases that you heard yourself and throw them in when you are in a discussion. You will be more likely to steer them your way than with logical arguments. People that love processes will never talk about what makes sense, but what the process is we have to follow. You can very well cherry pick something out of the processes and use that to your advantage.

As a simple example, the only times I had good conversations with the Iqua boss was when I started a conversation asking: "how did you do that at Nokia?" It was predictable and worked every time. A funny sport. You scratch their back and they say "oh that's the spot." Try it, it works.

Roger Fisher's *Getting to yes* from 1981 is a bestselling book by the Harvard Negotiation Project. It is a standard work on learning how to negotiate well. The *Harvard Method* focusses on leading conversations. But Fisher himself admits that in "the discussion around *getting to yes*, we might forget something what often weighs much more than a difficult negotiation: not talking at all." In our everyday life, at work, at home, with friends, there are always moments in which we do *not* talk. Possibly, because we try to avoid the conversation or we just don't get a chance for it. Maybe we don't want to talk. Or when we start a conversation that is very difficult, many feelings start to escalate, like anger, frustration, hurt, or sadness.[52]

We assure ourselves that we disagree and sometimes lead a virtual conversation with the other person. Something the other one said gets stuck in our heads, like if *he says that then I will say this*. By recalling past conversations we think about what we should have said to counter better and this goes on and on. That can even lead to an explosion when you meet next time, before a conversation as even started or continues.

It gets more difficult when you try to deliver a difficult message or opinion. Imagine you disagree completely with your group of best friends on a very important topic, the son of pacifistic parents wants to join the army, the only child in a conservative and deeply religious household is coming out gay, you have to lay someone off that worked for you for 20 years, or you have to tell your wife that you just lost your job when she wanted to go to part-time in hers; the list of difficult topics is endless.

No matter how tactful you try to be, the famous advice to *be diplomatic* doesn't really help if the news that you deliver or the argument

---

52 Fisher, R. (1999)

that you believe that you need to have is unexpected, unwanted or otherwise not comfortable for the receiving party. It will still be an explosion, no matter how diplomatic you are trying to say things. The dilemma is should we avoid or confront the difficult topic? On the one hand we would love to get it over with so we don't have to carry the burden of the unsaid around with us. On the other hand we know that it might shake things up and we are afraid it could harm the relation for a while or forever. Finding the right timing seems to be mission impossible.

Any conversation will come down to a few separate things. One of them, the most obvious is the argument about what the truth is, what has to be done or what has just happened. It's the *"what happened?"* conversation. Who said what, who is right, what did he mean by that, whose fault is it?[53]

The other part of a conversation is not about what is being said, but how we feel about it. Human conversation has always something to do with satisfaction or dissatisfaction. A good conversation makes you feel good, winning an argument makes you feel strong, but also distances you from the other person. And vice versa losing an argument can weigh heavily on you for a long time. There are always feelings involved and people debate with themselves and with others what feelings should be valued, and which ones should not be part of *this* conversation.

I have spent a lot of time observing people on how they act in front of co-workers, supervisors and executives. I watched their body language, analyzed the spoken language and the method and the outcome of their work. You can always see a pattern that people follow and what it's influenced by: their position in the hierarchy, their cultural, geographical and ethical background, their education, their life and work experience, and their ability and willingness to reflect and to use their own reasoning.

Any company's strategy will be more successful if it's communicated well and the employees can identify themselves with the goals.

---

53 STONE, D. / PATTON, B. / HEEN, S. (2010), P. 9

Because people have all different backgrounds, the way people hear, reflect and understand communication differs a lot. The way you communicate will trigger feelings of approval, disapproval, sympathy, excitement, anger, indifference or interest.

The art of good communication is to adapt your style to your audience without changing your story.

Depending on the people you deal with, you may want to keep some things rather simple, dive into complex details, have a long discussion or just go through a to-do-list.

With the understanding how the others might feel about situations and adapting to their personality, it doesn't mean that you should say things you don't believe in. Immanuel Kant described it precisely in a letter to Moses Mendelsohn:

"Although I am thinking about many things with clearest belief and my great satisfaction, that I will never be brave enough to say loud; however never will I say something, that I do not believe."[54]

In other words, just tell the same story, but adjust the wording and the emphasis of certain aspects to your audience. Don't try to flatter people. Besides the ego-centric personality that feeds off that, most people will realize and call you out on it.

The larger the corporation, the more randomly the people are mixed together. You can have the neat order taker that does all by the process, the intellectual thinker who only has this job for the paycheck, the go-getter with a ton of travel experience who can relate to any issue, the tunnel view people who only see the world from one perspective, the optimists, the pessimists, the pathological liars, the lazy ones, the joker, and the worker bee. Some people stress quickly, others are more laid back. The people are after all the sum of their experience. Adapting to the other person's conversation style doesn't mean to say things they want to hear, but to speak a language that they can relate to.

As an example, people who are less educated or aren't using their own reasoning are easier to predict, because they will always repeat

54 Störig, H.J. (1962), P. 487

the same sentences often with the exact same wording. Conversations though are difficult, because the lack of intellect often makes any discussion unfruitful. Especially if you don't have the background to argue and live in your own filter bubble you are just reciting pre-defined opinions that fit into your world view. Those people often won't even listen to your explanations and line of arguments, because they either don't have the intellect to reflect or they are simply ignorant. Keep it short and simple; avoid arguments, because they can be tedious and frustrating.

Opposites to those are the ones who are very good at arguing about anything, without having an actual opinion. They just like to take everything apart that someone else says, it's like a sport. They can be people with an all negative attitude towards everything or they feel powerful by shooting down other people's ideas. Whatever you suggest they will find something to argue against it. Talking to someone who doesn't want to agree as an attitude is just as exhausting as someone who doesn't understand at all.

With all types of people you have encounters and Sun Tzu's recommendation applies: choose your battles wisely. With some people you better do not discuss anything, it will only exhaust you. It draws the energy out of you that you need for the important things.

Conversations create the best feelings if two of a kind speak to each other. Two or more people who love to talk about politics, people who have traveled the world, people with the same hobbies, follow the same sports, exercise the same discipline, or are fascinated by the same art or literature. When the level of knowledge and genuine interest about a topic is similar, the conversations are often interesting, fruitful and leave lasting impressions. If you have topics of common interest, feelings don't get hurt that easily, even if you disagree in certain aspects.

Finding a common ground will always make it easier to become friendly with each other. The goal of a conversation should be the same as with negotiations: all parties leave and feel better than they would have without the conversation. It should lead to the satisfaction that you just came closer to someone, enjoyed a good time with an old friend, learned something new, or reached an agreement on future joint activities. No-one goes into a conversation with the intention of feeling worse after it. With this attitude you can anticipate reactions and take steps to influence the outcome. The more you know about the person before you have a conversation, the easier it will be to find common interests. This way you can have an interesting and respectful conversation at eye-level with anyone.

Although we are looking for good conversation the difficult ones are inevitable. Mostly it's the ever returning assumption about truth which causes endless distress: To be convinced about being right and the other one being wrong. Difficult conversations usually aren't just about what the truth is, but misunderstandings. Common reasons for misunderstandings and affliction caused by conversations are that intentions stay in the dark. We assume we know what the other one wanted to say based on how they said things and the way they lead a conversation. Some people attack *how* you said something in order not to talk about *what* you said. It's a common defense tactic of people; distracting from the real issue, because it turns the blame frame around. It can change focus on who is to blame for the current situation. Difficult conversations are essentially all about feelings.

Most conversations are emotional, even if they don't seem to be. Other people have feelings and they usually differ from yours. We forgive ourselves easier and accept explanations quicker than we are willing to grant the same to others. If we feel a certain way during or after a conversation we assume that the other person's intention was to create that feeling in us. Let's say in an operation room (OR) there is a drug missing that had to be given to the patient during surgery. The surgeon asks the OR nurse where it could have gone, and the nurse might think that the surgeon tries to blame her for the missing drug and becomes defensive. Even though he just tried to solve an imminent problem. A couple might be driving in a car and she wants to take a break and asks her husband: "do you want to take a break?" and he replies "no, I'm OK, I can still drive." She might feel that he is not considerate, because he doesn't want to stop. He feels good because she asked him about his well-being and is a glad that he's still awake enough to make a little more distance in the car before taking a break.

We also apply different rules to ourselves than to others and let ourselves get away easier with our own mistakes. If the husband doesn't get the car cleaned from the inside before a family vacation he's irresponsible, but if she forgot to do that it's because she is overworked and stressed. If we are late to an appointment we have an explanation and our justification is OK with us. If someone else comes late we ask them to be more punctual next time. They should be more respectful of our time.[55]

By analyzing how conversations happen and what feelings can be triggered you can be prepared for that from both sides. If someone asks you for something, take a breath and think about what their intentions are. If you are unclear, rephrase the question and ask if what you heard was correctly understood.

The best question to ask every time is: *What do you mean?*

Your communication towards others can trigger certain responses. If the other one abruptly becomes defensive, don't attack, but rephrase, be inclusive, explain your intentions. Reacting to tension with tension will not lead to a good outcome. Don't assume the other one knows your intentions and don't assume you know theirs. Time it right when you have a conversation to lead or an announcement to make. Self-control also means to find ways to store a thought for a while and let it out when it is appropriate. It might make us feel better to let something out, but it can trigger bad feelings. For example you shouldn't tell your friend that you were promoted when he just lost his job. If your car breaks down and you don't have money to repair it you don't need to hear that you still owe your friend a thousand dollars. Being tactful will always pay off on the long run, karma will thank you.

Most people tend to think that the others are the problem; they are ego-centric, naïve, don't think rational, or try to control. Our counter-

---

55 Stone, D. / Patton, B. / Heen, S. (2010), P. 46

parts probably think the same thing about us. The *truth* is what makes sense to *us*. Sometimes you can tell that the other person doesn't understand complex situations, cannot or does not want to see facts. Yet, that is still the world as the other person sees it and it makes perfect sense to him. That *is* the truth of the other person.

Listen carefully to what people say, even if they try to avoid comments about politics and/or religion, you can certainly tell after a while where they are coming from. Think like the other, understand their world view. This can help you to stay calm in a difficult conversation, because you understand it from their perspective. Even if you completely disagree. Avoid certain topics for a while in order to stay on friendly terms which will also prevent you from getting a reputation that is unintended.

Many things are not said. You cannot be sure that people know what you want unless you say it. They will assume they know and that may well be different from what you think. Others might easily believe that you are perfectly happy if you never say a word. Therefore you have to be persistent about what matters to you and communicate it well. Most people prefer when you speak your mind. The challenge is often on how and when to say things that might upset the other person's feelings. Understanding how conversations happen will help you to grow a thicker skin in difficult discussions and help you to improve your communication style. Reactions of others are triggered due to what is said, how it's said, how the other is feeling about it, if the content is perceived as fair or not, or if the listener is attacked or maybe feels as if he has to defend himself. Will there be an immediate excuse or blame game? These reactions will be triggered by the listener's character and background. The more you know about the other person, the more you can anticipate those feelings and adapt your communication style accordingly. It will help you to speak to others about easy or difficult things. You will be able to deal with a colleague or manager who is difficult to have a conversation with.

At work, we have the impression that our direct managers are the problem or someone who's work your own progress is depending on.

They can be the obstacle that we have to overcome to be happy at work or to proceed in our career. You will always end up having to report to someone: your boss, then your next boss, your investors, your customers, or your spouse. An independent person that requires little supervision and is allergic to micro-management, will need a boss that is similar to good technology: if it's good, you will not notice it, because it's all smooth. If technology is developed badly, you will feel it. You don't complain or praise your computer when it's running the way you expect it to, but you will swear a lot when gets stuck, especially if it's the same problem over and over. At work, many things are assumed to be normal, until they aren't anymore. Every time a new player enters into the game, the dynamics change: a new boss, a new colleague, or a new process.

It's not difficult to thrive with empowering managers or motivated and helpful co-workers. The challenge is about what to do with the others. In their book *Working for You isn't working for me – the ultimate guide to managing your boss* Katherine Crowley and Kathi Elster sum it up precisely: "unfortunately, the untrained or inept leader seems to be a far more common occurrence. And then there are the individuals who either abuse or misuse their power: supervisors who hire smart people only to micromanage their work; executives who encourage the free flow of ideas and then shoot the ideas (and the people who offer them) down; board members who are absent, complacent, or resistant."[56]

Reading their book reminded me of a story from my times at Digital Chocolate. I had a customer who became a good friend. He managed the content for T-Mobile Austria, anything you could see and download from the operators' mobile site. That was before iTunes and Google Play took over the world of mobile content. At work he had met his future wife, who was in a public relations position at T-Mobile in Austria. She wanted to change to the T-Mobile's US entity based in Seattle, to pursue work and life experience abroad. They came to visit me in New York in 2006 after I had just relocated there the first time,

---

56 CROWLEY, K. / ELSTER, K. (2009), IX

right after my gig in Brazil. They told me that everyone in the chain of decision makers was supporting her move, until it came to her newly appointed boss. He didn't want to be bound to promises that were made before him. And he was jealous of having his report leaving for a big career step abroad and was working behind her back to make the deal go bye-bye. It was pure jealousy of a manager towards his reports. She ended up quitting her job, they moved to Dubai where they had been offered new endeavors for their careers and an exciting experience in another country. The ego of a manager made two good people leave. It's not an isolated case, it happens quite often in the corporate world.

This is only one of many examples I know of, when a direct manager is not working in the favor of his report, but based on his or her own feelings and needs, ego, career plans and benefits. That had happened to me at Digital Chocolate, and again with Iqua/Savox.

Main stream career literature ignores that in most cases your success does not depend on your skills, but on whether or not you have a work environment that enables you to grow. A bad manager can outweigh all your talent and become your biggest obstacle for career progress and also the largest motivation killer to even go to work.

I wish I had read more around the topic of "managing up" before running into my challenge with Iqua/Savox. Had I learned how to deal with a power-abusing and yelling manager, it would have been much easier to handle. Not only because it helps to get a more relaxed attitude towards the behavior of your manager, but anyone in general. Crowley and Ester's work stands out, because they call people's behavior by its name. Most of the literature talks about *management styles* and work around terrible supervisors in a political correct manner, calling them detail oriented, instead of micromanagers, and visionaries, instead of all-strategy-no-execution, much-ado-about-nothing, or no-sense-for-what-has-to-happen people. Similar to career guidance, literature on managing up is packed with top-down approaches oversimplifying the topic down to different styles of leading, never mentioning that some managers are just in the absolute wrong position and should be fired.

We will still have to deal with our managers. Not, because we are extremely gullible and need guidance and people lead us in different ways, but because otherwise they might drive us completely crazy. In order to stay sane and a good performer we need to analyze our boss's behavior and adjust. Categorizing different types of bosses – and colleagues – helps you to understand how some of them work and is of enormous importance to detach psychologically from them. It will otherwise keep you up at night, bring a bad mood home, make you continuously angry and clench your teeth. Not everyone wants to kick and punch a heavy bag daily for anger management. Inept leaders are wasting your time and energy.

The good news is: You can to learn how to deal with difficult people and use the patterns of their behavior in your favor.

Your boss's type of management isn't a *style*, but human behavior. Disrespectful behavior, abuse of power or micromanagement aren't styles. They are bad manners and bad leadership. People say that you cannot argue about taste. I agree, because some people just don't have any, hence the word *tasteless*. In analogy there are managers who don't know how to manage. That's it. Some people just have no skills for anything else so nature puts them into middle management. Unfortunately the main stream literature on business always talks about how to manage people when the most challenging part in corporate life is how to deal with people who *cannot* manage. In most cases people do better the less you manage them. A good executive doesn't have to find better leaders for his company, but find better methods to detect and fire inept managers, in order to ensure success. Don't try to hire leaders that ensure that people do their work, but remove the ones who keep people from doing what they are best at. The economic costs of inept leadership is tremendous: People slack, leave companies, turnover increases, inefficiencies increase, mediocrity is worshipped, and getting by with the minimum becomes the norm. No company that wants to thrive can afford that. The foul apple on top of the pile can spoil the whole basket. Lost productivity that is caused by mediocre management cost the economy multiple times on what many savings plans and streamlining do. Some people say that from time to time you have to cut the fat. It's true. But for a long-lasting effect you should also get rid of the source of motivational morbid obesity.

There are many things a CEO is in charge of. But if there would be only one thing, it would be to make sure the key people in his company are left alone to do their magic. Top performers have to be able to do their jobs, because they have the tools to do so and the right motivation. They share the strategy goals and get paid according to their capabilities. But most of all, they need managers that are like the best waiters in a restaurant: they only come to serve when they notice that you need them and don't annoy you by constantly asking how it's going.

The misleading top-down leadership literature assumes that leaders are somewhat different creatures who have a particular unique knowledge that is needed to guide a gullible workforce to do their job. That may be right in a 19th century factory, but it's not applicable today in white collar work environments. A good leader is the servant of his team. A good leader has to remove roadblocks instead of being one. Trickle-down theories neither work in the world's economy nor in a micro-economic scenario.

There are managers who proofread your out-of-office-reply before you are going out on vacation; others encourage you to spend countless hours on presenting new ideas, only to shoot them down. There are managers who have something to correct at your work no matter how good it is. I once had a manager who I could have presented with his own work pretending it was mine and he would have found something to correct, just for the sake of having the last word. And to make sure everyone knows who was the boss. Another one only cared that your desk was cleaned up, no matter if you had to work yourself through a pile of paperwork. The list of ridiculous micromanaging anecdotes about bosses is endless.

There are numerous ways of categorizing the behavior of a person in charge that drives you crazy. Crowley and Elster show a good analysis on how to detect and deal with the chronic critics, rule changes, yellers, underminers, I'm-always-right-bosses, micromanaging control obsessed bosses, such as ego-centric bosses who are terribly in love with themselves. If you have to deal with difficult managers, it's worth getting a copy of their book and read a few related articles. In this book I won't go into that level of detail, but I recommend to keep two of Musashi's rules in mind:

1. Learn to be unmoved in the heat of battle.
2. Become the opponent.

First of all: it is never about you. A manager who drives you crazy doesn't do that to bother you or purposely against just you. To that person it's all normal. They go home and sleep well and think they have done a great job, while you go home and talk about how much you hate your boss. You wake up in the middle of the night recalling some discussions. You are angry and sleep deprived on your way to work the next morning. You dream of driving over him, throwing his laptop out of the window, pinching his tires, hold his head in between the closing elevator doors, or sending two bull-necked Mafiosi with a baseball bat to pay him a visit. And the fact that the person doesn't even see how he is driving you nuts riles you up even more. That is the moment for role play, when you have to put yourself into his position. If you were him, how would you expect people to act? Put yourself into the role of a power-abuser or ego-centric person, or someone who plays favorites and yes-men. Think about what you would like your reports to do if you were that creature? When would you yell and scream? Study those trigger points through thorough observation.

Remember that a terrible manager is only a passenger on your life's train. Don't become distracted, control your temper, ignore your moods and concentrate on what your goals are. Grow a thick skin and adapt for as long as it's necessary. If you have a yeller as a boss, he yells at everyone, so don't take it personal. Just open both ears so the sounds can leave your head as fast as it entered. Think about what music would go well with it. If you have a rule changer, don't go crazy to follow any process too diligently, because he will change it anyway, focus on what needs to be done. The moody ones and rule-changers are probably the most difficult to deal with. The power abusers or yellers are way more predictable.

How often do people say that their boss drives them crazy because he *always* does x, y and z in certain situations? Always, that's the key here. It's very likely that there is a pattern to the behavior of your boss. That is your advantage. Analyze the behavior, detect the pattern and adjust your sparring style to it. Many people recite their beliefs over and over. The more people are stuck in immovable ways of thinking, an invariant approach to work, and a single way of doing things, and the more robotic they are, the better you can prepare for it. All of a sudden even the most difficult boss you may have, becomes a sport for you.

I love the outdoors and back country camping. There is a funny analogy to fly-fishing and dealing with the pattern of another person. When you are fly-fishing in a river, you have different ways of catching a fish. Most of the time you are either imitating a fly that is floating on the river (dry fly) or you are imitating a cocoon that is rising from the bottom in order to hatch. The fish usually swims in an inner curve or behind a rock, where the current is less. They also like to hide underneath overhanging branches or other things that provide visual protection from predators. Because the fish is swimming in the current using a lot of energy, it needs to eat frequently to stay nourished. In most cases the fish reacts to a fake fly. Whenever there is a fly swimming by, the fish rises to the top. Next time your yelling boss is outraged about something, try to find out what's that fly that makes his temper rise, just like a fish. And if you think about the expression of a fish as your boss's temper rises, it can be quite amusing. I recommend not to start laughing out loud in such a moment. For most people who never think about controlling their temper, just like people who constantly use foul language, it comes due to a habit, almost instinctively.

Most people who yell, only yell at their reports, not at their managers. Find out when that usually occurs; I promise once you can call it before it happens next time it becomes a fun game. Three, two, one and explosion. You have to learn to detach from other people's behavior and take it with a good sense of humor. They all come and go. You can't get rid of them just like this, so the only alternative is dealing with them.

The reason why some boss behaves like he wants to is usually because he can. Most people who treat their reports without respect cannot be found doing that in public to strangers or speaking to their own supervisor in that tone. In this small and connected world it is very likely that your paths will cross again in the future. The way you treat people in your first encounter will have a direct impact on how they treat you the next time you meet under different circumstances.

Study the behavior of the people that surround you, like a great general studies the terrain he is leading his army into. In martial arts you can see that everyone is moving to a rhythm, study that rhythm. Good close combat fighters do not waste a lot of energy attacking, but try to fake attacks in order to get the opponent to make a move. Any time your opponent throws a kick or punch at you, their defense is open and you can strike. This can be timed. Be aware of everything your opponent is doing without getting caught that you are observing him. What is it that your boss always does? Use that in your advantage. Stay out of the line of sight when he's angry, talk to him when you know something excites him, feed him the bait that triggers him to rise from behind the rock. If you have a boss that drives you nuts and you finally got behind what it is that drives you crazy, you realize that you can put a carrot in front of that donkey and he'll do whatever *you* want him to do. Even though you are the report and he's the boss. It's fun and also it relives the stress from being micromanaged by someone who is less skilled than you are. Had I only figured that out earlier, I would have talked half my time at Iqua about Nokia.

With this method you can begin to detach from a person. You realize it's not about you. He treats everyone the same. Sometimes we still build up negative energy, which is often inevitable. Initially, before we cool our head, we are emotional about how people treat us and we tend to think it is about us. It's not. Some of your colleagues or supervisors might rob you of your last nerves and you just can't help, but be angry about it. There are a couple of things you can do that will help you before having many sleepless nights:

1. Exercise. Too much energy? Go let it out.
2. Find a mentor. Someone that is able to see beyond your current emotional challenge and set your mind straight. That is the person you need to find to talk to. That mentor can be a former manager of yours, a former University professor, a friend who is good at analyzing these types of situations. Basically someone who knows you, but is not emotionally involved in the same way as you are. Your alter ego.

Usually, after you have let out some energy and talked to the right person, the mind and body find a balance again. You will focus on what's important and do not get distracted from someone who spoils your party. Most of the time when I had a discussion with a manager who made my life difficult, I started to day dream about the day when I have already moved on. He will still be living in his bubble and continue to do the same he always has. People come and go in life. Make sure that the people that are not helpful for your cause are the ones that go quicker. Your life is not about them, so don't let too much of your energy and time be wasted by such people. This takes practice and focus. It often feels like having unfinished business with some of those. It is hard to be as indifferent about them, as they are about you. Their behavior is normal to them, not to us.

When it crystalizes that there is a person who represents an obstacle for you to move forward with, you have to make sure to plan your next step ahead of time. Treat him like one of your weaknesses in your strategy, something that needs to be eliminated from your list in order to get closer to your goal. Try to learn to handle a difficult manager like an operational obstacle, like a flat tire or a burnt out light bulb. Just take it with the attitude of an engineer.

Some literature suggests that it might help to find others who suffer from the same problem and maybe jointly file a formal complaint or talk to the supervisor about the issues in the team. My advice is not to fall for that. Many people complain when the majority of a current group is doing so and they all say that something should happen. But when the day comes they the majority ends up siding with the other one, because they either get cold feet or spontaneously believe they might get some advantage by not backing the mutineer.

Most people are pack driven and side with the majority. In the game theory this is called the *paradox of voting*: Individual preferences are passed to collective tastes, and therefore rationality as we would otherwise expect, is not fulfilled. In those cases it can occur that an outcome that is no-one's preference will happen, because the individuals are willing to go with the majority and seek their 2nd best option. Don't try to be a hero and spokesman for a team that complains to their boss. You might get crucified, even though you wanted to do something good. Maybe everyone is with you, but on judgment day they don't feel strong enough and will fail to support you. In the question whether to let out your feelings or actually change something, a better method is to become a person whose opinion your boss values. If you are able to speak face to face to your manager you can always say that *the team seems to believe*, or *some people say*. Open confrontation doesn't work in your favor. In close combat it is better to stay close to the opponent to minimize his ability to maneuver and move. Think about boxers who run out of energy: they hug the opponent, so they don't get hit. Getting closer to a boss that you don't like can simulate that tactic and makes it difficult for him to strike against you. Do so by conducting a good *esprit de conduite*, not flattery. Keep your friends close and your enemies closer. Give your micromanaging boss some hugs.

If you don't like your boss it might show and he might not like you back. That is a weakness of yours that you need to deal with if you want to maintain good enough terms. Simple measures can start to improve a relation. Be at work before your boss arrives, always greet him friendly and make sure he recognizes that you have been there earlier. Be attentive in meetings, do not read your emails or stare at your phone when other people speak. It is a respectful behavior that anyone deserves. The little details make the difference, because in the accumulation they will get noticed.

Now comes the flipside: Although it often it seems that the mediocre managers are in the majority, don't blame your boss too quick. Do not lean back on criticism and say your boss is terrible. Maybe you cannot take criticism right, maybe your boss has a rough way of telling you how to do your job. In the first place look at the content of what people say to you, not the how. Maybe your feelings were hurt, because your boss was pointing out to you that you were lazy or you made lots of mistakes. Maybe the truth hurts your feelings and you can't handle it? There are many foul apples in managing positions. But just like anyone has to lead by example, you have to apply the same rules to yourself as well, otherwise you are no better. Maybe you needed to get yelled at, because you ignore it every time someone says something in a friendly tone? Maybe you need to be micromanaged, because you do not pay attention to details? I hope not, but there is the possibility. People sometimes overreact, maybe your boss should not have yelled at you, but he could be right and you are wrong? Give that option a thought as well, before making a judgement. And if you look for another opinion, look for a mentor, not the person who will just approve and confirm your impression to make you feel good, and right.

Sometimes it can be that you have a problem with your boss, because of an impression that your boss has of you. Find out what your manager expects from people and see if that is just his so called style, or if it has more of a strategic nature. Maybe there is something that you can learn and what can be very valuable. It's a weakness on your list that you have to deal with, either way. If you change your way of behavior, you can change the way your boss sees you. The best way to do that is by learning what is important to your boss.

In an economic model you call this the ex-ante circumstances, the given rules before entering the game. In the economic model of you vs. your boss, his behavior and expectations set the rules. You have to move according to that. Learning how these rules are set makes you superior in strength, because your boss does what he does out of natural behavior and his usual pattern. You are using calculus and playing chess. Sometimes it means to bend your principles a little, sometimes it means to become better at your job, sometimes it means wasting your time at work with things that don't matter to the business, but your supervisor. Either way you will always learn something and you are always serving your own purpose alike. As long as you do it because you want to do it and it's part of your strategy, there is nothing bad about it.

I have learned some of these lessons the hard way, because I am a thickheaded Bavarian of stubborn nature. I have a hard time not to bang my fist on the table when others are wasting my time. I can't keep my mouth shut if someone is clearly an idiot. I have extreme difficulties respecting authority if the person who holds the position has no visible skill that would justify it.

I have learned about this insight only *after* I had made all possible tactical mistakes. It made me eager to analyze what had gone wrong. I know that Iqua wasn't in the best financial situation and today the company doesn't exist anymore. When I was laid off I was told the typical political correct stories of tough financial times. Whether it was ego, the financial situation or the fact that we had so many fights that there was no more way to work together was irrelevant at that point. At that point they were useless mind games. I was out. That's it.

It was disappointing because I really enjoyed the industry Savox was in. Critical communications technology excited me and I believed that there were plenty of opportunities. I had built a lot of good relations around the world, the product idea was meeting a big demand. If only done right, it would be a good business. Maybe it was something I should pursue on my own? Indeed I should, I said to myself. This was another inflection point.

6 MAGNA CARTA

"Every man possesses the right of self-government."

THOMAS JEFFERSON (1743–1826)

The dog and the wolf is my favorite among the fables from ancient Greek philosopher Aesop (6ᵗʰ–7ᵗʰ century B.C.):

One moonshiny night, a wolf, almost skin and bone, met a dog who was as strong as he was fat. The dog said to the wolf that it would be easy for him to be as fat as he was, if he liked. The dog said: "I know with your irregular life you will soon die of hunger. Why don't you work steadily and you will also get your food regularly, just like me. Follow me, and you will be much better off". "What shall I have to do?" asked the wolf. "Almost nothing," answered the dog; "only chase away the beggars, and fawn upon the folks of the house. You will, in return, be paid with all sorts of nice things – bones of fowls and pigeon – to say nothing of many a friendly pat on the head." The wolf, imagining the comfort he could be living in, and they trotted off together. On the way there the wolf noticed that the hair on a certain part of the dog's neck was worn away, almost bare. "What is that mark?" the wolf asked. "Oh nothing," said the dog. "That is only the place where the collar is put on at night to keep me chained up." The dog assured him that soon he would get used to it. The wolf made a sudden stop and asked: "Chained up? Can you not always, then, run where you please?" "Well, not quite always," said the dog; "but what can that matter?" "It matters so much to me that your lot shall not be mine at any price. Good-bye to you, Master dog."

The moral of this fable is: *Non bene pro toto libertas venditur auro* —
Freedom cannot be sold for all the gold in the world.

Anything in the world has some value, but nothing is worth anything without liberty. Only freedom can lead to happiness. Freedom is
as much an activity as it is a natural right: It has to be exercised. Some
people think that they are free, because they live in a free country.
That is only true to an extent. If you let others think for you, others
guide you, others tell you what is good and bad for you and accepting it
without reflecting upon and questioning their intentions, how free are
you then? If you live in a free country, but you are buried in financial
obligations, because you have a car that you can't afford, a house that
you will never pay off, no disposable income to save for retirement or
have to pay overwhelming tuition for education, you will become the
slave of your paycheck and a dependent citizen. And if one puts all this
financial burden on oneself in the belief that this is the way it is, then
one hits the last nail on the coffin of personal freedom. The more people are enslaved in that cycle, the less free they will ultimately be. By this
standard, a person living within his means has more freedom than the
one with a high-income-high-debt ratio. It becomes a matter of being a
free person and independent. Having no income at all can put you into
just that situation as well: having to settle for a job that may neither be
fulfilling nor a stepping stone to a better life. This was the dilemma I
was in when I was let go. I was thrown into a dependency against my
own will, like being innocently thrown into jail.

The one who always lives within the limits of what is expected
from him, will also think within these limits.

The world expects the hard working and dependable person who
will in return be rewarded with success. That expectation includes a
life style of a disciplined person who goes to bed early, eats healthy,
works hard, and exercises. A person that doesn't argue and avoids
open conflict. A lifestyle of a person that executes tasks consistently
to the fullest satisfaction of the demander, without arguing.

Society and economy needs the independent thinker to progress.
Starting with artists, they are the ones who act as a mirror on society.

Artists can be somewhat rebellious to society and live like hippies. Therefore in addition to that society needs the rebels within the yuppie system. If you live in a box of expectations it's hard to think outside of it.

Some creative ideas were borne late night after too many drinks in a bar. If they were written down to remember they inspired the creators for times to come. Maybe the ones who stay up late reading books and articles irrelevant to their job, will find a parallels to his job's challenges and will show up tired at work at times, but with new ideas and full of motivation.

Isn't it the unadjusted and inadequate person who is driving innovation? Isn't the leader distinguishing himself from the follower by making things happen, a person who thinks and acts based on his own will? Breaking the rules and breaking taboos is what brings innovation. Otherwise we'd still believe that the universe was circling around the Earth and we'd travel with horse carriages. People who follow the perfect life-style doctrine may survive, and sometimes easier than the rebel, but they won't change the world. To say it with Frederick II the Great, King of Prussia (1712–1786): "Let them all find happiness in their own fashion."

Freedom also means the liberty to make dumb decisions, take a chance, and follow a gut feeling. Try and err is what creates true experience, the ability to reflect upon one's life, and derive consequences accordingly.

If you don't want to wait or leave it to others to do anything on your behalf, the only choice you have is to take control of your own life. Today, not some day. Be an auto-mobile: self-driven. Don't be the donkey chasing the carrot. Your personal can-do-attitude is want counts. That will lead you to success. It's not the others' fault if you don't move on.

Happiness is based on the freedom to choose a happy life. Success and happiness are something unique to every person and cannot be measured by outside standards like the position in a hierarchy, or money. A freedom based success level would be measured to what extend a person's way of living is based on his own free will, and the capacity to make up one's own mind free from biases. Freedom means to be the master of your own life. And to be responsible for it. When you get to a point where you cannot praise or blame anyone else, but yourself, for success or failure you know that you are on the right track.

I was born in Augsburg, a city in modern day Bavaria. It's Germany's second oldest city, founded in 15 B.C. by Nero Claudius Drusus (38 B.C.–9 B.C.) as a Roman colony and named Augusta Vindelicorum. Drusus was the younger brother of Tiberius (42 B.C.–16 A.D.), who later became Roman Emperor. From the 13th century on, Augsburg was a free imperial city for over 500 years and had its heyday during the Renaissance as a trade hub between Italy and all major cities north of the Alps. The most prominent mercantile family were the Fugger who were running their international business from Augsburg in the 15th and 16th century. The city's peak time lasted until the 30 year war which took place 1618 to 1648 all over Europe. The vast majority of city's population was decimated through hunger and disease in 1634, after a the Swedish army refused to surrender to Catholic troops besieging the city. In the following time the city was never able to recover its previous glory. The 30 year war had initially been a war between Catholics and Protestants who fought their battles back and forth across Europe. Later it turned into a war of nations emerging from it, like the independence of the Netherlands from the Spanish crown in 1648. During that war Augsburg was an important strategic post.

Not far away from Augsburg there is a place called the *Nördlinger Ries*. The Ries is a large impact crater formed by a meteor over 14 million years ago. Celtic people were among the first people to cultivate the fertile lands of the Ries that had always brought good harvests. One of the most fascinating part of the Ries' history is that the small self-sufficient farmers were never part of the feudalist system, meaning they did not have a landlord; they weren't bond-slaves. While my grandfather's family comes from a mercantile family in Augsburg, the one of my German grandmother's is dating back to the free farmers of the Ries. They never had a landlord and they also never really affected from the warring parties of the 30 year war. As if someone had forgotten about them, the armies always passed by at a distance. Within catholic Bavaria, it is one of the few protestant oases that retained their religion throughout the 30 year war.

One may say that maybe they were just lucky to be free people and it is not the same is if you would have gained your freedom through a revolution, a battle, hard work or other means. They are wrong.

Freedom is nothing that people earn: All men and women are born free. An unfree person can therefore only regain freedom, not win it like a prize or a trophy for bravery. Freedom is also indivisible; you can't be a little bit free. And one can't be more free than another one. One might just be happy in his nonage, and mistake it for great freedom.

Freedom is priceless: there is no freedom that is worth more than another freedom, because there is just one and that is universal.

On a personal level, one may value freedom more than others if they had experienced dependency, arbitrary rule and oppression, yet the universal value of freedom itself doesn't change through that.

My ancestors were free people for hundreds of years, because they had not lost their freedom that was given to them by nature. Maybe they were lucky, but that is irrelevant. They were poor, but they were free. None of that has anything to do with your financial situation. Everything has some value, but nothing is worth anything if you aren't free.

The question on whether you are and feel like a free person depends a lot on your personal situation, not only the political system of your home country. In a feudal system there were people that were free, despite the political system. In corporate feudalism you can achieve the same. Maybe you don't change the world's economy and the laws of business, but you can still free yourself from it to a good degree.

Maybe in return for a false sense of security you have voluntarily given up your freedom, so how can you regain it? Or is it nothing that concerns you? Do you think you are a free person because other people say you are? Maybe because people say you live in a free country that means you must therefore be a free person? Some people accept things the way they are, because they don't want to bother about anything? People who never lacked comfort also tend to mistake it for freedom?

In the bible, Psalm 23 says:

> "The Lord is my shepherd. I lack nothing."
> In some older versions the same is phrased as:
> "The Lord is my shepherd. I shall not want." [57]

Since all humans are born free, the biggest quest about being a free person is not about gaining it. The quest is how to keep it. It is so easy to give it away for comfort or false sense of security.

For centuries, people were ready to give their lives for their Freedom. Today, most people mistake Freedom for the size of their flat screen TV and the number of shows they are free to record at the same time. People grow comfortable in immaturity very quickly. If things are easy, why make it difficult. As long as my job pays me to have a lot of things, why should I think about anything? As long as someone else tells me what products to buy, what political views to have, or where to go on the perfect vacation for, why do I have to bother?

Freedom doesn't mean the liberty to be as ignorant as one wants to be. Unlimited opportunities are not equal to unlimited bigotry. To fight for something in the name of Freedom is the same as to fight in the name of God; it's interchangeable. To stand up for your *own* Freedom is what counts. It's not about chanting to a leader who says Freedom in every other sentence. To be a free person is not about *believing* in Freedom, but to *act* like a free person.

Laziness and cowardice, as Kant said, are the reasons why such a large part of mankind gladly remain minors all their lives. "They are the reasons why it is so easy for others to set themselves up as

---

57 HOLY BIBLE, PSALM 23:1

guardians." I have no need to think, if only I can pay, is what Kant observed. This is as present as it was when Kant wrote his essay on enlightenment over two hundred years ago. How often do you hear people solving problems by suggesting: "Just pay someone to do it." You get used to pay others to do the things you don't until you cannot do them on your own anymore. And if then you lose your source of money you are completely dependent.

I had a colleague once who paid a pool cleaner and a gardener, because he didn't want to deal with it himself. He was bragging about how he didn't need to do those things because he could pay someone. He also occasionally went jogging with some of my team mates. I heard he wasn't a really good runner, very slow and not in the best shape. In general that wouldn't matter, but with his bragging style I could not keep myself from commenting that "it's because he can't pay someone to run on his behalf".

The same methodology of using one's brain is what makes people putting freedom equal to having a lot of things. The next step is having to keep up with the Joneses and it turns into a vicious spiral. That is when life becomes driven by others: your job, your necessity to pay bills and to live according to standards that are set by others. Having a job which provides nothing in addition to income is therefore empty and idle. And as long as the money comes you want to believe this is how the world goes round.

In 2010, a year of major emotional rollercoasters, I was able to attend a once-in-a-lifetime event at the Fraunces Tavern in New York: a private invitation to see one of the only four existing original copies of the Magna Carta alongside an original copy of the American Declaration of Independence. They may well be the two most important documents in human history for Freedom and Democracy. A moving moment to be able to see them in person, both documents in the same room! And I still enjoy it just thinking about it.

The building at the southern end of Manhattan dates back to the year 1719. The tavern has been in there since 1762, which makes it New York's oldest. This place of pre-revolutionary popularity, owned by the Sons of the American Revolution since 1904, was the perfect setting for this event. Everyone was dressed up in tuxedos; it was a historic moment for anyone attending and treated with the respect it deserved.

Almost 800 years earlier, in 1215 A.D. the Great Charter, also called the Magna Carta limited the arbitrary power of King John of England. It marked an important moment in human history, in which the power of a King was not arbitrary anymore, but that he too, was bound to the law. Probably the most important piece was clause 39 of the charter which stated that "no freemen shall be…imprisoned or disseized….except by the lawful judgment of his peers or by the law of the land." The idea that no man should be held in jail without a trial found its way into the Constitution of the United States of America over half a millennium later.[58]

The most powerful message from the Magna Carta is that law and law enforcement must not be arbitrary and everyone has a right for a fair trial.

At the time I saw these documents of liberty, my recent lay-off experience was still fresh and very much alive. The arbitrary handling of agreements, rules that don't apply to everyone in the same way, and the person in power deciding over my fate, in absence of fair and independent judgment. And a management that is backing him in a dispute that had been as fair as a trial in the Spanish inquisition.

How far does law and granted freedoms really go? Does free market mean that companies are free to do whatever they want and whatever happens inside a company is not bound to at least laws of morality?

Any company, institution or political movement needs leadership for direction and execution. But leadership shall be bound to the same rules as everyone else. A leader should be respected for the example, not the rules, he sets. William Shakespeare (1564–1616) said: "I think the king is but a man, as I am: the violet smells to him as it doth to me:

---

58 ENCYCLOPAEDIA BRITANNICA, MAGNA CARTA

the element shows to him as it doth to me."[59] In a company, shouldn't the same rules apply to everyone in the same way then? Why is it that some are able to bend the rules, others not, if in the end we all work for the same cause? And if there are rules in place, but they don't apply to all employees equally, why make contracts and agreements at all?

The King has been bound to the law for 800 years and counting, but a power abusing boss can get away with it? I had enough of it. I was angry and sad, disappointed and motivated, spiteful and hopeful, desperate and full of energy at the same time.

The introduction of the American Declaration of Independence from July 4th 1776, has very powerful words for this; universal to mankind:

"When in the course of human events, it becomes necessary for one people to dissolve the political bands which have connected them with another, and to assume among the powers of the earth, the separate and equal station to which the Laws of Nature and of Nature's God entitle them, a decent respect to the opinions of mankind requires that they should declare the causes which impel them to the separation. We hold these truths to be self-evident, that all men are created equal, that they are endowed by their Creator with certain unalienable Rights, that among these are Life, Liberty and the pursuit of Happiness..."

Natural Law, to which the Declaration refers, is a philosophical system of justice which is universal and common to all humans, and derived from nature rather than from rules of society. It stands in contrary to positive law, laws made by a political community or society, or even a company. Aristotle believed that what was "just by nature" was not necessarily what was "just by law". The idea is that natural law is independent and exists regardless of "people's thinking this or that."[60]

The State, as Machiavelli describes, was justified by the mistrust towards the people. Positive law, the rule of opinionated men, has found its way into the *reason of corporate*. Rules and bureaucracy in prac-

---

59 SHAKESPEARE, W. (1599) HENRY V, 4.1.155–7

60 ENCYCLOPAEDIA BRITANNICA, NATURAL LAW

tice can serve to control people or in the opposite ensuring their liberty to exercise their skills to the fullest extent. The absence of rules can lead to a reckless corporate turbo-capitalism, or to unleash creative entrepreneurial energy. The opinions and intentions of people is what can create a tipping point into one or the other direction.

Many people believe that what is right is what the law says, but forget that the law has been made by people, based on the world view and interests of the original law maker. That is why natural law will always stand above positive law, and the free minded man will always unshackle himself from wrong-headed rules made by believers or the lobby for preservation of special interests.

Friedrich Schiller (1759–1805), German poet, philosopher, physician, historian, and playwright, and name-giver to my high school in Frankfurt, is sometimes attributed to as the founder of German idealism. He believed that it matters to act and do something based on what one has been made for. Schiller's idealism was the conviction that it is possible to master things, and not to become dominated by them.[61] It felt like Newton's apple falling onto my head and I realized what I had to do.[62] I decided to unchain myself. I was firm in my decision to become an entrepreneur. Maybe it is a risk to become an entrepreneur, but looking at the odds of the past years, I thought, it can't be a greater danger than working in a mismanaged company whose fate I cannot influence. I mentally joined William Tell to swear the *Rütlischwur*, the legendary oath of the Old Swiss Confederation:

> *"We want to be a single People of brethren,*
> *Never to part in danger nor distress.*
> *We want to be free, just as our fathers were,*
> *And rather die than live in slavery.*

---

61 SAFRANSKI, R. (2016), P. 11–15

62 Isaac Newton (1643–1727) allegedly sat under an apple tree in front of his parents' house as an apple fell on his head. He thought as the apples always fall straight to the ground, never left or right, it must be because there must be pulled towards the ground by the earth; and there he had discovered gravity.

We want to trust in the highest God
And never be afraid of human power.[63]

Never be afraid of human power. Take a minute to digest this sentence and a life to embrace it: Never be afraid of human power.

Kant said in 1794, only eight years after the Declaration of Independence, and five years before the French Revolution that "enlightenment is man's emerge from his self-imposed immaturity". He claimed that this "immaturity is self-imposed if its cause lies not in lack of understanding but in indecision and lack of courage to use one's own mind without another's guidance."

How free am I when I am dependent on the good will of my boss? Do I have to fear just that, human power? How can I pursue my happiness when I am dependent on the skills of an executive to make the right decisions? What if that person is not as smart as he thinks he is, but my livelihood depends on it? I have experienced too much lack of integrity and intelligence, it had cost me a lot of money and many years of my life spent on things I never wanted to do.

I lost two jobs over bad company management. Fool me once, shame on you. Fool me twice, shame on me. Not a third time. I am not going to do that again! If my life is screwed up, then at least I want to be the one who screws it up. I don't need a mediocre manager for that. Why should I give the control of my life to others if I can never be sure that they have the same commitment to *my* future as I have?

My experience may have biased my vision. At the same time I came to realize that maybe I wasn't just made to be a corporate mercenary.

Man has flown to space, cracked the genetic code, invented x-ray and the automobile. How difficult can it be to start your own business? It's not rocket science. In my situation I had no money and no investors. To start a business out of my position in 2010 looked like a mission impossible. It required indomitable spirit, determination and

---

63 SCHILLER, F. (1804), ACT II, SCENE II

perseverance. In a world that suffers from attention deficit disorder and expects quick success, patience and focus have become the most difficult state of mind. If it takes years in the making, you will harvest lots of malice: "Oh you are still working on that?" People belittle your goals if they look too ambitious or if they take years in the making. Gottfried Ephraim Lessing (1729–1781) had a precise answer to this: „*Der Langsamste, der sein Ziel nicht aus den Augen verliert, ist immer noch schneller, als jener, der ohne Ziel umherirrt.*" – The slowest, who doesn't lose his goal out of sight is still faster than the one who runs around without an objective.

Always finish what you start, and "whatever you do, do it heartily".[64] But it's not all about getting somewhere, but also to improve constantly on the way there. The *Do* – the way – to achieve something is just as important. In Taekwondo practice, Grand Master Suk Jun Kim once explained to me, the Asian *Do* or *Dao* emphasizes the way, not the goal. In Western society we always think about doing this, to achieve that, while in many Asian cultures the end result isn't always the focus.

Today the time from an idea to success is expected to be lightning fast. If I start my own business, and the business is not successful, then I still improved as a person. And maybe it takes a second or third try to become a successful entrepreneur. What matters is the decision to do it and to do it for the right reasons. Becoming an entrepreneur is not about proving your skills to others. It's about putting them into action and it's part of a process to become self-sufficient. Don't expect to get rich, but to become self-determined and the master of your own destiny.

I went back to building a strategy. My new target mission was:

I want to become an entrepreneur, to be in charge of my own life and pursuit of happiness, while making enough money to feed my family.

I wanted to turn all my unheard and ignored ideas, that I had for a business entity at Savox, into my own business. I had a good head start, because I had seen all the things that Savox was doing wrong, from research & development, to operations and sales & marketing. I had accumulated a lot of knowledge in the critical communications

---

64 HOLY BIBLE, COLOSSIANS 3:23–24

industry. It can be an advantage to be 2nd or 3rd on a market, especially if the 1st mover on a market is not able to seize his advantage to capture it. In a high-tech market with critical customers, the quality of your product is outweighing any marketing budget. I wanted to do everything different.

Many companies are borne out of a former employment. People leave or are let go from a business. They believe they know how to do it better. There are some multi-billion dollar companies that started like that.

The two most typical ways to start a business are:

1. You start a business in an industry that you work or have worked before by leveraging your expertise and existing network.
2. You turn your hobby or interests into a business.

It doesn't mean that it's all fun. It's not. I recall a conversation that I had during some backpacking time in South America many years ago. I chatted with the instructor on a white water rafting boat on the Rio Urubamba in Peru. As we had some breaks from Class IV and V rapids, I said to the instructor how great I found that he has a job where he can go rafting every day in beautiful landscape. He said: "yes, that's the fun part, but think of this: I have to get up and check the boats, get the trailer hooked to the bus, make the lunch that's included in the rafting tour, then pick everyone up, drive an hour to the river, instruct different people in the same things every day, and after the fun I have to drive everyone back, clean up the boats and store everything safely before buying food for the next day's tour. That makes it at least an eight hour day, out of which I am only two on the river. Even though this is what I love doing, it's not all just rafting on the rapids."

Applying an 80–20 rule, in a good job you probably love 80% of the things you do. That will make you stay and continue working for a company. Starting your own business the ratio may well be the way round. Yet, for the entrepreneur this is often the price he's willing to pay.

In my starting position it wasn't relevant. I had no money whatsoever to start anything in 2010. Rousseau said: "As long as people is compelled to obey, and obeys, it does well; as soon as it can shake off the yoke...it does still better...to yield to force is an act of necessity..."[65] In 2010 the world's economy was in bad shape, just moving out of a recession. Needless to say it wasn't the time to shake off the yoke, the opposite was the case. All the dreams of Freedom and entrepreneurship had to go on the back burner. I had more immediate worries: I needed a paycheck. Very badly.

It made the job hunt even harder. On the one hand I really, really wanted to become an entrepreneur. My thought was that any job would just be temporary until I could come back up. On the other hand, the decision to become an entrepreneur doesn't mean that you'll be successful and can make a living of your business. So I also needed to plan for the eventual case that I'd never be able to fulfill my dream. So I couldn't just be foolish to do just any job to survive. The next job needed to fulfill several purposes. Firstly I needed to make money, secondly I needed a job that would be a career step in absence of any entrepreneurial plans, and thirdly should be a job where I could learn something different, rather than just executing and stepping on the same spot. Not the easiest of all job hunts that I had set myself up for.

Many people have reasons why they have set-backs that make them interrupt their diet or their attempt to quit smoking. Learning how to deal with setbacks is what ultimately leads to success. Having a lot of will power on days that you feel great is easy. The mind has to win over the body on the other days. That's what determination and perseverance is about.

In those days I remembered an interview with Christopher Reeve (1952–2004) on the BBC shortly before he passed away. It was the first time I had been on a difficult job hunt, right after graduation. Reeve had been the actor of Superman. He had suffered an injury after falling off a horse that left him almost completely paralyzed. He

---

65 ROUSSEAU, J.-J. (1762), CHAPTER I AND III

had the dream of walking again one day. One part of his daily routine was going for an hour into the swimming pool every morning. The interviewer asked Superman on how he makes himself go on all these days when the chances for healing are close to zero. Superman said: "90% of it is just getting there." He added that the most important was to "ignore your moods."

After ten months of being number two and number three in numerous job interviews, I finally landed a job in Global Strategic Alliances and Partner Management at Dell in Central Texas. Neither of which were places of my preference, but it was going to fulfill all three requirements. Working for a big company would secure a good paycheck, mark a step forward on my resume in case I needed it for a new job hunt, and I was going to learn how big corporations function. From all places I found that kind of job was in Texas. For my long term career and my financial situation it was certainly a better move than being a junior salesman or a marketing program's manager at some no-name company. Given the nature of the job market, I felt that a big name in the resume would be more likely to land a job elsewhere after some time, especially since I had worked for smaller companies before already. This would balance out the experience. It wasn't really what I wanted to do, but I knew it could help me to get out of my troubles. It was purely instrumental: Be at a well-known company for a while, get a good pay and retirement savings, have a disposable income for an easy job, and stay out of trouble until I recover from my mess.

I didn't know how I would like it at Dell or in Texas, but at that time it was the best option I had. After starting my new life in Central Texas it crystalized quite soon that it was like taking a time out from life and skills.

My quest from the first week on was how to get out of this state of dependency. Working for Dell was a mean to an end. Getting into Dell was a way to get out of my mess. This is how I saw the purpose of my job and it was the most important reason why I never got excited about it.

Meredith, had a three year commitment with the federal government to work at a hospital in an underserved area in return for a subsidy of her student loans from graduate school. The cost of living in Texas was far more economical than in New York. On top of that, Texas does not collect a State Income Tax, therefore we earned more, paid less taxes and spent less money. It served the purpose quite well.

We missed a lot of things though: more variety of things to do, city lifestyle, four seasons and the vicinity to friends and family. Our financial situation started to be more comfortable, but money alone wasn't just going to cut it since the other things weren't what we wanted. I wanted to do something extraordinary.

Being there, I had ended up doing what I never wanted to do. I love big cities, I like small companies, I like to be in charge and I love to speak my mind. None of the above was going to happen for the next three years. I was doomed to walk through life with my head hanging low, due to the Texas heat and the motivation on extremely low flame. The career outlook for the future was very uncertain. We moved to a small town north of Austin, the State's super hip capital.

Georgetown, Texas lays in Central Texas, a short drive north of Austin. Driving on the same highway further north for three more hours, you get to the Dallas Fort Worth area. In between there are small towns and villages along the way. Georgetown felt like the closest livable place to us, which was still commutable to Temple, Texas, where Meredith worked. It was a 45min commute north for her, and a 20min commute south for me. This meant we weren't able to live in the open-minded capital of the Lone Star State, but in one of the largest retirement communities in the United States. I missed the four seasons, I missed an abundance of intellectual people, and the infinity of things to do in a city. Life is easy and laid back in Texas. But it's boring. Some people like not to have to stress out about anything at any time. Maybe that's why Texans are so nice and friendly all the time. To me though, it was monotonous and it it felt like every day was the same. It felt like I am wasting precious time of my life doing something I don't want to do, when I could spend it doing something I want to do. That ticking clock was what concerned me the most. I could not relax over the fact that despite everyone around me being really nice and laid back, that I just didn't want to be there. I had to take a job that I wasn't excited about, working in a large corporation. I always tried to avoid working in big companies and now I was making a pact with the devil. Necessity is the mother of invention: I had to make money to pay for things that I had already spent. I knew that I needed money more than anything. From now on I couldn't afford to be right, to say what needed to be said, to stand up for what I believed in, to question the status quo or to challenge wrong decisions or unethical behavior. Basically I needed to suppress my natural character in order to fix what I had gotten myself into. There is nothing worse in life than the feeling to be dependent on another person's or company's good will. It was depressing.

I decided that I was going to be what I needed to be to get through this. I decided to say yes a lot to, stay out of trouble, not to challenge anything. I had to put up with the job and the location. This constellation required more self-discipline inside and outside of my job than I ever had to deal with in my life. The hardest part in a situation like this is not to let yourself go, bury yourself in self-pity and blame the world for your situation. I knew that it would take quite some time to replenish my enthusiasm, to analyze what had just happened and to derive the right actions for the future. I wasn't going to become a yes-man, I was a mercenary. I just did what I was paid to do without trying to question the reasons behind it.

Every challenge is an opportunity. Living and experiencing, activity and reflection, go hand in hand. I didn't want to blame the broken contracts with my previous employer as a reason for self-condolence, but rather as a motivation to make my dream happen. I took the broken pieces of glass in the attempt to build something shinier and brighter.

The question that followed was: "Now what?" John Lennon said that life happens while you have planned something else. I had planned to be in New York City and found myself in Georgetown, Texas. I did realize that in the end it is neither Georgetown nor New York where I want to live. Maybe that was the most valuable aspect of the experience. A good friend of mine always says that if you don't get off the beaten path you will stay on the way. Side-tracking can help you find your own path to happiness. Confucius said: "The way is made by walking it – 道行之而成" The attitude you have while living your life is what matters to its outcome.

Many people give up on their dreams before they have started. Often people are afraid of the unknown or uncertainties, or because it seems so big at first. That can then be ornamented with an unlimited amount of nice sounding explanations of why *their* circumstances do not allow to go for something. I can say one thing upfront: You can try as hard as you want, you will never break my optimism. Many have tried, all have failed. The only thing in life that I am not too optimistic about is that the obstinate pessimists will ever smile and stop trying to warn me of possible negative outcomes. Or the ever returning advice that one may be better off to adapt to a comfortable and stable situation rather than taking risks. Why not take the risk to try to be happy? You can always be a miserable conformist accepting fate. It's the easy choice. The tough choice is to put action to your pursuit of happiness, especially when you realize that the status quo and your default future are nothing close to it. At the time we moved to Texas I was excited about the new start. It felt like my next chance. I was so excited about getting my life back on track that I underestimated the heat of Texas and how horrible it is to work in a corporation of a hundred thousand people with just as many processes.

Nevertheless, it was no reason for pessimism. I don't believe in pessimism for the simple reason that it doesn't help to get things done. One has to believe in his own capabilities. Let others call it naïve or *too optimistic*. A pinch of naivety can be helpful when aiming high, otherwise you may lose motivation in the sight of the dimension of your dream. Some dreams are so big that you need a good sense of humor and a great spirit of adventure to get started. Ninety percent of it is just getting there. There are always people that like to say *now you are dreaming a little too big*. Pessimists have frown faces and make sunny days look like they were foggy and rainy.

Optimists don't err more often than pessimists, but they live happier. Pessimists of course never admit to be one. They say: *I'm not pessimistic, I'm just realistic.* How often have you heard that in your life? In Economics there is a simple formula for inflation that applies to pessimists alike:

Inflation is a function of the expected inflation. If everyone expects prices to rise by 3% over a year's time, then businesses will adjust prices accordingly. Inflation is considered a self-fulfilling prophecy. If you see your chances to get anything done in life as a function of the expected chances of that, you can easily derive how successful pessimists can become. Courage and risk are calculable; entrepreneurs for example are no foolhardy risk-takers, but adventurous freedom loving people who take calculated risks. Someone who tries to climb Mount Everest after thorough preparation and help is taking a calculated risk. Sailing around the world knowing how to navigate without computers is a calculated risk. It is foolish to go into any adventure without preparation, not because the act itself can be dangerous.

In Finland there is a saying called *tekevälle sattuu* – the active person also makes mistakes sometimes. The homo faber, the blacksmith, as he prepares the metal with a hammer may at times accidentally hurt himself. Staying away from the hammer may keep him from that type of harm, but he'd also not make anything. You can't make mistakes if you don't make anything, but then you don't make anything.

Contemplating pessimism as the mistaken description of realism is the self-condolence of the timid. Reality and realism is something very subjective describing how reality looks from the eye of the beholder. Optimism has nothing to do with foolhardiness, risky impulsive action or absence of reason; it is simply the pure exciting feeling of *YES!*

The time from 2011–2014 in Texas was time to get dusted off, put the Iqua/Savox chapter behind me, pay off my debt, and look forward to a new venture. My encounter with the Magna Carta and the Declaration of Independence were not the ultimate trigger point; that would be stuff for a movie. But they certainly gave a philosophic meaning and a call to action for something I had been contemplating with. Never losing my goal of entrepreneurship out of sight I knew that eventually my sentence at Dellcatraz would be over and I could be a free man again. It was the day I was working towards without knowing when it would come nor how I could get there. At that point I didn't have a clear picture how to reach the post-Dell life, but I was determined that it was only a stop on my train of life. I knew that I had to start working on that immediately. Otherwise I'd be at risk to get a Stockholm syndrome.[66] How can you get out of a situation that you got stuck in and there is no-one but yourself who can help you? This was the quest I was about to go on.

---

66 The Stockholm-Syndrome describes a psychological phenomenon by which the victim of a hostage situation begins to create a positive emotional relation to its kidnappers. This can lead the victim to sympathize and co-operate with the kidnappers.

7 NEVER LET YOUR ARMY REST

"The art of waiting is to make good use of your time."
CONFUCIUS (6ᵀᴴ–5ᵀᴴ CENTURY B.C.)

Living in New York City was a fantastic experience. Millions of people, a culinary heaven, museums, great Jazz, a world class Opera, cocktail bars, happy hours, art galleries, giant rats, and many other things. It is never boring in New York, it's addictive. I had a great time. It's also very expensive and life is passing by quickly while you are living in that Oasis, this microcosm of the world. There are many reasons to love the Big Apple with all the hustle and bustle. And everyone you speak to has their own reasons why they love it.

There is a moment for everything in life and I'm glad I lived in New York when I was young and I was able to afford it; at least two out of the three years. I would not want to miss that experience, but I'm also glad that I moved on from that city, and in life. In New York time is flying, because you are so busy to work and live hard. As I had time to see my life from a distance again I found that there are other places that are exciting in their own way, and maybe more livable in the long run. I had time to think of what the place was where I'd like to settle and raise children. Put an end to the nomadic life of a hunter and gatherer. Maybe this thought came to me after finding myself in a place where I definitely did not want to grow old.

It was the first week of January of 2011 when I packed my things to be on my way to a new adventure. Moving to a different place for a while is always exciting. I have lived in many cities around the world, moving to Austin was just another new place. After a while you learn how to adapt and embrace into any new culture, how to fit in and have fun. It doesn't scare me to set up camp in a new unknown place, it excites me. It was a great road trip from New York to Texas. My brother, Sebastian, flew in from Germany to "help me move". In other words, he came to join me for a fun road trip. Meredith was going to follow me down there three months later. The day we left New York, there were still piles of snow everywhere from a storm that had stopped by just a few days earlier. We left at 6 a.m. in the morning to beat the traffic through Manhattan and as the sun was slowly rising we had left the lights of the skyline behind us. That chapter was over. Something new was about to come.

Country-Singer Willie Nelson (*1933) wrote suitable words: "On the road again. I can't wait to get on the road again…..goin' places that I've never been. Seein' things that I may never see again…" A lot about being on the road is to be open about what's happening next and embrace every moment, because it may never come again. And even the boring times will pass eventually, like the scenery goes by as you are driving.

We visited the battle field and museum in Gettysburg in Pennsylvania and spent a few hours learning about the history of the American Civil War. We stayed overnight in Columbus, Ohio and celebrated my birthday the next day in Nashville, Tennessee. With live country music and eating good barbeque I started to prepare mentally for the lifestyle of America's South. A day-drive later we stopped in the sleepy town of Natchez, which is the first settlement on the Mississippi river, established 1716 by French colonists. We thought everyone was already in bed as we arrived. Only the Under-the-Hill Saloon right on the Mississippi river, probably the oldest Saloon at the shores of the river, was open and alive. We made friends with the long-bearded local Harley Davidson riders, listened to the live band and drank Budweiser out of bottles until they closed the bar on us. What we had known about the South from TV was real all of a sudden. The best about road trips is that you never know where you end up. It's a little bit like your whole life in a time lapse, you have times when it's fun, sometimes you have to get through it with a terrible headache, and most of the time you meet interesting people. And the journey is what you in there for, not only the destination. I felt neither like a New Yorker, nor a Texan. At the check-in in Natchez the receptionist asked me where I lived. I said: "In the infernal red Dodge Charger that's parked outside." Yes, with Dell's relocation bonus I had bought a gas-guzzling muscle car. When it Rome, do it as the Romans do.

When we arrived in Houston, Texas to stay at a friend's place for the night, it was already t-shirt weather. It had been only a few days since winter. We had fast forwarded to the warm weather by driving south. We were able to sit outside in the evening with a cold brew and enjoy a good time, catch up with a friend. Arriving in Austin the next day and starting to settle I felt that compared to New York this was going to be life turned upside down. I had to drive everywhere since advanced public transportation almost didn't exist. It is more dangerous to ride a bicycle in Texas than in New York, because people don't expect anyone *not* to use a car. Initially the weather was pleasant, then it got extremely hot for a very long time. Life is a lot slower in Texas, more meat than sushi, bigger cars and larger distances. Almost everything was different, which made it exciting *at first*. Austin reminded me of my time in Córdoba in Argentina. I have spent a year and a half as an exchange student of Economics at the Universidad Nacional de Córdoba; founded 1613 the 4th oldest University in South America. The river that ran through the city, the vibe from thousands of students living there, the live music and the vicinity to the hills. All these are features describe Austin, just like it describes Córdoba. The only difference is that Cordobeses love to dance to their Cuarteto music, while the Austinites prefer Rock Music. This created a welcoming feeling in me and even though it was a new place, it seemed familiar and cozy.

During the three years I lived in Central Texas I had to be very active in order not to fall into an idle-state. It was to learn how to transform boredom into energy and desperation into excitement.

Compared to the amount of social life and opportunity for activities in New York, Georgetown was like night and day. Wherever I have lived in my life, in Augsburg, Frankfurt, Salamanca, Córdoba, Helsinki, Buenos Aires, San Francisco, São Paulo, or New York, I was always right in the middle of it. Not anymore.

In Georgetown, Texas I could set my clock by the time the elderly couple from down the street went on their morning walk. I had put my home office into a room with a view to the street. Any day I worked from home at four p.m. in the afternoon the school bus stopped across the street. At the same time the neighbor's door already opened as if they had an automatic timer on it. Their dog ran out and did the exact same circle sniffing the grass it always sniffed. The children ran to say hello to their mother. Every day it was the same picture. While this all sounds like the idyllic life of the country, it was driving me insane. Those were the moments I wanted to play Russian Roulette with myself. Every day was exactly like any other day. It was the opposite of what the renaissance taught us, to remember that one day we will die. If one day in my life was like any other day, why bother to live it up and make it special? It felt like the mid-evil life in the ban of eternity. In the corporation during the week, everyone was only waiting for the weekend to come. Only that on the weekends there wasn't too much to do, because it was too hot to have any energy. Going to work on Mondays was only a welcome change, because it *was* actually a change. But it was like coming out of the frying pan straight into the fire. Given the summer temperatures in Texas, quite a fitting image.

My life felt like that of weatherman Phil's in Groundhog Day.[67] In this movie, the main character Phil travels to Punxsutawney, Pennsylvania to cover the festivities of Groundhog Day for the news of a TV station. The weatherman finds himself condemned to experience the same day every day. Every morning at 6 a.m. he wakes up to the same music and soon realizes that he is cursed. All he wants to do is leave

---

67 GROUNDHOG DAY (1993)

the town, without any success. After going to bed and waking up the next morning, he notices that it's the same day he has already lived. In the movie at one of his repeating days, Phil says to himself: "What would you do if you were stuck in one place, and everything that you did was the same, and nothing mattered?" The moment in the movie, the realization that he is stuck, is the turning point for Phil to become a better person. He stops complaining and to face his situation only with cynicism and desperation. Instead he starts to become friendly with the insurance person, an old class mate of his, that he never used to like. He takes piano lessons, learns how to carve sculptures out of ice and many other things. He doesn't become a different person or suddenly changes his mind over the fact that he wants to leave the town of Punxsutawney. However, he brings out the good and positive side, he becomes a better person, more likeable and likes himself also a lot more. He shakes off the self-pity. And while he is stuck in the little town, he also improves many of his skills and discovers new talents in him. There is quite something to learn from the transformation of the *miserable*-Phil to the *carpe-diem*-Phil throughout the movie.

So what to do in these idle times? We all experience times in which we aren't happy about the status quo. It turns into a feeling of being stuck when you come to realize that at this point in time it may not be smart or possible at all to change your life. Maybe you love to travel for business, but you have a new newborn child in the house, which keeps you grounded for a while. Maybe the job you just started is nothing at all what you expected it to be, but you should probably stick with it a little. Maybe you attend evening classes and do not have time to spend your nights with job search until they are over. Probably you need the salary desperately – like I did – and you don't think that anyone else would pay you as much as you are earning now? Or maybe your spouse has a job in a place where you can't find anything in your profession and don't know what to do about it. While it's easy to say that if you are not happy in life, you should just change it, in reality there isn't always an immediate opportunity to solve that problem. And it seems to get harder with age. Sometimes we just have to get through it. And if your next step should be a step forward, it's very likely that you need some preparation time.

I learned it the hard way. I lived in a place whose climate I couldn't handle and worked in a company I didn't want to work for. Some people advise that in tough time you just have to adapt to your circumstances, although they may have never really experienced tough times. The lack of alternatives to the status quo is what makes adapting a chore. In reality it is much rather conforming than adapting. The biggest risk here is to get used to a situation that you dislike and to lose sight of your goal. You may forget or become complacent about your desire deep inside to have a different life. Under no circumstances did I want to get used to the new situation. On the other hand, a minimum amount of diving into and mixing up with the situation is necessary to live where you are and enjoy the life you have. It is a balancing act that has to be practiced every day. Don't worry, be happy. Integrate, but don't assimilate. I wanted to give it a chance, but I knew that I could not live without the four seasons in the middle of nowhere forever. It is tricky: you may grow comfortable with 2nd or 3rd best. After all, it-is-not-so-bad is just another expression for it-is-not-so-good.

Doing something you never wanted to do and getting comfortable with it is a good elixir for a mid-life crisis and age related regret.

Dell's company headquarters was located in Round Rock, a 20min drive south of Georgetown; half way to Austin. The Dell campus was a large corporate complex with various gray concrete buildings, at the time hosting several thousand worker bees stuck in individual honeycombs; since they came without the honey they called them cubicles. The only way to get there was by car. In the morning around 9 a.m. you could see lines of cars coming from everywhere heading towards the parking lot, like armies of ants going into their anthill. Every day, after parking the car and greeting the person at the front desk, I would swipe my security batch, and as I heard the loud clicking sound from the opening door was I walked into rows of cubicles with grey walls and artificial light. The grey cubicle walls where so tall that one had to tip-toe to look over them to see a colleague.

One thing that most intellectuals and artists will second is that a liberal and inspiring environment is a pre-requisite for any creative work. Day light, windows, and open space offices create transparency and creativity, team spirit and joy of work. Every modern work space is set up like that. There are studies about the effects of architecture on the mood and energy of people at work. Cubicles and artificial lights are probably at the bottom of the influential factors for hard work, excitement, creativity, and open-mindedness. In fact they are like blinders for horses. Observing the expression in people's faces every day was that of depression and anxiety rather than enthusiasm and excitement. Stress from the need to get a paycheck, frustration from mind-numbing work and anxiety from trying to find something to deliver to justify one's job position.

In a large corporation, people stroll into work around 9 a.m. in the morning, start their computer, and then walk to the cafeteria to get some coffee. On their way back to their desk they have a few chats with their colleagues about last night's sports event or the latest company announcement that came in the mail early in the morning. Using Voice-over-IP (VoIP) calls, everyone will join a conference call, slurping his coffee while browsing the Internet. When you hear your name and have to answer a question you quickly try to organize your thoughts, click with your mouse to open the microphone and then say "I'm sorry, I was muted." You'll repeat the question and find a standard response out of your three possible answer portfolio. While in a meeting, your status on your instant messaging software will show you as "in a call". If your boss happens to look if you are around on instant messaging software, your status shows that you seem to be working. After an hour of attending that conference call, it's time to use the bath room and ask colleagues about where you could be going for your hour lunch break. If you have some errands to run, maybe it will be two hours. Then you could call some automated number, like the weather forecast with your VoIP software, and our online status will show you as busy. There are many ways to kill the time in a corporation without actually working. And most people do. It's a place to hang out until it's time to go home.

In the meantime you try to get by with the minimum while looking extremely busy. Some are more sophisticated than others. The day you have your weekly one-on-one with your manager you usually spend an hour or two talking to colleagues to get something going and maybe work a little bit on a presentation, so that you have something to report this week. Once you are done with your meeting you are done for the day. It's a pretty laid back way to make money. Only that you easily get complacent and your brain calcifies.

There is an Austin based startup named Zello. They are an instant-voice messaging software company that offers a push-to-talk walkie-talkie style app for smartphones. Yesterday, there were walkie-talkies, today there is an app for that. Zello's app has been downloaded over a hundred million times. I knew one of the founders since I had established the business relation between Savox and Zello in the past, when the company was still called Loudtalks. I called their CEO, Bill Moore, and their CTO, Alex Gavrilov, to meet up for lunch one day. Before heading to eat we met at their office at the Capital Factory in Austin; a co-working space used by several startups. You can rent a desk or an office and use the joint kitchen, meeting rooms and other facilities. The vibe there was the extreme opposite of the grey assembly line rows back at the corporation. A glass front along the entire office let real light in, people smiling and laughing in the kitchen, others were concentrated at work or engaged in meetings. This co-working space filled with start-ups was a picture telling the difference between a creative mind factory and a corporate mill. My first thought was: "This is where I want to be. Where people care about what they do. Where your work is more important than your title. Where your ideas are valued based on their content, not the place in the hierarchy you possess. Where people only laugh about a joke if it's funny, not because your boss told it." It wasn't just eye-opening to see that contrast in such a short time-period, it was a bucket of ice cold water in the face. After a nice lunch and good conversation I drove 25min back north to the Dell Campus and sat in between the grey walls of the cubicle cell. Just staring at them for a quite a while.

Years later, in December of 2016 I visited Zello in Austin and told my friends there that maybe if I had lived in Austin and worked at Zello, my life would have been very different than living in Georgetown and working for Dell. Any place in the world can just feel so different depending on the circumstances you are in. It's important to recognize your own situation.

But that came in the future, in 2012 I was still very much stuck in my present desperation. My current present, which was then future, would have never come had I not started to work on change in that moment. What now? I asked myself. I didn't have the motivation to make a career at Dell from the start, but my encounter with the alternative life over lunch cleared any possible doubt. Just thinking of spending more years than necessary in my cubicle made me sick to my stomach. It is still an all-depressing imagination and I am glad I went to the source of the ice cold water and decided to jump in it to find out if that was any better. I had a movie split screen scene in my head. On one side a startup and it's hands-on spirit, and self-driven people. On the other side of the screen it said: "meanwhile in the large brand name corporation". There I saw rows of cubicles under artificial flickering light, where people counted the days until the next pay check, pretended to be very busy and just couldn't wait for the clock to hit five. I thought that even if I wanted to make a career here, and get a cozy corner office with a window, the view from there would be a 50-50 chance of either seeing the parking lot or the highway. Hierarchies, corporate language, slow processes, some people working really hard, others hiding in a lot of meetings, and some try to get by with the minimum. No thanks.

I purchased a *bobble head* for my desk. It's a small statue of a famous person with an oversized head that wobbles around when you push them, as if they are constantly nodding. It symbolized the best way to survive the corporate jungle. And it was an amusing thought among my colleagues and me to imagine everyone in a meeting having an oversized bobble head just smiling and nodding. My bobble head was that of Elvis Presley, who also seemed to sing the Jailhouse Rock if you stared at it long enough.

Another game that one can play in a corporation is corporate Bingo. Fill out different papers with the typical words that corporations use, including "align", "drive the strategy", "focus", "core competence", "buy in", "lead the conversation" and whatever corporate jargon yours is using. You mark off your words when they are said and call out "bingo" when you crossed them all off. When you play corporate bingo you realize that if you take away the corporate fill words everyone uses, there isn't much content left in the sentences. Cutting out all the words that are ruminated, you can reduce the content of any meeting to probably 3 sentences that are useful and add value. This would save a lot of time and nerves of the participants. But meetings are set up for an hour, so let's talk for an hour and mistake it for work. That is the preferred option.

People in Texas are extremely friendly and so they were at Dell. Fortunately during the three years there I never had a personal issue with a direct supervisor, they were all really nice people that left the team to do their job. We all knew what we had to do and the atmosphere was very professional. It was the overall atmosphere of that anthill which was weighing over me. From day one on at Dell I knew there was no way I could stay for too long doing this. It just didn't feel right.

I never really wanted to work for Dell in the first place. A recruiter had reached out to me if I was interested in a position in Global Strategic Alliances & Partner Marketing Management for Dell. I needed a paycheck and I knew that this was a position I would have a good shot at given my previous experience. I had tweaked my resume, my strengths and my target image in a way that after the signaling & screening process I was on top; picked out of a dozen candidates. The company paid for my relocation including a nice sign-on bonus. I knew I could do the job well, and during the three years I was there I think I did. I worked like it was the only thing I ever wanted to do. Corporate culture demanded from me a high level of self-motivation and discipline. I guess you would call that being professional. I even received an award for my performance once, a certificate in a plastic frame. I had no choice, I needed that job for a while. Nevertheless I thought: "Oh boy, what have you gotten yourself into?" It was the complete opposite of what I had in mind for myself.

The pay was good, I knew that a big name in my resume would help me find another job later if I needed one. Maybe the best experience that I still benefit from today was to learn how big companies work, or better said function. One day I'd be on the other side again, selling products to a big company, I thought. Might as well figure out how things are done or not done. Who makes the decisions, who can make things happen?

Today that it's over and the pain has eased, I must say that Dell was a good experience to have. Most people were very pleasant and that made it bearable. It was a mean to an end. I knew what I was going for and treated it accordingly. I disliked working at Dell very much, but that never had anything to do with the company itself. I'm just not made for big corporate.

Goethe said *"Man still must err, while he doth strive"*.[68] Close your eyes and get through, I thought. But how long would this take? What's next? I knew I wasn't in the position to walk away from my paycheck and I needed to get through it. But there seemed to be not even a glimpse of light in the tunnel.

I was used to making decisions, executing them, go on a business trip when I deemed it necessary, lead people, influence product road maps, define marketing strategies. I was used to wearing many hats. Now I had to wear only one. For every other hat I had in my skill closet, there was already another person's bobble head assigned to. In a large brand name corporation, the speed of adding new experience to your skillset equals molasses going down your back. The brand name feels good for a while and decorates your resume nicely in case you need to move on. To improve your skills it may not be the best place.

In Global Alliances and Partner Management we had a good place to position ourselves for internal politics. We were the team that han-

---

68 GOETHE, J. W. VON (1808), PROLOGUE IN HEAVEN

dled all major alliances partners of the company. We proposed joint go-to-market strategies, aligned technology stakeholders, defined budgets and co-marketing campaigns, and negotiated partner paid sales incentives. The challenge in a big company is that all teams are much bigger and communication is more difficult. I always wondered why so many people believe team leadership was equal to being a team leader. In a direct supervisor-report structure it is extremely simple to lead people, because there is an uneven distribution of power. One of you is the boss, period. It is much harder to lead people in a cross-functional role in which you have to pull many strings to move a project forward. The other people, on whose help you depend on, do not report to you and have their own incentives, if any. You have to influence other people to do something for you even if they don't *have to*. Sometimes the people that are the easiest to work with aren't the ones who are the most important for your job priorities. Very quickly you can get sucked into a lot of projects and meetings that are completely irrelevant to your most important tasks and you can get tangled up and forget to focus on what matters. Then you lose sight of the goal.

In finance, maybe the most basic rules is that an investment period should be equal or shorter to its amortization time. For example you should not finance a car over six years if you are only planning on using it for three. That way you would be paying for something that you don't use anymore. In high inflation countries, banks don't give out long term loans, because the high inflation would eat their return. This causes many developing countries with high inflation to lack important long term investments. You can apply this rule to individuals investing their time into work in exchange for a possible return in form of recognition, promotion and growing salary. If you can get the same results with short term gains, why risk a project getting thrown under the bus due to new corporate goals half way through. When fiscal quarters steer the actions of the players in this game, it creates the need for constant quick wins.

Big business suffer from a memory effect. This term is also called battery effect and applies mostly to nickel-cadmium batteries. These batteries "remember" an energy demand based on previous charge times. If a battery is constantly recharged after only 20% of the loaded energy has been used, the battery will gradually lose charge capacity. Eventually it will end up with a maximum charge capacity of about 20% of the original full capacity. The risk that I felt working in this quarterly business was that exactly that was happening. What you haven't done by the end of the quarter doesn't matter anymore. We just put it aside and think into the next quarter. After a year nobody remembers what happened in the past because it's already too many quarters ago. This quick return-on-investment, or better said hand-to-mouth use of energy adds to the low flame people work on in a fiscal cycle economy. This is what makes it mind-numbing.

Like in high-inflation country, it is hard to build anything in the long run in a large corporation. Strategies change often, there is big turnover of employees and the skills and motivation of the players vary significantly. With thousands of people attempting to stand out of the crowd, the ability to navigating corporate culture, dealing with politics and hierarchies is highly useful. It can be stressful. Every couple of months there is the next new big thing that should make the difference for the business and people drop their current projects like hot potatoes and run towards to next strategy meetings. It's a welcoming moment, because it seems to allow everyone to drop past responsibilities. Talking strategy is also a good tactic to avoid tangible work and accountability. Some people answer any tactical question by giving you "a high level strategic overview".

All of the above lead to shorter project cycles, otherwise nothing gets executed. It supports the mentality to take credit for other people's work. My manager at Dell called it a *hero culture*: "People look for quick success that can catapult them to the next promotion."

In 2013, Michael Dell took his company off the stock market and went private again. A private company doesn't have to disclose its finances or strategy. You can make long term decisions without being scrutinized by shareholders who want to see short term gains. You can also lay off a lot of people without informing the press about it. Your competitors can't see what you do either. With a decreasing headcount and many people trying to make their way up the corporate ladder, the competition for jobs is tough. The company was eliminating some teams and building out others. It was a shift in priorities that all companies undergo at times.

In this environment it can be a risk to look for a promotion. When two or more teams are merging, the excess middle managers are the first ones to be made redundant. If your next career step in the hierarchy would be to lead a team, a promotion would put you at risk to get laid off in the next round. Aiming for more pay is also tricky. Many people with long tenure were laid off. They simply made more money than their peers that did the same job. Under the prerequisites of the division of labor people at the same hierarchy level are considered equally skilled. Under purely financial consideration, when two people at the same skill level do the same job, the one with the higher salary has to leave. Everyone is replaceable. On the one hand HR wants to encourage everyone to do their best and make a career, on the other hand, at times that can be counterproductive. Like the colleague I mentioned earlier who negotiated himself into a team that was made redundant on his first day. Welcome to the team and good bye.

Over their life-span, large corporations are in a constant inflate-deflate process. Big companies usually don't drive innovation, but acquire new technology and integrate it into their business processes. Their ability to scale businesses is their biggest strength and the number one reason why all small businesses want to become their supplier; or acquisition target. With the amount of process, entrenchment, rows of cubicles and hierarchy it is already in theory impossible to be innovative. The only way to circumvent that is to build a separate think tank or innovation center for employees who are supposed to be creative. In most cases though, corporations grow, acquire smaller companies including their headcount, and after a while they need to cut costs and get rid of the departments that are no longer needed. Getting back to their pre-acquisition size. To get there, headcount has to be reduced, either at large by eliminating certain areas of business or maybe they just cut one per team. In the latter case workload is just getting shared by the ones who stay. Since most peers were previously already sitting in the same useless meetings, that is not a big deal. The remaining two hours of real work per day can easily be spread over five or six other people in a team. This is the natural flow in large companies. Everyone knows that lay-offs are a common habit in a large corporation. They constantly move, but slowly like a large naval vessel in the sea is adjusting its direction only little by little. Very common lay-offs in companies are somewhere between 5-10%. At the average team size being 5–10, you just have to be somewhere in the midfield in performance and the scale of how much you are liked by your manager and peers. It is the story of two people running away from a bear. One of them stops to change from hiking- to running shoes. The other one says: "Do you seriously believe that you can outrun a bear?" "I don't have to outrun the bear, I only have to outrun you."

This tactic of not causing too much attention, yet not too little either, can get you through to secure your paycheck. Only that it reminds me of being on an intravenous drip in a hospital: You are not moving a lot and you are dependent that there is enough left in the bottle.

You are idle and hope that nothing will happen that affects you. Following orders, not trying to cause too much attention, being a conformist for the sake of a paycheck is not much different to an animal that tries to survive. That process is driving alienation from work and cannot lead to happiness and success at work.

But let's assume you *want* to stand out? How can you stand out of the crowd if the crowd is huge? Maybe you are doing a great job in your team, but the executives deem your team unnecessary overnight?

What concerned me the most about working in a large corporation was the dependency on others and not being able to take full control of my own success. You can work hard, win awards, get a big bonus, praise from executives, and yet it might still be over any day. A friend of mine calls this the corporate feudalism: You are depended on the good will of others. The way up is hard, the fall down unprotected.

A large corporation is the extreme version of the division of labor. Everyone is a replaceable piece of the clockwork.

Large corporations have a lot more funds to pay you good salaries than smaller ones and you can do well for yourself financially. In addition, a lot of people are brand-focused. For your signaling and screening ritual on your next job hunt, it's beneficial to do well in a large corporation. If there isn't always a lot of intrinsic value in your work, at least it has an instrumental benefit.

If you do want to make a career in a big corporation, one way is to think like the CEO; read analyst reports and the news, listen carefully to what the executives say in company meetings and interviews. Read between the lines: What would you do if you had their job? Observing the competitive landscape and the trends in your industry help to identify which will be the future growth areas and steer your career that way. When you understand the big picture in which direction the company is going towards and which teams will be crucial to success, you have found the area where to look for an interesting position.

I was well aware of what I was going for and therefore the corporate culture itself didn't catch me by surprise. It was more astounding how many people could put up with it indefinitely. Many people have never worked in a different environment and have internalized the hierarchies, processes, and the lack of self-thinking. They have grown comfortable with it. That reality was normal to them.

What seems either dull or ignorant is often simply the lack of knowledge. They just don't know any better. If you are an order-taker, you are not allowed to make decisions and certainly not question any processes, how do you keep your mind and your intellectual brain sane and in shape? In a big corporation, following the protocol, you basically spend weeks in trying to convince your boss and his boss that they should order you to do, what you knew a long time that you should be doing. Getting approval for your actions is what many people spend their days, weeks and months with. I never quite understood what the manager approval is for in every little thing. People work better if you let them do what they are hired to do. Isn't that after all what the skill-matching with open positions on the labor market is about? Can't we assume that if a person is hired based on their experience and skills that they can also do the job with little supervision?

My opinion didn't matter. This was my reality and my life now. I was neither going to change that, nor did I have a way of leaving my reality. Complaining didn't help. I had to deal with it.

Two previously mentioned ancient Chinese wisdoms were my leitmotiv to get through it:

- "Never let your army rest" (Sun Tzu)
- "The art of waiting is to make good use of your time (Confucius)

Sun Tzu said: *"Never let your army rest."* If you let an army rest, they will start to plunder, drink, gamble and get out of shape. When the army has to be ready to march again and go into battle they are neither disciplined nor fit enough to battle, moral and spirit are down. Worse if they are subject to a surprise attack by the enemy.

A famous example for this is when Napoleon's troops conquered Moscow in 1812; after which he let his troops plunder the city for quite some time. The longer it took, the more the discipline went down. And the winter was about to come. By the time Napoleon was on his way back to France the *Grand Armée* was destined to be decimated in a disastrous way.

Some people say if you need an important task to get done in a timely manner give it to someone who is really busy. Usually we increase our efficiency when we have a lot on our plate, since we would otherwise not be able to get everything done. Even though we're busy, we want to get enough *play time*, to do the things we like. If we have only one thing to do, we manage to procrastinate forever in order not to do this one only thing. Keeping yourself busy and always work on your goal works as an accelerator: Everything will get more efficient. And your time off will also be more enjoyable, because you can see progress and start looking forward to Mondays instead of dreading them.

The Germans say: "Erst die Arbeit, dann das Vergnügen." – First work, then pleasure. The better and busier you work, the more enjoyable your free time will be. You earned it and it's more enjoyable.

Some people mistake spending their days in meetings with work. I sat in meetings and calculated the combined yearly salary in the room to about million US$, a single wasted hour would cost the company about 500$. It's easy to see how much time and money is blown out the window. On the flip side it's a good way to get your salary up. By skipping useless meetings and a fixed gross income, your pay per hour will go up immediately, without being less productive. On the other hand it helps to come prepared to all other meetings. Adding quality input to your work, clear action points for you and others and holding others accountable by documenting and following up. If you work efficiently for 2–3 hours per day on the things that matter to your boss, matter to your incentive plan to get your bonus, and that makes you shine in a good light, then you will be a good performer. Carve out the rest of the time for something else. You will be happier for only doing the meaningful things, and you are working better than at least a couple of colleagues, I promise. All without exhausting yourself in useless meetings.

With increased personal efficiency life in a corporation feels less wasted and less stressful. The more tangible work you create the more you can point to results. Working in a big corporation can feel like the life of a hamster in a treadmill, but it doesn't have to be that way.

We have to watch out not to be absent either. It's a golden mean. Out of sight is out of mind. And vice versa. I read about a market research company in Germany that conducted a study of likeability. For this field trial they put a group of people into a class room at a University. Some of the participants of the study attended class more often, others only a few times throughout the semester. None of the participants ever said a word in class. They only sat down to listen. At the end of the semester they showed students in the class pictures of their research-dummy-mates. It turned out that the ones who had attended very often were described as "very nice" even though they had never said anything. The order of sympathy went from the person who most attended to the person who was seen the least in class. The result can be summoned as: Continuous presence creates sympathy. It is important to show presence when it matters to be seen. It can be helpful to ask your boss and your peers out for lunch frequently, take advantage of moments that are non-business, casual environments. You don't have to try too hard to make good impressions, just be there, be yourself and be nice. Over time that drop will hollow the rock.

When the time wasters that also nag on your nerves are eliminated from your work day, you are still expected to be in the office most of the day; or at least reachable any time at your home office. So what should we do with all that time? Here we adhere to Confucius recommendation on the art of waiting: Do something useful with your time.

More time carved out will enable you to run all your errands during corporate time. Make phone calls to friends and family, go food shopping, or go to a doctor's appointments. If you have to leave for a few hours, just grab your laptop and some papers, make sure your desk looks like you are only gone for a meeting. Always have a jacket hanging over your chair and a notepad out with something work related scribbled on it on your desk. Maybe a few post-it's hanging on your computer screen. A clean work space, yet with clear marks of action going on. Neither a mess, nor clean as if you left the job. As you leave and return, it looks like you went to a meeting. And nobody ever asks where you were. You could go and sit in a coffee shop and read a book or meet some friends for a two-hour lunch. You can go twice a week to take a private lesson in a foreign language or go to a fitness studio every day to work out. If you are tired you can book yourself a meeting room, close the door and snooze for an hour. Then you return refreshed to your work space like you just had a good meeting. Always carry papers and walk determined. The ones who don't carry anything and wanders slowly are going to the cafeteria, not to work. If you walk into your boss or his boss on the way, try to say something nice and look busy, like you have to catch up on something a little later. Or ask him something related to work that you want to get back to at some point.

If you can do your job in 3 instead of 8 hours, then pick the 3 hours. Think of Musashi: "Do nothing that is not of use." The best way to get out of a meeting is to say that you have another meeting at the same time and that it would be important. Don't take over leadership over certain meetings unless they are part of your core-responsibilities. Work hard on anything that affects your reputation, your performance review, the tasks you are being paid for or that your boss asks you to do. Cut everything else.

I didn't want to keep my corporate job longer than necessary. I knew I needed at least a couple of years' worth of pay to get out of my financial mess though. Therefore the only choice was to get through my status quo and to plan and prepare for the time after. Having goals can keep you occupied and create quite some energy, despite a monotonous daily routine. And you may not even have a clear idea what the next move will be as long as you are determined there should be something else. You don't need all the answers at the start. The opportunity will come if you are prepared for anything. You can learn something new, study a subject through an on distance study program, take classes, start a bunch of new hobbies, read a lot, and meet a lot of people to get ideas.

I have met quite a few people who worked in a corporation who had a side business. They all had in common though that they did their job diligently. Then they collected pay and benefits, and used the rest of their time to work on their own stuff. Some people are able to run a business on the side and jump full time on it when the right moment comes. A lot of business start like that. Just be careful not use any employer resources or their computers to do that. Don't save any private documents on a work computer. Keep it strictly separate. Many companies use spying software to monitor what people are doing. Big brother watches you everywhere.

Don't avoid your paid job and try to get away with it, so you can do your own thing. Firstly it would be like stealing money, and secondly it can actually cost you your job and then you'll be in trouble. You need a financial cushion or a second income before doing any business on your own. It takes time. As long as you do your job, perform on what you are hired to do, you will never have to explain yourself. You just work more efficiently on what you are getting paid for than others. If they want to waste their time with calling a meeting for every problem, it's not your problem. Have your own style. Don't be afraid to make decisions alone.

One of my Taekwondo teachers once said that if you want to master something you have to practice it diligently and in isolation for an extended period of time. There is a saying of *going up to the mountain*. In the historic days of martial arts that meant to climb a mountain to practice in isolation by kicking down branches and trees. I certainly had the isolation in Central Texas, and I had time at hand. I imagined that to be my mountain top where I could practice improving both body and mind. In a big city you always have a lot of interesting things to do, but maybe because you are very busy you don't have time to cultivate and practice things that you really enjoy. Maybe your busy social life keeps you from taking a break to find out your true interests.

At times when I was extremely bored in Texas and imagined it to be my mountain top I wondered how I could do something useful with my time?

Necessity is the mother of invention: I needed to become a renaissance man ever more. During the three years in Texas I took private classes in Chinese every week. I learned how to smoke food and make real Texan BBQ. I learned how to bake crusty bread and how to stuff my own sausages. I should have started to brew my own beer. I don't know why that never occurred to me. It would have been the perfect setting for it. Make your own cold brew in a hot place.

We lived in a small house with a garage. Everyone in Texas has a "man cave". Some work on their motor cycles in the garage, others have big flat screen TV's and beer fridges to hang out with their buddies, others lounge on chairs with an open garage door watching the street as if it was a café. I turned our garage into my private Dojang with foam mats, a large mirror, a heavy bag, nun chucks and rubber knives. For three years I practiced on my own for my promotion test to a 3rd degree black belt. When I was promoted in 2013 I felt more accomplished about how I got there rather than the achievement itself. I had been able to maintain my practice despite the heat, the isolation, the lack of training partners, and teachers. I had to bite myself through it. The way to achieve my 3rd degree counts more to me than the actual belt.

When in Rome, do as the Romans do. I wore my new leather cowboy boots as my "going-out" shoes when we went out for dinner, I had fun going horse-back riding, or listening to country music while cruisin' through the Texas Hill Country in my fire red muscle car.

In Austin many people do triathlons, so we decided to do one as well. It was fun to practice with a goal in mind and a great feeling of accomplishment. Meredith completed the triathlon three months pregnant.

I practiced CrossFit and completed a *tough mudder*, a military style obstacle course over a distance of almost a half marathon, overcoming about 30 military style obstacles on the way. I helped a friend of mine to brew homemade beer which we served at a private Oktoberfest that Meredith and I organized in our house for all our friends, alongside German folk music and traditional food. And, after a 20-year-break, I bought a piano and picked up playing again.

My daily routine in Texas between work and the little town was monotonous. I faced my reality and prevented self-pity by becoming extremely active in fighting boredom and mental idleness. The abundance of free time combined with the urgency to do things led me to get a lot of things accomplished. There was after all a big benefit to spend some years on the mountain.

It was my counter balance to the low flame of brain power at work. Otherwise I would have intellectually and physically decayed in Texas. And maybe I'd weigh twice as much now, too.

Daily robotting for no real reason, entering into the indefinite row of grey cubicles in cheap artificial light felt like going to a halfway house every day. The only difference is that if you are sentenced to prison with an allowed furlough, you are locked up at night. In this case I felt imprisoned at daytime. I wondered sometimes why I had to be there, what was my wrongdoing? Was there a way out?

It can be a vicious cycle that is difficult to break, especially if you think that you can't see the light at the end of the tunnel. If your job is mind-numbing like mine was, making the change in your free time can have a positive effect on everything else. Arrange your free-time activities in a way that they stimulate mentally and physically. Watching TV is not an activity for example, it's passive brainless existence. Sometimes it can be just what you feel like doing, but it's not what you should aim to do with your free time. Exercise of mind and body is the key to the happiness of the soul.

There are moments in life when nothing seems to move forward, when boredom and desperation seem to be overwhelming. This can be combined or caused by general unhappiness about one's life situation and the missing outlook of a change in the near future. Facing a situation like this, words of wisdom can be found from Machiavelli: "A wise Prince, therefore, should pursue such methods as these, never resting idle in times of peace, but strenuously seeking to turn them to account, so that he may derive strength from them in the hour of danger, and find himself ready should fortune turn against him, to resist her blows."[69]

A single hour of "me-time" every day can lead to accomplishing great things. In the idle times in my career, when I had no choice but sticking to it, I have found the high-intensity free time the way to stay mentally sane.

If you are going through hell, keep going. Texas wasn't hell, but it was certainly at least as hot. I missed the four seasons and the city life with all its varieties. Sometimes you can't change your situation immediately and there doesn't seem to be a way out. Take it like Superman and ignore your mood. Just get through it and never let your army rest. Eventually there will be a way out if you don't lose sight of it. Don't become idle and lazy, don't feed yourself with self-pity. If work makes you unhappy and stressed out, load up on energy in your free time until you see an opportunity to change your professional life. Not everything

---

69 MACHIAVELLI, N. (1532), CHAPTER 14

can fly at all times, so just keep going and it will get better eventually.

Any line of growth in a Cartesian coordinate system will reach a point where the curve turns exponential. You don't know when the inflection point will come, but as long as you keep moving on, that day will come.

According to Abraham Maslow (1908–1970), each person has basic necessities that must be satisfied in a hierarchical order. He called that the pyramid of needs, in which one level of necessities has to be fulfilled in order for a person to aim for the next level. These range from physiological requirements to love, esteem, and self-actualization. With each level of needs being satisfied, the next higher level in the emotional hierarchy dominates conscious functioning.[70]

Maslow's Pyramid of Needs defines the following order of necessities:

1. The first need of humans are physiological: breathing, sleeping, nutrition, health, a roof over your head, mobility.
2. Security: Law & Order, Protection from dangers, regular income, insurance.
3. Social desires: Family, friends, relationship, love, intimacy, communication.
4. Recognition: Status, respect, acknowledgement, Prosperity, Influence, private and professional success, mental and physical health.
5. Self-realization: individuality, unfolding talent, perfection, enlightenment, self-improvement.

Having lots of love, a regular income and roof over my head was covered in Texas. But I was not happy. Social life and human relations are very important to me. And that doesn't only include having friends around, but like-minded people. I missed a culturally and intellectually environment that allows to have discussions and conversations about more than pickup trucks and BBQ, country music

---

70 ENCYCLOPAEDIA BRITANNICA, MASLOW, ABRAHAM

and guns. The German poet Christian Morgenstern (1871–1914) had precise words for this: "Home is not where you live, but where you are being understood."

In any place in the world it can be a lot of fun to enjoy the *local* way of life. But if you recognize that it's not *your* thing after all, you are better off making a decision to move on before it's getting harder and harder to do.

In order to reach the next level on Maslow's pyramid, self-realization, a change of scenery was overdue for me. I decided that I have to rise to the level of my competence at work, to be in charge of my own life, and live among a higher density of academics and entrepreneurs, global-minded locals and ex-pats, culture and history, artists and hipsters, four seasons and a variety of free time activities. I couldn't handle the monotonous small town life; I just wasn't made for it. I felt short of breath and locked up. In addition the fact that I had to drive everywhere, being a slave to my car, made me feel extremely isolated. I just don't want to be obligated to hop into my car if I need a liter of milk, a newspaper or a bottle of wine. It's nice to have a car and mobility, but when life without a vehicle wouldn't be possible it's not a mean of comfort anymore, but a tool that's essential to surviving. I was never able to get used to that. I love my public transportation, I love to be able to ride a bicycle to wherever I need to get quickly, whether it's the post office, the pharmacy, a museum or a local restaurant or beer garden. In Georgetown there wasn't even a taxi that I could call. It's great to have a car for mobility, like if I want to go on a trip or I have to buy a week's worth of food. A car doesn't make you independent though if you can't live without it. I like to be in charge of my life, including mobility. I needed to get out of there. There were many things though not only my corporate job, that I needed to unshackle from. When I finally recovered financially and mentally from my previous fall, I only thought: "I have paid my dues, can I please leave now?"

On my quest to leave Texas, as much as I had tried to find different opportunities elsewhere, I wasn't successful. Despite a few interviews that I had, nothing materialized. For the jobs I wanted I wasn't invited for an interview. And for jobs I was approached by recruiters for, I didn't care for. Maybe I was also half-hearted, because I was just dreaming of my own business. Anything else would have felt like a fowl compromise. How difficult can it be? Others have done it.

Great people are often small people who just happened to be the first ones to do something extraordinary. Many of history's success stories are circumstantial or people just followed their passion and accidentally became famous. The invention of the eye glasses, printing with moveable type or x-ray for example, have changed the world a lot, just like Martin Luther's translation of the bible into the language of the people. These people did what they believed in, they became celebrities because of their actions, their goal wasn't to be famous, but to do something meaningful. Let's focus on what we want to do instead of trying to copy other people. "Live your own life, the others are all taken", Oscar Wilde said.

Sir Edmund Hillary (1909–2008) and Tenzing Norgay (1912–1986) were the first men to climb Mount Everest in 1953, with 8848m the highest mountain in the world. Sir Hillary is getting all the fame, while most people don't know who Norgay was. Just like most people don't remember Buzz Aldrin(*1930) who was the second man on the moon, right after Neil Armstrong (1930–2012). To me the achievement is incredible and I would love to do both of those things: Climb Mount Everest and set foot on the moon. And I would not care if there had been others before me. The achievement is what counts. If you aim high, quite often you will not be able to manage the quest on your own. What is often forgotten when we talk about people who did something incredible: Usually they weren't alone! Whatever mountain you want to climb in your life, you need a Tenzing Norgay to help you. Meredith is my Tenzing.

Dell announced plans to reduce workforce in early 2014 and offered voluntary separation packages for the ones who'd leave on their own. Coincidentally with their announcement at the end of 2013, Meredith's contractual obligation with the Federal government had run out and we were free to go wherever we wanted. As a health care professional it was easier to for her to find a job than for me. She took a position in Boston, Massachusetts which allowed me to take Dell's package and we starting packing. Yeehah! Thanks to my wife I was able to take the risk of taking the Dell severance without knowing what would happen if I ran out of money. Only because of her we were able to get out of Texas. My wife was the partner in crime that I needed for my jailbreak. I was able to run away from the plague of reporting to duty at the concrete building next to the highway every day.

From my first week in January 2011 on, all I wanted was to leave. When Dell offered a voluntary separation three years later, it was no surprise that I jumped high shouting: "pick me!"

A few weeks later I handed in my security badge and my laptop. In the three years it might have been the only day that I saw a large meeting room full of *happy* people high-fiving each other.

I overheard other people's conversations:

"Hey, you are also leaving? What are you going to do?"

"I don't know yet, but it's not this."

My brother had flown in to "help me" move back to the Northeast again. Sebastian, who was waiting outside in the car for me saw another person walking out of the building screaming:

"Yes, I am free!"

If Dell had offered me a million dollar to stay another year, I wasn't going to take it. I am not kidding.

Money can only satisfy to a certain extent. When you have the basics covered in life, you realize that other things are more important. One might say: "but just for a year?" The issue is that I do not have an unlimited amount of years in my life, I can't just sell them away like this. It's a hypothetical question anyway, but in the moment we were done, all I wanted is to get out of there.

I don't think that Dell treats its employees bad or that the company is somehow different to any other large corporation. It's the nature of the beast. The sword of Damocles hanging over your head continuously. The pressure, the processes, and the hazy outlook for your career that comes with working in a large company. People hang on for the money, but when they unshackle the chains and make the move to get out, they are all happy.

With every hour that Sebastian and I drove further from George-town, my version of Punxsutawney, I felt happy and grateful about the life experience I had gained and at the same time I felt relief that it was over. Rumor has it that road cleaners had to remove a lot of iron rings and heavy rocks that had fallen of my heart with every kilometer on the road leaving my mountain.[71]

Moving to Boston was great, we were much happier as individuals and as a family together. In Boston I felt immediately comfortable and happy, inspired and enthusiastic, at ease and driven. In the US there are different start-up hubs. With New York being an area for finance, media and fashion, Silicon Valley is the place for social media, e-com-merce and games. Boston, with its Massachusetts Institute of Tech-nology (MIT) pops out one hi-tech hardware and software company after the other. Some call it the nerds, I call it the people with real skill. While my company idea wasn't borne out of MIT, maybe this was a good omen. Starting a company is like having babies, you can never really afford it and you never really know if it's the right time, but when you have it, you know it was the right thing to do regardless. My feeling though was not doubtful anymore. My Elvis bobble head changed it's tune to singing "it's now or never." After ten years in the corporate world the moment had come. As I was leaving Dell I finally had to jump into the ice cold water and become an entrepreneur. I knew at that point that it was my calling. And with at least some mon-ey in the bank now, a better moment may never come, I reckoned. There was no way back. Like Martin Luther I said: "Here I stand, I can do no other. God help me. Amen."[72]

---

71 In Grimm's fairy tale of *The Frog Prince*, the princess throws the ugly frog against the wall which undoes the spell on him and turns him back into a prince. When his servant, the *Iron Henry*, is maneuvering the horse carriage with prince and princess on board to their castle, they hear loud noises on the road. After wondering about it, Henry explains they were the iron rings around his heart that are popping off. Now he had no more worries about the well-being in the light of the regained freedom of his master.

72 These are the words that Martin Luther are attributed to during his justification of his reformatory actions at the Diet of Worms, Germany, in 1521. It is not proven that he actually said that, but studying Luther's biography it comes at least close to what he could have said or thought.

8 SISU

"Strength does not come from phyiscal capacity.
It comes from an indomitable will."

Mahatma Gandhi (1869–1948)

On November 30ᵗʰ 1939 the Soviet Union declared war on Finland. Stalin (1978–1953) dispatched 800 000 troops to attack the Nordic country which only had 4 million inhabitants at the time. Heavily outnumbered by the Soviets, Finland withstood the onslaught of the red army during this winter war reaching a peace treaty in March of the following year. "More attention was given Finland in the last three months of 1939 than in nineteen preceding centuries", The New York Times wrote on January 14ᵗʰ of 1940 in an article which titled: "Sisu: A Word that explains Finland."[73]

It was the attempt to explain a word that cannot be directly translated into any language. It is the "strong will, that carries its man even through grey granite." Aleksis Kivi (1834–1872) wrote in his novel *The Seven Brothers.*

Finland had only entered the world stage a few years earlier when Paavo Nurmi (1897–1973), a long-distance runner called the *Flying Fin*, had won nine Olympic gold medals and three silver medals out of his 12 races that he competed in. Sisu may be a compound of bravado and

---

73 The New York Times (1940)

bravery, tenacity and resilience, the ability to keep on fighting after most people would have quit. This Finnish spirit, as the Finns call it, is "patience and strong will without passion" as Nurmi described it.

The Sheriff of Ilomantsi, a town in Eastern Karelia close to the Russian border, told the New York Times journalist that "sisu is the Finn's minus as well as plus. It makes it impossible for him to compromise with his ideals."[74]

Sisu is therefore less about success and accomplishment, but the mental strength to face challenges with courage and determination.

As I left Dell to start my own business I certainly was determined, yet it also needed the perseverance. I had a severance package that would finance my life for somewhere between 6 and 12 months depending on how I could budget myself. But that would only pay my bills of living, not any physical investment into the company; only the time I'd put into it. The biggest weakness of starting businesses is the lack of money. What would you do if you had a thousand, ten thousand or a hundred thousand? The purpose is to find either an investor or a customer. Or both. But before even getting there you'll need a proof of concept, a prototype of a product or a beta version of a software. It is a chicken and egg situation. With limited funds of your own, any penny you put into your business will shorten the time that you'll be able to survive.

With a lot of creativity and time you can build a lot little by little. Easier said than done, yes, but other people have done it. It is possible. Nothing is easy at first. So don't give up, because you think without money you can't do anything. Today most people seem to expect hat a good idea would immediately find funding, and in the inverse, if there is no funding, the idea may not be good. I keep refusing to call my company a start-up, since we have been building it as a long-lasting enterprise from the start. If one day someone would make an offer to buy us that we cannot resist it would flattering, but if that day never happens, it's fine too. I am an entrepreneur, not a money multiplier

---

74 THE NEW YORK TIMES (1940)

for venture capitalists. I certainly never became an entrepreneur to become rich, but to be in charge of my life.

When I would have liked to raise money, I couldn't find any. By only using little money, one is forced to make smart decisions on how to invest it. People whose business idea has not yet ripened enough, with too much capital on hand, do not have the urgency to get things right the first time. The fact that I didn't have the money at first actually worked in my favor. I had to be a lot more detailed in every step. The former Managing Director of Lowe Electronics, Richard McLachlan, a UK based company that Savox had acquired, always says about investment decisions: "If it was your money, would you spend it?"

The lack of funds is one of the most difficult quests when building a business. But the exact same thing also unleashes a lot of creativity and gets you to think very sharp. If you can pay for anything you need you may never focus on what's important. You may have a lot of nice and shiny things, but mostly nice-to-haves. If you are able to get by with little funds and grow organically you can also keep investors out from messing with your company. Yet, there will always be the need to spend some money. Many things can be achieved through favors and maybe giving out shares to people that can help you build your company. However, for some things you'll need actual cash. If you have time and patience, you can start to work on a business for as long as you can while having a job. Start the business before you can run it full time. With a salary coming in, you will be able to pick up smaller costs on your own. Some of them you might be able to deduct from taxes. If you have to make investments of US$5.000 to get started on something, maybe instead you can use US$500 a month, or save the money up and then pay for it. Maybe it's not as much fun as it would be to start immediately, but if that's your only option, it's better than nothing. It depends how much you really want it? We can all think of what to do with a few hundred dollars money a month. Putting it instead into a venture that you don't know if it ever takes off may be a tough decision. Or maybe not. Maybe from all the bills to pay, that's the one you look forward to? Away from the hand-to-mouth. If you believe that your idea is good, then what does it matter if you do it now or in a year or two? As long as you start it with stoic diligence working towards it. Every long journey starts with the first step. For any product or service you will be able to find an audience, no matter how many other people are already selling something similar. There is no such thing as "someone else does that already." Competition stimulates the market. It is all a question of how you position yourself in terms of quality, price, and customer experience. No company can dominate a market by itself. You can always find a niche.

For three years in Texas I took private Chinese classes. As I was at the verge of becoming an entrepreneur, shortly before moving away from Texas, my Chinese teacher, Grace Xiaojia Chen, taught me an inspirational Chinese proverb called 愚公移山 *(Yúgōngyíshān)* – the foolish old man. Interestingly, despite calling the old man "foolish", it stands for willpower, or spirit (精神), and continuation. The story goes as follows:

Once upon a time there was an old man who lived with his children and grandchildren close to two mountains. Every time they had to leave their house or come back home they needed to walk over a mountain. It was starting to be very uncomfortable to deal with the mountains and it influenced their quality of life to the extent that the old man suggested one evening to his whole family that they should start moving the mountain. Everyone agreed that they could move the mountains rock by rock, stone by stone to the sea. They weren't afraid of the heat in the summer, the cold in the winter, or the rain on the mountain, every day they kept working to carry the mountain piece by piece to the sea, without stopping. One day a neighbor stopped by and asked:

"You foolish old man, how do you think you will be able to move a mountain?"

The old man said: "You don't have any children and grandchildren! Maybe I will die soon, and maybe one day my children will die, but then there will still be my grandchildren. If we keep carrying one stone after the other away, little by little there will be less rocks to carry, and eventually we will have moved the whole mountain one day."

Grace helped me to write a script for a Kickstarter campaign video that I created in several languages, including Chinese. Kickstarter is a crowdfunding platform in which companies and individuals pitch ideas they seek funding for. Among the crowd of people looking for interesting projects on Kickstarter's website, individuals pledge money towards a campaign. If the campaign gets funded, the pledge will get charged to a credit card, the campaign receives money and the supporters receive an award in return. If for example someone was seeking funding for a book called *Career Chess* on Kickstarter or any other crowdfunding platform, the supporters would receive a copy of the book after it has been printed.

Grace taught me Language and Culture between 2011 and 2014. We became very good friends, and our family was visiting hers and vice versa. We enjoyed tea ceremonies, cooked together, celebrated our birthdays together. She had posted a picture by her desk in her school holding my new born son in her arms. In 2014, about a month after I had left Texas, she became the victim of a random homicide by an unknown person. She was never able to see my Kickstarter video in which I am pitching my business idea in Chinese to the world. She would have been very proud.

I used to have season tickets to the Austin Lyric Opera. Since we moved away before the last performance that year I gave her my tickets. I was driving from Austin to Boston with my brother when I received an email from her thanking me, that she had had a good time and the music had been wonderful. I was happy to hear that and said to myself that I'd call her or e-mail her when I'm settled in Boston. I never had the chance to speak to her again.

She was a wonderful woman, a great teacher and a good friend. Everyone who knew her misses her. I miss her. Often when I look at the moon and think about her and the Chinese Moon Festival. This big Chinese festival is taking place when the full moon is the biggest and brightest of the year, usually in September. People gather to embrace the moon and think of their beloved ones who aren't with you, but look at the moon from a different place in the world. I think that she is watching it too, just from a better place. May her soul rest in peace. Dead is only what is forgotten. When I think of my friend and teacher, I never think about how she died, but how she lived. It is even more so an example on how quick life can be taken from you and there is no excuse to let life pass by without doing what you love. She did what she loved, that was teaching.

As I was moving out of Texas, karma was waiting for me. A major twist in my life's tale happened: Savox had gotten into financial troubles – again – a new round of layoffs came along. Savox' Chief Engineer, Pasi Auranen, was one of the victims. We had become friends during my time at Savox as he had designed the first Bluetooth speaker-microphone for Push-to-Talk with Cellphones for Savox. Freed from his obligations at Savox, he was full of enthusiasm to get this going together with me. He was quickly able to gather motivated people, to build a rough prototype as a proof of concept. For an audio- and hardware engineer that has built communication devices, mobile phones and developed military style communication in the past, building a prototype for our Kickstarter campaign, was a walk in the park. He had done that so many times, pulling this off was a pretty straight forward exercise for him. Just like many first time entrepreneurs we started with a major excitement and we had hopes into our fundraising campaign. Also, since we had no plan B how else we could be financing the business.

You never know if your business is going to take off. It is always very stressful. You can only be in it for the passion. The rest comes on its own or it doesn't. Therefore the 1st rule for entrepreneurship is:

Don't do it for the money.

Being an entrepreneur should not be a decision based on how much money one might make with it, but about the attitude to be responsible for oneself. Most entrepreneurs aren't rich. That can be a nice side effect, but the goal is to become responsible for your own destiny. Being successful without being passionate about it is very difficult, if not impossible. Most mentors of entrepreneurship advise not to invest or engage in a field that you don't have a particular interest in. Venture Capitalists usually invest in their own field of knowledge.

The same applies to us. We can spend our lives doing the things we love, success will then either come or not. In the meantime we are happy, learning and improving.

There are many reasons to become and entrepreneur, and there are some reasons not to become one. Some people just don't want to take that risk or put the burden of the responsibility upon them. It also comes with a lot of sacrifice for yourself and your family. There are uncertainties attached to it. It's understandable that many people cannot afford to take such a risk. Personally, I'd rather work double the time for half the money if it's my own, because I have experienced just as many uncertainties in my life working for other people. I don't want to risk again having a boss who will ruin my mood and may cost me my job again. I don't want to run the risk of not having tried. I don't want to regret it when I'm old.

The 2nd rule is: Don't start a business with your best friends. Good friends don't disagree easily. It's difficult to find a decision maker, but someone has to decide, otherwise nothing will get done.

I was determined to become an entrepreneur and I was going to be back into the critical communications business. I wasn't going to try to compete with Savox, but to create a technology that would make theirs obsolete. And that as well totally independent of them. I simply believe that this type of technology has to become a lot better in order to succeed. The industry and the customers are the same, yet the technology has evolved. The products that have a potential to be sold changed significantly. At this point in 2014, I was neither spiteful about Savox anymore, nor did I want to use anything they had created to my own benefit. Even if I had wanted, four years had passed since my lay-off at Savox. In hi-tech, four years are lightning years. Starting the business was a business from scratch in all aspects. There were some old contacts, but they had to be refreshed, too. One of them was the turning point.

Soon after starting our Kickstarter campaign, Pasi and I realized that there was no way to get even close to our funding goal of 225.000 US$. We had barely reached a few thousand after two weeks into the campaign. We knew that it would have been a waste of time continuing this battle.

Another way to finance a company is by having a customer who would place an order or a strategic alliance that has an interest in a product or service like yours, yet without having the ability to create it. But maybe they have funds. I looked up my business contacts and reached out to a person that I had never met in person, only over a few conference calls many years ago. He was still working in the same Fortune 500 company in the public safety industry. Boldly or desperately, whatever you want to call it, I emailed him asking if he knew someone on their Push-to-Talk Software team since I had just built a rugged and loud speaker-microphone which they may be interested in. The device was built to remote control these apps over Bluetooth while keeping your phone at a safe place. Within a couple of hours I received a response that he was back on that team himself. He was keen on seeing our product, since they had an immediate need for it. I couldn't believe it. I had not expected a response this quick.

A week later I traveled to their office to meet with their team to demonstrate our working prototype. With some cautious interest in our device he asked me:

"When can we get this?"

"I still need to be able finance the full development and production of this device."

"When do you think that will happen?"

"I'm not sure, but you may be able to help me, help you."

"This may be a possibility, I think we have done some financing with non-recurring-engineering (NRE) costs for small companies before. It's nothing that we really like to do, unless it is a technology that we cannot get from anyone else."

"This is the only device on the market that works with the iPhone."

"This is why we are interested in it, so far what we have seen only works for Android."

"How could we move this forward?"

"Can you come again in two weeks when some senior folks will be in this office location? You should show this to them."

Opportunity had just met preparation. I was lucky to have so many savings in my karma bank. In this moment it seemed that the Kickstarter had not been in vain. It led to create a working prototype, a website, create a company logo, e-mail addresses, business cards. Most of our material was basic, but it was enough to start. What mattered was that we had a working product, not just an idea. We were able to show that we can do it. We named the company AINA Wireless. AINA (in English pronounced as *eye-nah*) is a Finnish word which means "always". It is easy to pronounce by anyone in the world since it is short with mostly vowels. At the same time it stands for the focus of the company to make wireless products and it's a reminder of its Finnish roots.

The fish had taken the bait, now I had to reel it in the boat. The reason they were interested wasn't just because the product was good. I was able to give them something they were enticed to take.

Big companies have their own strategy and priority. In the Global Partner Management team at Dell I deleted many emails daily from small companies claiming to have a product that would really benefit us. Some of that was interesting, but it would be too tedious to get anyone in the hierarchy excited enough about it, unless it was already on the strategy roadmap. The only time a big company cares for what you have is if you offer them what they are currently looking for.

Many small companies try to convince big companies through sales efforts that they have what the big player needs. That usually only works if it's a must have item for them that you are selling. Most large companies focus only on their core business and source everything else from other suppliers. For example a car-maker doesn't make its own tires. There is your starting point. What is it that they need, but don't do on their own? With "what they need" is meant from *their* point of view. The little startup that hopes to land a big deal often only sees how they benefit from it. We always tend to like our own ideas. In our world view they make a lot of sense and if executed they will probably benefit us as well. How nice. Unfortunately not every large company sees it that way. In the same way as you learn to read the trends of a large corporation from within, in order to keep your job, you can also read the trends from outside in order to look for an opportunity to do business with them.

The second important issue is that big companies like to work with big companies. Any project for a large player will always include many people from different teams, including legal, finance, procurement, engineering, quality assurance, marketing, sales and some in corporate leadership functions. If there are 10 people working for a year on a project with a supplier, they don't want to take the chance that the other one runs out of business. It is a financial risk to work with a startup. Most big players shy away from that, unless there is something they really want.

If they actually intented to deal with you, be prepared for a year in negotiations until everything is decided and signed. Everyone wants the big deals, but in the meantime we have to eat. It's important to have a bread and butter business, some other source of income or enough savings, so you can hold on. You may need fallback plans in case it doesn't work out. Large companies may suddenly get an investment stop ordered by their management, or a major re-organization is happening and you have to start all over again. Many people have to sign up for any kind of investment or formal partnership. Even if everyone loves your product, it will still take a long time until it's all agreed and signed.

For AINA Wireless I needed the deal desperately. Without the deal with the big client I wasn't going to be able to get any bank, foundation or institution to give me the needed funding, in addition to any NRE. I ate my entire package from Dell and maxed out my credit cards. At one point I had 0.02 US$ in my bank account a week before my phone bill was due. I plundered my private retirement account which wasn't overflowing, since I had only saved during my three years at Dell.

In their 1940 article on sisu, The New York Times wrote that "when a situation looks particularly dangerous or grim, the Finn laughs and says, "Oh, well, nothing fiercer than death can come of it."[75] This is not everyone's attitude, but the times Pasi and I had to go through weren't made for people with weak nerves.

In the negotiations with a large company it is extremely helpful to visualize the division of labor again; and to remember to use guerrilla tactics. If everyone on the other side sat down at the same time at the negotiation table, the big company could force almost any terms on you. They are paying, they are the big ones. You are small and you need money. In theory it seems that a big company can demand anything. However, you are always dealing with individuals. Their attitude is also positive, and collaborative. In the end, they do have an interest that you are doing well as a company since they need you as a supplier. If you receive a supplier contract of somewhere between 50 and 100 pages it will cover anything from payment terms over quality assurance to product specifications. For each item the responsibility lies with a different department. The legal department will need the input of each department to see if they can make concessions and where they have to stay tough.

If you can find out who the different stakeholders are you can set up meetings and phone calls one by one. Once you are on a personal level with one person at a time the big company vs. small company has gone. Then there are just two people doing their job, discussing the terms of a certain portion of an agreement. Instead of sparring one against 10 you are sparring one on one. None of the others have to look tough in front of a crowd or impress a manager. The discussion becomes fair and most people are very reasonable. It's not about a big company trying to force terms on a small one. It's about doing what makes sense and what helps both parties. Give and take. It takes a lot of time to work through all the details with so many different people. It is worth every minute of it. You will end up with a contract that both parties can walk away with and be happy. At the same time you've already built a personal relationship with all the people in the

---

75 The New York Times (1940)

corporation you will be dealing with in the future. It doesn't hurt to start building those personal relations early on.

All of these are exercises in which one has to stay "unmoved in mind even in the heat of battle" as Musashi said. There are so many battles one has to fight and because a business that you start is your own baby, you are very emotional about it. You also may feel impatient and desperate at times. Desperation is a bad agent for a cool head in a negotiation or a sale. You will have to learn to ignore that emotional rollercoaster when you have to perform. Ignore your moods. Deep inside you may know that you need a deal, one has to stay cool and act as if you didn't need it that bad. Otherwise they will notice and may take advantage of it. It's when you change the hats between being a sales person who gets the other side excited and a CEO who needs to see the impact of anything to his business.

It can help to look into the mirror and think who do you have to represent today. Closing a deal is not just about closing a deal, but to make a good one. Once its signed, that's it. You can't change it anymore. Therefore one has to see not only the financial aspect of it, but the operational, and strategical. How do your concessions affect your ability to act as a business in the future. Where are the areas that you can give in, and where not. Building a business and having to face many challenges, especially the financing part of it, requires a long breath and a cool head. Everything takes time to learn. What if your business idea is the only good idea you think you'll ever have? Is it worth ruining it by trying everything too quick and without thought? One of the biggest challenges facing me was to pace myself in order to make the right decisions without delaying firm decision making. Starting out as an entrepreneur one can't wait for it to get going, yet it's the focus that gets you to the goal, not the speed. A day before any meeting, Pasi and I prepared for hours what our position was going to be, anticipated the other side's expectation and what we could offer as a solution to satisfy their needs and move a step further.

Taking a break can sometimes get you forward quicker and better than trying too hard every day. Many serial entrepreneurs need a few companies to make it right. And they say that the earlier you make mistakes within a company, the better. It's an entire process of learning what you have to do right. That's why we have to make mistakes. Mistakes are the mother of all improvement. Mistakes are not the end, they are the beginning. Don't be afraid of doing something wrong, but avoid making unnecessary mistakes that can be prevented by thorough preparation. Just like Sun Tzu said: "He will win who, prepared himself, waits to take the enemy unprepared."

It took until January of 2015 until we could eventually sign a deal and started the project to build our speaker-microphone for real. Eight months after I had reached out the first time. And eight months was quick for such an agreement. Since our first customer only paid for a portion of the funds we had yet to get the rest from somewhere else. However, it worked like a booster detonation and got everything rolling. We were able to use the agreement to get more funding from different financial sources in Finland.

A startup has three main phases:

- Development stage with no revenue.
- A product in the market, making revenue, but losing money.
- Making revenue and being profitable.

The alternatives to finance a company are:

- Your personal savings and any cash you can find.
- Some say family, friends and fools. I would personally stay away from that, but for completeness I mention it.
- A bank loan. It's difficult to get and very risky. If your business fails you will sit on a lot of debt.
- Government: Small business innovation & research funds, Almost any country in the world has these types of funds. They always have a different name, but basically governments fund research and development to support innovation in the hopes to create jobs at home. This was the way how we financed large portions of our company.

- Foundations: there are public and private institutions that support almost anything in the world. Maybe your business idea can help one of them. Do your research.
- A customer or business partner that is willing to pay for the development. Maybe in the entire supply chain of the industry you plan to be part of there is a bottleneck that keeps companies or the entire industry from growing. If you can solve the bottleneck, you can a) find a way to finance your business and b) prove that what you are making is actually needed.
- Venture Capital (angel investors, wealthy individuals, serial entrepreneurs, incubators, investment firms and industrial funds), and
- Crowdfunding. A project on a crowdfunding site like Kickstarter or Indiegogo can possibility finance your project.

For each startup idea and environment one or the other way of financing might be more suitable for you. The size and scope of the investment also differs depending on your situation.

There is a plethora of information to be found on the Internet on this topic. And finding a good mentor and good advisors is invaluable.

Investors always want to see the next step. If you have a working prototype they want to know when you will be ready. If you have a product, they want to see a customer. If you have a customer, they want to see another customer. Even if you don't have an investor or don't want one, it helps to think like one. From a birds-eye view you can ask yourself the same questions they would ask you:

- Why would anyone pay for this?
- How do you make money?
- How much does it cost you to make money?

Money is a commodity, it's everywhere. The necessity to finance a company can make someone unwary. Watch out for the wolf in the sheep's fur. Some companies try to make themselves look very interested in working together with you, only to steal your idea. They may be counting on your desperation for funds and therefore making you an easy target, knowing that you wouldn't have the money to sue them if they stole your idea. This happened to us at one point. We were able to walk away when we smelled it. The same applies to investors who try to take away too big of a portion of your company in return for funding.

There are a lot of different types of investors, just like you can have a lot of different types of bosses. The moment you need to raise money it's like picking your new boss. There is:

- the dumb money (someone who just spends money on investments, because they can),
- the passive money (someone who invests, but leaves you alone),
- the mentoring money (someone who can help you with a lot of expertise, contacts and previous experience in building companies) or
- the sell-out money (venture capital firms who not only give you money, but also take over most decision-making power).

Don't change your passion for a business for the glory of a press release that you were funded by someone well-known. Maybe you just get yourself an investor who will completely take over. I like to think that if this was the only idea I had in life, then I'd better not sell it out too fast, only because I'm going through some tough times. A good mentor of mine once said to me: "You have the idea, they only have money."

When you start a business you can find many great mentors. Successful entrepreneurs love to help others who try to do the same, they are excited for others. It's a live-and-let-live culture and most successful entrepreneurs are delighted when you ask them for advice. Some might even invest into your business at some point. Sometimes all you need is to ask if they'd listen to your business idea and to give you a brutally honest feedback.

The more unpleasant questions you have to answer, the more homework you will have and the more you will improve. The learning curve can be very frustrating, but it's a very good one. You need someone that can disagree with you, set you straight or help you focus on some of your weaknesses. You might be the smartest and brightest, but you still need a coach. The best athletes in the world have one. Therefore the feedback of a good mentor, no matter how harsh it may sound at times, is probably the best you can ever get.

Theodore Roosevelt (1858–1919) said: "Have your eyes at the stars, but remember to keep your feet on the ground." Many people dream of running a business and eventually making millions. Over this they forget to execute, scale and operate many tactical steps on the way. Others get lost in too many details and forget the big picture.

You dream about how amazing life will be, when everything is up and running, and successful. You imagine the stage in which everything will go smooth and you are making money and you'll be your own boss. That is a dream that all entrepreneurs share. That is what you need to get started and to keep going. You have to find the happy medium between dreaming it and making it happen. Over the nice dreams that every entrepreneur has we should not forget what your own company doesn't do for you:

Firstly, it doesn't take away financial troubles, they may get worse at first and by taking a chance to build a business you always risk ending end up sitting on your debt and working in a cubicle again.

Many successful businesses that rose to global fame weren't founded by people like you and me. Many famous founders never had financial troubles, they were able to start a business, because they didn't need to worry about income too much. They talk about the challenges of finding the right team and build a great product and how much of an uphill battle the selling was. The real struggle for most people that want to start a business is how to pay their own rent, buy food and worries about the future. If you are looking for examples of successful entrepreneurs, also look at their biographies on where their journey started. How to start a business with no money is the story that we want to learn, not how the rich kid became an entrepreneur.

Secondly, as an entrepreneur you will still have to deal with difficult people. You might have an investor or strategic business partner, sales channels and customers with plenty of demands. There will be channel conflict, and conflicts in the team. The necessity to interact with people and influencing their decisions in your favor will never change. Especially if you want to be respected as a leader, not feared as the boss.

To be an entrepreneur is neither about money nor total independence, it's about being in control of your own life. You can't launch a business overnight. The most important part of cooking is the preparation, the action happens in the frying pan, and yet nothing gets eaten as hot as it was cooked. Prepare, be diligent and don't let others discourage you. Take some chances, break the rules, follow your gut feeling, and don't take anything – including yourself – too serious at all times.

For key people in your company it is wise to share parts of the ownership, especially if they are people that you cannot replace overnight. Having others who sit in the same boat can uplift everyone to go above and beyond. Maybe you had the idea, but you can't make it yourself. Would you rather own 20% or 30% of a lot or 100% of nothing? In a complementary skill-partnership everyone wins. In difficult times it helps to cheer each other up to keep going. To be alone with no money is a difficult position to motivate yourself at times. If there are two or three of you, one always has a drive and pushes or pulls the rest.

All of this takes a lot of time, trial and error. It can take months or sometimes years to figure out how to get going. Quitting a job to start a business is usually not an option, even though many people dream of that. Maybe you have to start a business while you are working somewhere else and hop on when the time comes to do it full time. You will know when that moment is there. It requires a lot of perseverance and also self-discipline to stay patient until you recognize the inflection point.

From the moment I left Dell until the launch of AINA Wireless' first product, the PTT Voice Responder, our company has an undergone a lot of progress from being a two man show that more than once looked as if it could fail. Yet, neither for Pasi nor for me was failure an option. We had no alternative, we need to make this work.

At product launch in late 2016, our company consisted of 11 people with an office in Salo in Finland and in Boston, Massachusetts in the United States. One piece at a time we have built a network of resellers, partners and customers from California to the Kingdom of Tonga in the South Pacific. Our supplier agreement with our first big customer was key to getting funded by a mix of different sources including research & development funds and bank loans. Once there is one who believes in you, the snowball starts getting bigger. And if you do not lose sight of your goal, you can achieve anything. In 2016 we applied and were granted 1.74 million Euros (US$ 1.92M) through the Horizon2020 project funding by the European Union. We received funding for a two year research & development project, aiming to build an IP based communication device for public safety with potential to entirely replace the need for Land-Mobile-Radios and Smartphones in professional communication. The years from building a prototype to getting a big amount of funding could fill a book itself, with good and bad times, and lessons learned. When it comes to building a business the challenges and the situations in which they are built are circumstantial. Yet in the end they don't differ much from building a career within a company. Defining a goal, a mission statement, analyzing the circumstances and working on achieving your goal(s) are tantamount to success. You'll eliminate weaknesses, playing out strengths, while still maintaining likeability, dependability and honesty, which are also the requirements for succes. The reasoning and methodology which I have described throughout this book can be applied in the same way. This is why here I want to refrain from writing about *this-is-how-I-did-it*. Let's just say it this way: It needed a lot of sisu.

9 THE MAGIC FLUTE

"God gave us the gift of life; it is up to us
to give ourselves the gift of living well."

VOLTAIRE (1694–1778)

Should we aim to achieve great things in life or live the moment and enjoy the here and now? Can we constantly just plan ahead? Can't we just live the moment and not worry too much about the future? The golden mean may be yet again the right path. Obviously I haven't been the first one to think about this and we find, as so often, inspiration in the arts.

With *The Magic Flute*, Mozart created one of the most popular and most re-enacted operas in the world. It is only one of the many things he composed which made him immortal. Premiered in Vienna in 1791, it is in my opinion one of the most perfect operas ever written. It is easy to listen to and you never get tired of it, yet a musician has his challenges with it and it seems that one can never play it well enough. As it was written to be a people's opera, it has something entertaining, that of a musical comedy, yet it's equally full of wisdom. It's the work of a genius.

The two main protégés in the play are Tamino and his acquaintance Papageno. Tamino doesn't fear death to find his path to wisdom, Papageno is of a simple and happy nature who appreciates the things he has; without aiming for anything different.

The story line follows that of a fairy tale. It starts simple, yet romantic and turns out to be full of enlightened thinking. Equipped with a magic flute and a carillon Prince Tamino and his new friend Papageno go on a quest to rescue Pamina, the Queen of the Night's daughter who was abducted by Sarastro. After finding Sarastro's temple, one of the priests convinces Tamino that Sarastro is benevolent, far from evil and that the Queen of the Night should not be trusted.[76] Realizing the real spirit of Sarastro, Tamino decides to undergo the ordeal seeking friendship, wisdom, enlightenment and love in order to join the group of wise men. The prize for passing the ordeals for Tamino is that he will be able to be with Pamina with whom he had fallen in love. Papageno, who is asked to undergo the same three trials initially declines. He claims not to care much for enlightenment and wisdom. What he cares for in life was good food, enough wine, a beautiful woman, and sleep. When he learns about a woman named Papagena he decides to go for it anyway.

Part of the trials are being able to keep a secret, not talking to others when asked not to and not to fear death. Papageno fails the tests and wants to commit suicide over the desperation of having lost his Papagena. The three child-spirits warn him that you have only one life and he should not take a defeat that hard. They suggest to play on his magic bells from the carillon, which he does and makes Papagena appear again to be with him forever. They sing happily ever after about their future life together and the amount of children they will have. Happy with just themselves. While Papageno wasn't able to pass the trials, Tamino, with Pamina at his hand, uses the magic flute to get through chambers of fire and water. After mastering the final probe, the Priests invite the two of them to enter into their temple. Monostatos, the traitorous servant of Sarastro, the Queen of the Night and her three ladies appear at the end plotting to destroy the temple. However, before they are able to do so, they are magically banished into eternal light.

---

76 WIKIPEDIA.ORG, THE MAGIC FLUTE

People who are involved with classical music often ask the question: which of the two characters would you rather imitate in your life?

The right answer is: both. People who can be happy with food, wine and love, have an ability of being very content with themselves and their situation. They live the moment and enjoy the beauties of life. These people don't worry too much, and live with less stress.

Wine, love and music are the most imminent and central aspects of life since the emergence of humans on this planet. It is a great gift to be able to enjoy the basic things in life. Many people wish they could cultivate that, but they are too worried about what others think and feel the need to conduct a life that they believe is expected by others. Many people also constantly stress about money and financial obligations, hoping that if one day they didn't have to worry about it, life would be better and easier. Yet, nobody will ever be entirely stress-free, no matter how full the bank account is.

On the other hand, throughout history humans have always been striving for knowledge, wisdom, and enlightenment. People want to overcome obstacles, challenge themselves, discover unknown land, become better persons, learn about the planet and the universe, educate themselves in any aspect, and learn to reason. Since there is no black and white in the world, the truth is in the middle. You cannot be a free man or woman if you cannot reason like one. But you cannot be happy if you only try to find enlightenment and forget about wine, love and music over it.

It is when Aristotle meets Confucius: Following the idea of finding truth while being able to make the best out of one's circumstances; striving for enlightenment while being able to be-happy-with-oneself. The golden mean between Tamino and Papageno.

Waylon Jennings (1937–2002) sang in his song Luckenbach, Texas: *"We've been so busy keepin' up with the Jones. Four car garage and we're still building on. Maybe it's time we got back to the basics of love."*[77]

---

77 JENNINGS, W. (1977)

Winning the jackpot in the lottery could not solve all our problems and lead to indefinite happiness. The social standards of who is successful, ergo happy, are an assumption by the scale on how low your preoccupancy with bill paying is. A fast lived celebrity culture is only pouring oil onto that flame. If you randomly ask people what they would do with a lottery win, the vast majority will talk about buying a house, quitting their job, going on a long vacation and possibly buying a nice car. However, once you have quit your job and moved into that house after your long vacation, what then? What is going to make you happy then? Good examples of how quick success can turn into a sad existence are successful artists or athletes who never learn to deal with fame and money and gather the wrong people around them.

Maybe people are too busy keeping up with the Joneses and attempt to portray a happy worry-free life on social media for others to see. This type of peer pressure has been globalized. The need for money, a lot of it, in order to keep up with others is what forces people into a vicious cycle of having to perform. Reality on the first view may not be as exciting as the virtual things around us. But it has a main advantage: It's real! With a conscious taste for pleasure, life has more content than any online database.

"Less is more." This is a quote from Ludwig Mies van der Rohe's (1886–1969) that my mother has been reciting to me since I was a little child.

Mies van der Rohe was a pioneer of modern architecture. His ideas of more open space, less framework, more glass for more light and against anything that is too much, has revolutionized architecture until today. Beyond that, it has a very universal character that one can use in almost any aspect of life. Starting with childhood, it's better for kids to spend more time with less toys, to increase the time-per-toy and therefore the room to learn and live in a child's own imaginary world. It's better to have less friends that are close to you than hundreds on the Internet that don't care for you. It's better to focus business on a few areas and do them well, then trying to be in everything.

One of my Taekwondo teachers, Master Kathryn Yang, went to Harvard Law School and worked afterwards in a well-recognized law-firm in New York. After a few years as an attorney she decided to just teach Taekwondo for a living. I don't know any of her former colleagues, but I bet there are plenty who can only shake their heads not being able to comprehend such a move. It takes courage to say what you believe in and it takes courage to use your own reasoning, and it takes courage to do what you always wanted to do. Not only because your desires may be difficult to achieve, but also, because you will find yourself in a situation in which everyone around you has advice, comment, judgment, sometimes rancorousness, sarcasm, or dismissal for what you do.

I have derived from my experience in the corporate world, that my only alternative was to start my own business. This may not be the option or aspiration for everyone. After all, since everyone's life is very circumstantial, one piece of advice I can offer from the way *I did it* is this: Have the courage to use your own reasoning: Sapere aude! Recognizing inflection points in life and reflecting upon your life and environment is the one universal thing that anyone can do in the pursuit of happiness.

Pity has never really harmed a man, except when he pities himself. Life doesn't always work out the way we were hoping, but that is no reason to fall into idleness. No defeat is ever the end. It's the beginning of something new and part of the whole. If one door closes, another will open. The time to start thinking about what you always wanted to do starts now. Every day is the first day of the rest of your life. Carpe diem! Enjoy it to the fullest extent. Love, drink, dance and sing. Do crazy things, like it would be the second last day of your life. The second last day, because it makes us appreciate life's finiteness, but the people you meet today, may cross your path again tomorrow. Believing in your own capabilities and put a big dream into practice!.

I aim to become like Lessing's ideal of a free person, to be no one's master or slave. As a CEO of AINA Wireless I try to be the manager I always wanted to have. Set expectations and step back to let people do their magic. And I certainly invite people to question my logic and to remind me if I'm living up to my word or not. This has its own challenges. Founders are always at risk to micro-manage, because the company is their baby. I have a strategic vision in mind and I want to set the marching orders. At the same time, I trust my colleagues that they are able to do the right things. In the end that's why they are part of the company. This is not always easy to remember and maintain.

Pasi and I, while building our company, tried only to create jobs that are absolutely needed, and use software or outsourced services and sub-contractors for anything else. It is borne out of the necessity for the lack of resources, but the shortage of funds forces a growing company to follow this approach. Yet, it creates team spirit. It makes everyone's work tangible, creates sense of responsibility and accountability. In return this gives a great extent of personal freedom to everyone to do their job to the full extent of their capabilities. And they also get the credit for it. It helps to create pride and sense of ownership and prevents alienation from work. Keeping it this way is the challenge of any growing company.

I am not a friend of team meetings set up to define company values which are then hammered into people's heads. Only if you are inspired yourself can you inspire others. Excitement and enthusiasm, respect and communication have to be lived by example. Otherwise they are worthless. Therefore I am just myself and live and support the same tenets practiced in any Taekwondo Dojang in the world:

1. Courtesy
2. Integrity
3. Perseverance
4. Self-Control
5. Indomitable Spirit

With this a long chapter in my life is closing and a new one begins. In 1997 I left home for the first time. I took a train from Frankfurt to Salamanca in Spain to learn Spanish for a few months. As I was leaving, someone asked me if I wasn't going to settle one day? I laughed and asked: "I am only 20 years old, don't you think that a man should be a hunter and gatherer before he settles down?"

On a Finnair flight from New York to Helsinki in June 2016, I read a quote on the plane from the Irish novelist George Moore (1852–1933): "A man travels the world to seek what he needs and returns home to find it." It was a funny co-incidence to read such a quote on my way to Finland. I am grateful that through decades of trial and error I have found what I want to be as a man, and where I want to live as a father of a family. In medieval Europe, especially in Germany, craftsmen who had completed an apprenticeship left their home to travel for three years and one day, working for room & board. During this time these fellow craft would learn their trades, becoming masters. By traveling the world and seeing many places a man matures and learns to take care of himself and his family. Then at the end of his journey after three years, he as the one day left for him to return home.

Germany is my native home and I am very German in many ways. Though ever since spending my childhood summers in Finland, I felt a strong bond with the country. There are many beautiful places in the world and many places where I enjoyed living for a while. The place that I call home is in the land of a thousand lakes in the north of Europe. At the age of twenty I started my travels around the world. At the age of thirty I started to search for individual development. In 2017, at the age of forty my journeyman years ended with a single day to return to where I belong. A few years back in Texas as I was home-sick and commiserating about my life, Meredith asked me why I wasn't looking for a job back in Europe then. I said before we leave I wanted to build a company and publish my book. On the one hand because I want to finish what I start, and on the other to have something to point to what I have done all those years as a journeyman. I thought that I didn't want to return to Europe after years abroad and the only thing I did was being some manager of something working for some company. For my own pride I needed to do a little more. Building a company was is mean to happiness. While it isn't always easy, it is yet rewarding. And it is instrumental because it continues and it helped me to move back to Finland; to do what I love in a place that I love. Settling down in Finland in the spring of 2017, I have not left anything behind. I have all my experience with me and I continue to build my house of happiness on top of that foundation.

The first time I moved to Finland, in 2004, I had two bags, a hat and a radio. I still have the same hat and the same radio, but also a family and a few bags of experience.

And if I ever make good money with my company, I will buy myself a really nice bicycle. And I will not post a picture of it on the Internet. I will just enjoy riding it.

10 SOURCES

ADAMS, SCOTT (1997)
The Dilbert Principle – HarperCollins Publishers New York

ARISTOTELES (4ᵀᴴ CENTURY B.C.)
Die Nikomachische Ethik – DTV Munich

BENIGNI, ROBERTO (1997)
La vita è bella – Drama film – Italy

CLAUSEWITZ, CARL VON (1832)
On war – Woodworth Editions Hertfordshire

CROWLEY, KATHERINE / ELSTER, KATHI (2009)
Working for you isn't working for me – Penguin books New York

DAIMLER AG (2014)
Annual report for 2014. https://www.daimler.com/investors/
reports/annual-reports/2014/ (retrieved Mar. 3ʳᵈ 2017)
Euro to US$ exchange rate on Dec. 31ˢᵗ 2014 was 1€=1,2101 US$

ENCYCLOPAEDIA BRITANNICA (2010)
32ⁿᵈ edition – Chicago, London, New Delhi, Paris, Seoul, Sydney,
Tapei, Tokio

GINTIS, HERBERT (2009)
Game Theory Evolving, 2ⁿᵈ edition – Princeteon University Press
Princeton and Oxford

GOETHE, JOHANN WOLFGANG, VON (1808)
The Tragedy of Faust

GROUNDHOG DAY (1993)
Comedy movie directed by Harold Ramis

HOLY BIBLE

HOMER (8–7ᵀᴴ CENTURY B.C.)
Odyssey

JEAN-JAQUES ROUSSEAU (1762)
The social contract, Or principles of political right

JENNINGS, WAYLON (1977)
Luckenbach, Texas (Back to the basics of love) – American country song

KANT, IMMANUEL (1784)
Beantwortung der Frage: Was ist Aufklärung – Berlinische Monatsschrift"

KNIGGE, ADOLPH FREIHERR VON (1788)
Über den Umgang mit Menschen – Insel 1977 Frankfurt

MACHIAVELLI, NICCOLO (1532)
The prince

MARX, KARL (1844)
Economic and Philosophic Manuscripts

NOBEL PRIZE LAUREATES (2016)
https://www.nobelprize.org/nobel_prizes/literature/laureates/2016/ retrieved Nov. 16 2016

PETER, FABIENNE (1996)
The possibility of justice: aggregation vs. deliberation in social choice
Dissertation No. 1905, Difo-Druck GmbH, Bamberg

SAFRANSKI, RÜDIGER (2016)
Schiller oder die Erfindung des deutschen Idealismus –
Fischer Frankfurt

SEN, AMARTYA (1999)
Oekonomie für den Menschen – DTV Munich

SHAKESPEARE, WILLIAM
Hamlet – prince of Denmark (1603)
Henry V (1599)

SCHIKANEDER EMMANUEL AND MOZART, WOLFGANG AMADEUS (1791)
The Magic Flute – Vienna

SCHILLER, FRIEDRICH (1804)
Wilhelm Tell

SHUBIK, MARTIN (1954)
Readings in Game Theory and Political Behavior – Doubleday &
Company New York

SINOWAY, ERIC (2012)
Howard's Gift – St. Martin's Press New York

SMITH, A. (1776)
The Wealth of Nations
German edition: Der Wohlstand der Nationen – DTV 2001 Munich

STONE, DOUGLAS / PATTON, BRUCE / HEEN, S. (2010)
Difficult Conversations, Foreword by Roger Fisher (1999) – Penguin Books New York

STÖRIG, HANS JOACHIM (1962)
Kleine Weltgeschichte der Philosophie – W. Kohlhammer, Stuttgart

THE NEW YORK TIMES (1940)
SISU: A WORD THAT EXPLAINS FINLAND – The New York Times, Jan. 14th 1940

TRAUB, RAINER (2013)
Laboratorium der Neuzeit – published in SPIEGEL GESCHICHTE: Die Renaissance, No. 6 2013 – SPIEGEL-Verlag Hamburg

Lightning Source UK Ltd.
Milton Keynes UK
UKOW01f1305280118
316946UK00001B/28/P